RALPH TAILOR'S SUMMER

Ralph Tailor's Summer

A SCRIVENER, HIS CITY, AND THE PLAGUE

KEITH WRIGHTSON

YALE UNIVERSITY PRESS

NEW HAVEN AND LONDON

For information about this and other Yale University Press publications,
please contact:
U.S. Office: sales.press@yale.edu   www.yalebooks.com
Europe Office: sales @yaleup.co.uk   www.yalebooks.co.uk

Set in Century Schoolbook by IDSUK (DataConnection) Ltd
Printed in Great Britain by TJ International Ltd, Padstow, Cornwall

Library of Congress Cataloging-in-Publication Data

Wrightson, Keith.
  Ralph Tailor's summer: a scrivener, his city, and the plague/Keith
Wrightson.
    p. cm.
  Includes bibliographical references.
  ISBN 978–0–300–17447–2 (cloth: alk. paper)
1.   Tailor, Ralph. 2.   Plague—Social aspects—England—Newcastle-
upon-Tyne—History—17th century. 3.   Scriveners (Law)—England—
Newcastle-upon-Tyne—Biography. 4.   Notaries—England—Newcastle-
upon-Tyne—Biography. 5.   Newcastle-upon-Tyne (England)—Biography.
6.   City and town life—England—Newcastle-upon-Tyne—History—
17th century. 7.   Material culture—England—Newcastle-upon-Tyne—
History—17th century. 8.   Newcastle-upon-Tyne (England)—Social
conditions—17th century. 9.   Newcastle-upon-Tyne (England)—Social life
and customs—17th century. I. Title.
  RC178.G72N49 2011
  942.8'76062—dc22

                                                                                                2011008251

A catalogue record for this book is available from the British Library.

10 9 8 7 6 5 4 3 2 1

Contents

Illustrations

MAPS

TABLE

Preface

THIS BOOK IS A STUDY OF A SOCIETY UNDER IMMENSE STRESS: THE city of Newcastle-upon-Tyne during the devastating plague of 1636. It is also a study of what that experience reveals about an urban culture in this period: the attitudes and values of its people, their material culture, and the social and institutional bonds that shaped their world. Unlike most studies of the plague in early modern Europe, its perspective is primarily "from below". The focus is less on the response of magistrates and public health officials, on the demographic impact of epidemic mortality, or on its religious interpretation (though all these figure) than upon how ordinary people responded to, and coped with, a devastating threat to their families and their community.

The project began with an accidental archival discovery, described in my prologue. It developed as I tried to elaborate upon that initial find; as chance gave way to purposeful research. It was still developing as I began to write the book, as the attempt to address one question triggered others, prompting me to return to the sources repeatedly; rereading, sifting, and combining them to provide answers. I was able to do that more readily because I was working on a relatively small scale, on the records of a particular event in a particular place, and on the role in that event (and in the making of its records) of a single individual. In short, I was engaged in what has come to be known, since the late 1970s, as "microhistory".

Microhistory is not so much a school of history as a distinctive approach to history. Its practice is much older than the label, but the label is useful in drawing attention to certain characteristics of this approach. First and most obviously, it involves a reduction of scale:

the "analysis, at extremely close range, of highly circumscribed phenomena – a village community, a group of families, even a single person".[1] This in turn facilitates closer scrutiny of the sources, the "patient attention to small details" that is its second characteristic.[2] Such intensity of focus can not only provide a more vivid sense of the "lived experience" of the past, but also, by revealing things previously unobserved, discover new meanings that expand the interpretative potential of the evidence.[3] This deserves emphasis. Microhistory is undertaken not to illustrate a preconceived argument, but to explore things otherwise inaccessible. If it is concerned with the close examination of the particular, that is precisely because such specificity can illuminate larger issues. The particular is not in opposition to the social. Close study of a place, a person or an event can help to reveal "the invisible structures within which the lived experience is articulated", or, put more directly, "people making choices and developing strategies within the constraints of their own time and place".[4] It is a way of observing and trying to comprehend the networks of relationships and the webs of meaning within which they lived their lives. For that reason, a third essential characteristic of microhistory is its concern not only with specifics, but with context. "The discipline of history," as E.P. Thompson observed, "is, above all, the discipline of context."[5] It is knowledge of its larger context – institutional, social, economic, political, ideological – that enables us to understand the significance of the evidence that survives, and permits its meaning to be teased out.

These, then, were the procedures that guided me in this study: looking very closely at the records generated by a particular event; exploring the potential of those records (whether individually or used in combination) to answer questions; contextualizing the evidence (in terms of both the available historical literature and additional primary sources) in order to understand it better. In writing the resulting book, I have also worked in the microhistory tradition in a further way. For a fourth characteristic of microhistory is that its practitioners tend to be both reflective and remarkably open about what historians actually *do*.

By this I mean two things. On the one hand, microhistorians tend to involve their readers in the conduct of the analysis and in the construction of arguments. They are sensitive to the role of imagination, conjecture, and interpretative decisions in the writing of history, and there is a certain transparency about the way they introduce the evidence, explain procedures, pose questions, and involve the reader in the dialogue between the historian and the sources. Ultimately, of course, the author usually advances a particular case, though rarely in a very assertive manner; more often as the best interpretative option, with some possibilities left open. Second, microhistorians also tend to be self-conscious about what historians do rhetorically when they engage in persuasive argument. They frequently adopt a narrative form: often because the evidence itself is that of an event, a case, a life; sometimes because it can be used to reconstruct a process. But these are not the "unproblematic" narratives of historical advocacy and polemic, cheerfully papering over cracks and rugosities, skating fast over thin ice, and shouting loudest when the argument is weak. Rather, they tend to be analytical narratives, proceeding step by step through an explanatory process in which alternative readings are clearly on the surface, and carefully crafted in order to explore and assess them.

This book derives its somewhat unusual structure from an attempt to provide such an account of a particular moment in the history of a city and in the life of a man. The overall structure is provided by the course of the epidemic itself, and by the life and activities of Ralph Tailor, who did much to create the records of that event. Both of those interconnected stories, however, are punctuated with explanatory and contextual discussion. The many short chapters, and the alternation of narrative and analysis both within and between them, result from my efforts to sustain the momentum of those narratives, while at the same time explaining events, exploring particular dimensions of the experience of the plague, and reflecting on their meaning. The chapters are intended to be "units of sense", by which I mean stages in the gradual unfolding of a meaningful analytical narrative.[6] This structure seemed to me to arise naturally out of my efforts to make sense of the evidence of the plague. I hope that it will carry my readers with me through that process of exploration, reflection, and interpretation. It is a sombre story, to be sure, but, as I hope will become apparent, it is also one that gives grounds for optimism.

In researching and writing this book, I have benefited from a great deal of help, and it is a pleasure to acknowledge it. I must thank the staffs of Durham University's Department of Archives and Special Collections, of the Tyne and Wear Archives, of the Northumberland Collections Service, Durham County Record

Office, the Local Studies Collection of the City Library, Newcastle-upon-Tyne, the National Archives, and the Huntington Library. Annual visits to the north-east of England were facilitated by the generosity of the Universities of Northumbria, Newcastle-upon-Tyne, and Durham in appointing me to visiting or honorary professorships, and by the North East England History Institute (NEEHI), comprising also the Universities of Teesside and Sunderland, which appointed me a visiting Research Fellow.

Involvement with the research communities of all these institutions, and in particular the activities of NEEHI, renewed some old friendships and established many new ones. I owe special thanks to Bill Lancaster, who was instrumental in making all this possible, and to Helen Berry, Adrian Green, and Diana Newton. But I have also benefited greatly in the course of this project from the encouragement, advice, hospitality, and conversation of Joan and Richard Allen, Scott Ashley, Jeremy Boulton, Chris and Sharyn Brooks, Martin Dusinberre, Francis Gotto, Margaret McCollum, Maureen Meickle, Gwenda Morgan, Tony Pollard, Peter Rushton, Avram Taylor, Natasha Vall, and the many graduate students of the five universities associated with NEEHI. Parts, or all, of the first draft of the book were read and commented upon by Mark Dawson, Francis Gotto, Adrian Green, Steve Hindle, Lucy Kaufman, Matt Lockwood, Craig Muldrew, John Walter, Gordon Wardman, Phil Withington, and Andy Wood, all of whom made valuable suggestions for its improvement. Pamela Edwards helped me to resolve problems of interpretation at two moments of indecision. Durham University Library, the Newcastle Libraries and Information Service, the Syndics of Cambridge University Library, and the Yale Center for British Art kindly granted permission to reproduce documents, contemporary maps, and photographs from their collections to illustrate my story, and my own amateurish maps were expertly redrawn by Stacey Maples of the map department of Sterling Memorial Library. At Yale University Press, Heather McCallum has proved a supportive and understanding editor. I am grateful to them all.

One final debt; the largest. My wife, Eva, as always, has been closer to this enterprise than anyone, and more important to its shaping and eventual completion than even she can know.

K.W.

9 December 2010

Prologue

Iᴛ ᴡᴀꜱ ʜɪꜱ ꜱɪɢɴᴀᴛᴜʀᴇ ᴛʜᴀᴛ ꜰɪʀꜱᴛ ᴅʀᴇᴡ ᴍᴇ ᴛᴏ Rᴀʟᴘʜ Tᴀɪʟᴏʀ: ᴀɴ elaborate and distinctive signature placed at the bottom of a deposition made before the Consistory Court of the bishop of Durham in February 1637. The "R" is large and confident, almost brash, with loops to the side, one of which extends boldly to the right to become the horizontal line of the first letter of his surname. It seems the product of one elaborate swirl of the pen. Then the stem of the "T" is executed as a skein of swirling loops. The "l" sweeps up to touch the horizontal before curling around it. The final "r" extends down into a further eddy of loops. The effect of the whole is arresting in its extravagance.

This impressive display of penmanship lies a quarter of the way down one of the folios of a fragment of a deposition book, in a box described by the Archives and Special Collections Department of Durham University Library as "Box of loose depositions, 1633–4,

1. Ralph Tailor's signature.

1637, 1662–6".[1] I was examining it simply because it was a collection of fragments. The series of large bound volumes of Consistory Court depositions ends in 1631. I was short of time and thought I could best use this afternoon in the archives by skimming these fragments to see whether they contained anything useful for the project on which I was then engaged: check them out; eliminate them from the research plan. So I thought.

Historical records have a way of confounding such complacent expectations. They reveal unanticipated things. They disrupt the progress of attempts to sweep too purposefully through the evidence that they provide, to commandeer rather than heed it. I was finding a few things for my then purpose, but was more or less on automatic pilot when I encountered Ralph Tailor's signature. It caught my eye simply because it was so very different from the stiff and laboured autographs, or more often the simple marks, with which witnesses usually signed their depositions in this period when only a minority knew how to write, and even those who had the skill to do so might use it rarely and sometimes clumsily.

My curiosity aroused, I turned back a page and began to read the deposition. The formal heading identifying the witness told me that Ralph Tailor was from Newcastle-upon-Tyne and that he was twenty-six years old. I read on, and the story that he told soon captured my full attention. He described how, "upon the eight of August last", having been "sent for" to come to the house of Thomas Holmes, he climbed up "upon the townes wall of Newcastle adioyning of the key nere the river", and standing on the wall "over against [Holmes'] window where he then lay, he the said [Holmes] speakinge through the same window did by worde of mouth declare his last will". This Ralph "did presentlie after comitt to writeing as now it is and after the writeinge therof . . . he redd the same to the said testator whoe very sensiblie did acknowledge the same for his last will and testament". Also present "and hearinge" were John Hunter and Hugh Ridley, both of whom "subscribed their hands and marks thereunto". Pressed on a couple of points by the court, Ralph added that Holmes, "being then extreame sick", had retired after he had "declared himself", but "after the writeing therof he came againe to the same window and acknowledged it". Ralph also admitted that since the writing of the will he had indeed said "that he was not certaine whether the testator was of perfect mynde and memory at the makeinge therof yea or noe". That was scarcely

surprising. The man declaring his final wishes from an upper room
to the scribe and witnesses on the wall was confined there because
he was dying of the plague.[2]

Intrigued by this vivid scene, I checked the search room's card
index of probate records to see whether the will of Thomas Holmes
survived. It did. I filled out a request slip, and a few minutes later
I was looking at the document that Ralph Tailor had written that
day upon the city wall. It is short – only eighteen lines – and bears
some signs of the circumstances of its composition. The hand is
clear but seems hurried. It is certainly less neatly executed than
the accompanying inventory of Thomas Holmes' goods, which was
also prepared by Ralph Tailor (along with John Hunter and two
other men) some two months later. I thought I could detect a slight
slant to the lines, possibly occasioned by using a writing board
awkwardly propped on the parapet of the wall, but perhaps that
was fanciful. The signature of the scribe, however, is a beauty: just
like that beneath the deposition, but executed with yet more
panache; three times the size of the simple signature of John
Hunter, and starkly contrasting, in its elegance, with the wobbly
mark that Hugh Ridley managed to scratch beside his name.

The will describes Thomas Holmes as a "yeoman", a term
implying middling social status in this urban context, rather than
his actual occupation. In fact, he was a keelman. He made his living
transporting coal in a keel boat from the pits that lay close to the
Tyne, downriver to the colliers that shipped it to supply the fuel
needs of London and other coastal cities, or to the urban markets of
continental Europe. He left his half-share in "the cole bote I goe in
my selfe" to Hugh Ridley, "my cozen", "if he live soe long"; a telling
qualification. Modest bequests in cash were made to two married
daughters – suggesting that he was around fifty years old – another
cousin, and a brother and a sister, and "all the rest" went to his
wife, Ann, who was also named as executor. The will was of course
"nuncupative", made "by word of mouth" and unsigned by the
testator. The inventory specifies the contents of a three-room house
consisting of a hall, kitchen, and loft room. Holmes was surely in
the latter when he declared his will through the window.[3]

I took some notes, thinking I would certainly find a use for
this striking material one day. It had refreshed me. I moved on. On
the next folio, however, I came upon another reference to Ralph
Tailor – mentioned by a witness in a different case. There was yet

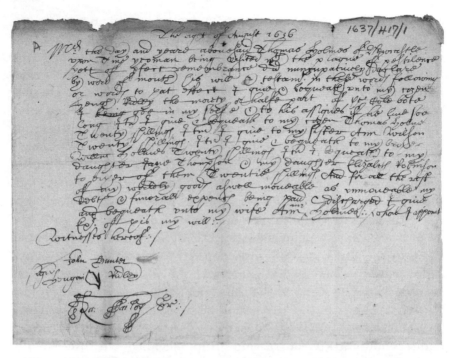

2. The will of Thomas Holmes, written on the city wall on 8 August 1636 and witnessed by John Hunter, Hugh Ridley and Ralph Tailor.

another on folio 12. On folio 13 he popped up again, giving evidence in a further cause, and I now learned that he was a scrivener, a writer of documents by trade. That explained the superb signature: this young man was a professional penman. On folio 23v he appeared again in yet another case, and when I opened the next folder for 1637, I soon encountered him once more. This fragment of a dismembered deposition book begins on folio 84; he appears on folio 85, giving evidence a few months after his first appearance. "Ra: Tailor, 26 – our old friend," I pencilled in my notes, before reading another peculiarly arresting deposition. By now I also knew that his name was pronounced "Raiph" or "Raph": that was how the court scribes took it down phonetically when other witnesses referred to him.[4] All of the incidents recorded related to an outbreak of the plague in Newcastle in the summer of 1636, and I now knew that the records contained a good deal more of the same. Given their fragmentary nature, a lot had probably been lost forever. But much survived, and Ralph Tailor's presence seemed to run through it like a connecting thread.

I left the library that afternoon preoccupied with Ralph Tailor. His recorded words, and the stories told by him and his fellow witnesses, had caught my imagination. There was still time to walk down Palace Green and slip into Durham Cathedral, turning right into the Galilee Chapel at the cathedral's western extremity. It was quiet, as it usually is, and bright; the warm light of late afternoon soothing the severity of the elaborate dog-tooth chevrons decorating the arches that spring across the chapel on clusters of slim columns. I knew that this was probably where Ralph Tailor had made his depositions to the Consistory Court in the late winter and early spring of 1637, 368 years before. The court met here. What would he have seen? There are faded medieval paintings on the inner wall. He would not have looked at them: they had been whitewashed out almost a century before his time in the destructive zeal of the Reformation and not yet been rediscovered. From the two small windows in the west wall one can look across the wooded gorge of the river Wear to South Street on the other side. He might have glanced at the view as he waited for the court to hear the causes in which he was concerned. But perhaps there was more to distract his attention. It would have been busy here on court days. There were probably chairs and desks for the court officials in the space before the present altar; clerks; proctors to plead cases; witnesses waiting, whispering nervously; tables piled with papers exhibited before the court; wills, inventories, and recorded testimony. One thing he might have observed, though. As a visitor to the cathedral noted in 1634, "in the Galliley, or Lady Chappell . . . is . . . the marble Tombe of venerable st. Bede".[5] It is there still, and there is an appropriateness in the fact that the dust of the eighth-century author of the *Ecclesiastical History of the English People* lies in this space where so many documents were made and exhibited; the records from which history can be created. "Time, then, is locked in this place, but its passage is also recorded. Its presence, whether still-stand or passage, contributes to a spirit of reflection and quiet."[6] I felt as I sat there that I had stumbled on a job to be done. I would put to bed the project on which I had been working and come back next year to dig deeper into the records generated by the Newcastle plague of 1636. And I was already pretty sure that Ralph Tailor would be at the centre of it. He seemed to have tugged at my sleeve.

CHAPTER ONE

Stories of the Plague

THE THREAT OF PLAGUE WAS ONE OF THE DEFINING CHARACTERISTICS of the early modern period in European history. From the devastating incursion of the Black Death in the late 1340s to the last significant outbreak at Marseille in 1720, plague constituted a live and present danger. When it struck it was "both a personal affliction and a social calamity", "decimating communities, destroying families, bringing pain and grief to individuals".[1] Even when dormant, its menace, and the anxiety that this entailed, gave it a "central place in the social imaginary" of the age.[2]

In consequence, plague has been much studied. Analyses of parish burial registers and of the "bills of mortality" compiled and published by urban authorities have revealed much about the incidence of epidemics, their seasonality, their characteristic patterns of mortality, social topography, and demographic impact. The records of national governments and civic magistrates have enabled historians to chronicle the developing governmental response to plague: the elaboration of public health regulations; the imposition of quarantine; the measures taken to sustain food supplies, to relieve and police the poor, and to restrain the desperate.[3]

Historians have also addressed the vast contemporary printed literature on plague, elucidating how the people of the time understood (or rather misunderstood) the nature of the disease, how they justified efforts to combat or contain it, and more broadly how they interpreted its meaning. The fact that, medically, plague was "shrouded in mystery and evoked immense fear" made non-medical texts particularly important in what has been called "the socio-cultural construction of a disease that effectively rendered the

physician ineffectual", and the outcome was its "extreme moralization".[4] Colin Jones has suggested that there were three interwoven
"scripts" for understanding plague – the religious, the medical, and
the political – all of which contributed to a fundamentally "dystopic
vision". Plague was a judgment of God upon a sinful people; a
sign of mankind's estrangement from the divine. It was also "an
aggressive, ravaging force" attacking both individual bodies and
the social body.[5] In the cities most at risk, "plague signifie[d]
urban catastophe, a vertical slice across the horizontal trajectory of
normal existence", "an inexplicable, cataclysmic wrenching of a
society".[6] As one contemporary put it, plague "cuts and severs all
ties of blood, duty and friendship". Outbreaks of plague were represented as "catastrophic collisions with the life and values of the
Christian community", in which personal, religious, and community life were "violated and inverted", and "the very principles of
collective sociability seemed threatened".[7]

This image of the plague remains powerful. And yet, as Jones
also argues, we cannot assume that the accounts presented by
the plague tracts are a full or wholly faithful reflection of what
actually happened in an epidemic: "the texts are just too heavily
freighted with pedagogic or persuasive intent, with symbolic meanings, and with metaphoric interplay." They arguably elaborated a
dystopic myth that laid the ground for a further myth of "salvation
and integrity refound".[8] Many aspects of the actual experience of
plague, in fact, remain relatively obscure. Above all, as Paul Slack
observes in his magisterial study of the impact of plague on Tudor
and Stuart England, "the reactions of the common people to plague
are the most difficult of all to reconstruct".[9]

Personal narratives of the plague might appear to be our best
point of entry to that experience. In contrast to the "routine imper-
sonality" of the public records of epidemics, they offer "testimony
to the direct experience of plague", our best chance of recapturing
the "emotions, attitudes and behaviour of common people, which
all too often remain in the dark corners of history".[10] Yet even
these rare texts, written by unusually literate individuals, tend to
reflect their writers' familiarity with the conventions of the plague
tracts of the times. They "drew upon a a shared vocabulary",
"a common stock of metaphors and narrative devices", "a shared
stock of images and rhetorical devices" – "sufficiently shared, in
fact," concludes James Amelang, "to lead the disease-weary reader

to suspect that if you've seen one plague account, you've seen them all".[11]

This should not surprise us. While each is in one sense unique, the authors of these memoirs of the plague almost inevitably employed the language and narrative forms deemed appropriate to their subject within their own culture. They followed familiar scripts because they were concerned to reinforce the same messages as the plague tracts. Thus, while Miquel Parets' narrative of the Barcelona epidemic of 1651 has distinctive features, and breaks, in its account of the deaths of his wife and children, into a deeply moving "memoir of acute personal crisis", it is shaped for the most part by the dystopian conventions emphasized by Jones.[12] As Amelang argues, Parets was concerned to depict how plague produced "the *breakdown* of the normal relations of friendship, neighbourhood, and family and kin obligations which had previously united and bound the urban community". "The triumph of plague becomes the triumph of egoism" – "the sordid victory of private interest over the public good . . . at all levels of society", "the abandonment of the most sacred of social obligations", "the suspension of relations of mutual trust and assistance within the family and the abandonment of obligation within society at large". The pervasive trope is that of abandonment.[13]

Similarly, the letters of Father Giovanni Dragoni from his Tuscan township in 1630–1 depict a threatened "disintegration of social life in Monte Lupo".[14] The most widely read account of the plague in England, Daniel Defoe's fictionalized *Journal of the Plague Year*, published in 1722, but based upon records and memories of the great London outbreak of 1665, is deeply coloured by the same tradition.[15] And the dystopian vision continues to influence historians' attempts to assess the social and psychological impact of plague. In his account of the social response to plague in early modern England, Paul Slack is cautiously pessimistic. "Plague was especially destructive because it was divisive. For most men the impulse to preserve self and family necessarily triumphed over other loyalties and obligations." The threat of contagion placed immense strain upon ties of neighbourhood and friendship, the bond between householders and their servants and apprentices, the obligations of kinship. While acknowledging exceptions and sensible of the likelihood that much may have depended on the pre-existing state of social relations – holding out the hope that "a desperate sense of community" might have survived among the poor – Slack's picture is ultimately sombre. "Above all, the sick themselves were shunned. Fear of the plague produced fear of its victims."[16]

That grand fact can hardly be gainsaid. Thomas Holmes' isolation in his loft room bears it out. Yet the dystopian vision elaborated in contemporary plague tracts, and shaping even personal narratives of the plague, distorts as well as illuminates. It exaggerates the undoubted human capacity for betrayal and abandonment. More, it neglects the role of the social in the imperative of survival. Ralph Tailor, John Hunter, and Hugh Ridley kept their distance from Thomas Holmes, but they were there. They listened to him. Ralph wrote down his wishes "in these words following or words to that effect".[17] Slack hints at the continuing importance of such realities. Giulia Calvi's work on the Florentine epidemic of 1630–1 suggests ways of exploring them. Her histories of a plague year are not carefully composed narratives, but vignettes, culled from the trials of those accused of breaches of the regulations laid down by the public health authorities of the city. They are nonetheless deeply revealing of the attitudes, values, motives, social ties, and, above all, survival strategies of the people concerned.[18]

To the best of my knowledge, there are no equivalent English records of comparable richness. But we have alternatives in the records of the ecclesiastical courts pertaining to probate (validating a will) and to testamentary litigation. Death always generated documents. Plague mortality generated many. These, too, provide stories of the plague – stories that have very largely been neglected. Some are simply brief scraps of information. Others are surprisingly full descriptions of particular moments in the unfolding of an epidemic. Taken together, contextualized, and where possible linked, they enable us to look again at the experience of plague in early modern England; to adopt a different perspective; to find alternative meanings in the evidence pushed up from inside that experience. That is what this book attempts to do: to explore how far the records of the Newcastle epidemic of 1636, and Ralph Tailor's part in it, provide an opportunity to think again about "what we learn in time of pestilence".[19]

CHAPTER TWO

The Destroying Angell and the Eye of the North

THE YEAR 1636 IS NOT USUALLY THOUGHT OF AS A PARTICULARLY significant date in the history of the plague in England. The experience of London tends to set the standard, and the surge of plague mortality in the metropolis that year has been characterized as a "lesser outbreak". To be sure, it killed more than ten thousand people out of a total population of some 313,000, which might be considered bad enough, but it pales in comparison to the truly devastating metropolitan outbreaks of 1563, 1603, 1625, and 1665.[1]

Newcastle-upon-Tyne, however, like other major east coast ports such as Hull or Yarmouth, had its own epidemic history. Outbreaks of plague in the northern city tended on the whole to follow those in London, implying the spread of infection through the close trading links between Newcastle and the capital, above all those maintained through the coal trade. This was the case, for example, in 1544–5, 1570–1, 1576, 1579, 1604, and 1625. Nevertheless, it was also open, by virtue of its extensive trading connections with the Netherlands and North Germany, to other sources of infection. In 1588–9, for example, Newcastle was afflicted a year ahead of other major English cities, while London was in fact spared. Moreover, the mortality of 1588–9 was peculiarly bad in Newcastle, suggesting perhaps the direct importation of a fresh and virulent strain of the plague bacillus.[2]

Sixteen thirty-six was another such year. In the final decade of the sixteenth century and in the first third of the seventeenth century, Newcastle had suffered relatively lightly from the plague. Outbreaks in 1593, 1597, 1604, and 1625 were alarming, but limited in their impact.[3] In 1636, however, it returned, and with a severity that, as the city's puritan lecturer Robert Jenison put it, was "never the like with us to that it is like to doe now".[4]

In Jenison's view, the infection was introduced directly from the Netherlands: the first warning came with the news of "how it raged in *Holland* and in other parts beyond the seas".[5] This is consistent with other evidence. In 1635, outbreaks occurred in Hull and Yarmouth, both leading North Sea ports, but plague was not evident in London until early May 1636, by which time it was already erupting in Newcastle. Since it clearly did not spread north from the metropolis, it is likely to have reached the east coast ports independently.[6] Jenison, in fact, is quite specific about this. He states explicitly that the plague "arrived our Port" of North Shields, at the mouth of the Tyne, in October 1635, "and made its abode there a while chiefly, yet so as that it sent up the river to us some few messengers of death".[7]

These, however, were only the first intimations, acquiring significance largely in retrospect. Thereafter the plague seems to have lain dormant throughout the winter, probably smouldering and diffusing among the rat population of the city until the advent of warm weather, which favoured the development of the rat fleas that ultimately transmitted the disease from dying rats to humans.[8] The fact that plague requires a temperature of 70°F (21°C) for several weeks in order to accomplish that process of transmission may have been one reason why Newcastle, with its temperate northern climate, had escaped relatively lightly in most of the plague years of the preceding generation. But 1636 was unusually hot. The young John Evelyn recorded in his diary: "This Yeare 1636, being extreamely dry, the Pestilence much increased in London and divers parts of England."[9] Newcastle was chief among the latter. As Jenison put it, "after some few moneths intermission, it hath broken out fearefully", offering in a marginal note "May 6, 1636" as the precise date upon which the severity of the outbreak was first realized. Since then, he added, "it increaseth, rageth rather, runs and spreads like wildfire". Nationally, it was a sideshow. Locally, it was catastrophic. As Jenison put it, the "*destroying Angell*" was "gone out" in the city.[10]

It was a city much admired by contemporaries. Robert Jenison, in an earlier work dedicated to the lord mayor and aldermen of London, deferred to the primacy of the "Metropolis or Mother-Citie", but did not omit to claim that his own town was one "of good note, being as the eye of the North".[11] Others were less restrained

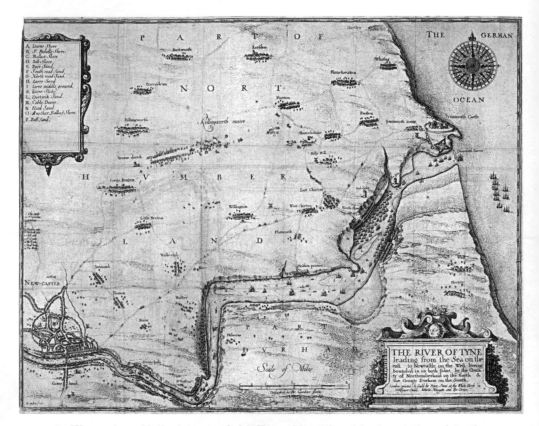

3. Wenceslaus Hollar's map of the Tyne. Note the shipping gathered in the river between North and South Shields.

in their praises, and they included visitors no less than proud citizens. To the well-travelled Cheshire gentleman Sir William Brereton, visiting in June 1635, Newcastle was "beyond all compare the fairest and richest towne in England: inferiour for wealth and building to noe cittie save London".[12] The approving adjectives used by Brereton and other visitors and chorographers, notably William Gray, who published his survey and description of the city in 1649, bear out that strongly positive assessment, and also reveal the criteria on which it was based. Newcastle was "ancient". It was "strong". It was "faire", even "stately". It was "rich" – "exceeding rich" – and it was "populous".[13]

The city was indeed ancient: it claimed to be of Roman foundation, situated upon the "Picts Wall" that marked the "outmost confines of the Roman Empire", and was replete with physical

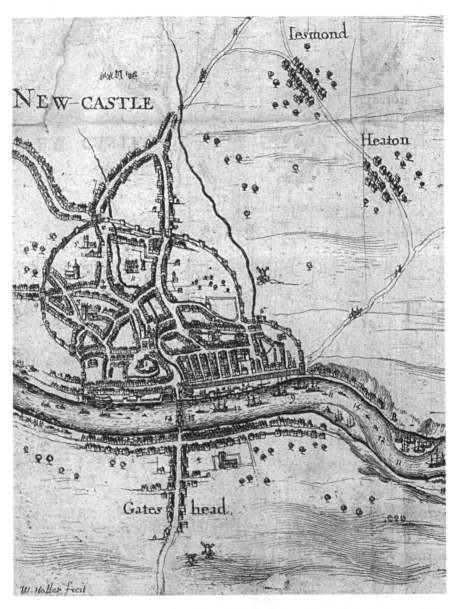

4. Newcastle-upon-Tyne *c.*1655. Detail from Wenceslaus Hollar's map of the Tyne. Note the keel boats carrying coal on the river, the shipping by the 'key' (quay) to the right of the Tyne Bridge, and the straggling housing of Sandgate along the riverside.

monuments to its medieval past.[14] It was also a place of strength. Its modern name derived from the New Castle built "out of the ground against the neighbouring Scots" by Robert, son of William the Conqueror, which still stood, now rebuilt in stone, at the heart of the city. It was "environed about with a strong thick stone wall", with seven gates and many towers, which both testified to its continuing strategic importance and embodied its civic identity. Each of the twenty-four wards into which it was divided was still charged with the defence of a specific gate or tower.[15]

Newcastle impressed contemporaries as "faire" in both its situation and its built environment. It was located "upon the . . . side of a steep hill, upon the North side of the River Tine", the "upper parts" on the plateau gently descending towards the escarpment of the river valley, the lower parts tumbling down it towards the Tyne and further dissected by the deep denes created by a number of burns, or streams, running down to the river.[16] In consequence, it was a city of inclines, some gentle, some precipitous. One traveller described the lower town in 1634 as "seated in a vale betweene two mighty Hills". Brereton considered it "placed upon the highest and the steepest hills that I have found in any great towne: These so steepe as horses cannot stand upon the pavements", an inconvenience countered by the laddering of the streets with "the daintiest flagged channels . . . that I have seen: hereupon may horse or man goe without danger of slideing".[17]

Three principal arteries traversed the city. Of these, the most important began at the New Gate near the north-west corner of the walls. From this, "the ancient and strongest" of the city gates, Newgate Street curved down past St Andrew's church, "ancientest" of the city's churches, and an area of "many old houses and cottages" known as "Hucksters Booths", to join the Bigg and Oat market, a broad street "adorned with good houses".[18] Here the street began to descend more steeply, dividing eventually into three, the Flesh Market, the Groat Market, and, between them, Middle Street, "where all sorts of Artificers have Shops and Houses". All three converged on the church and churchyard of St Nicholas', the principal city church, standing, as Gray described it, "in the mid'st of the Towne", and crowned by a stately lantern tower, which "lifteth up a head of Majesty".[19]

From the "Amen Corner" of St Nicholas' churchyard, the descent to the river began with The Side, initially a narrow street

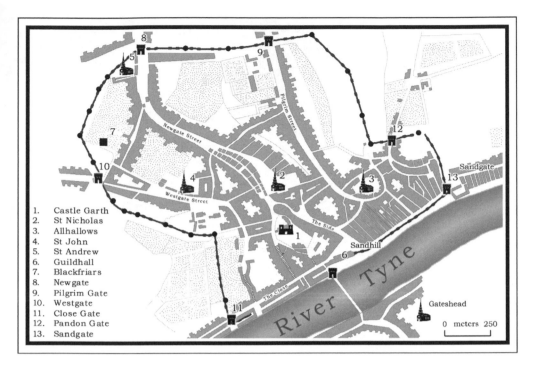

1. Castle Garth
2. St Nicholas
3. Allhallows
4. St John
5. St Andrew
6. Guildhall
7. Blackfriars
8. Newgate
9. Pilgrim Gate
10. Westgate
11. Close Gate
12. Pandon Gate
13. Sandgate

Map 1. Newcastle-upon-Tyne in the seventeenth century.

of "very great descent" cutting down beneath the Castle Garth or yard (to which it was linked by the precipitous Dog Leap Stairs). Broadening as it went, it became a substantial thoroughfare, lined with "shops for Merchants, Drapers and other trades", and graced at its lower end with "a faire crosse with columns of stones hewn, covered with lead, where is sold milk, eggs, butter etc".[20] Thereafter it turned into Sandhill, "a spacious Place . . . adorned with buildings very high and stately". Sandhill, located by the river, from which it had originally been reclaimed, was "a Market for fish and other commodities; very convenient for Merchant Adventurers, merchants of Coales, and all those that have their living by shipping". It contained "many shops and houses for Merchants, with great conveniences of water, bridge, garners, lofts, cellars and houses of both sides of them". It was also the seat of city government, containing the Guildhall, where the courts met, the Weighhouse beneath it, and the adjacent Town House, "where the

5. Merchants' houses in The Side, photographed c.1880. The Side still descends between St Nicholas' church and the Castle, leading to Sandhill and the river.

Clerke of the Chamber and Chamberlains are to receive the revenues of the Town".[21] From Sandhill, the Tyne Bridge crossed the river to Gateshead in eight arches, "high and broad, having many Houses and Shops upon the Bridge, and three Towers". Brereton thought it "one of the fairest bridges I have met with in England".[22] To the west of it ran The Close, a long narrow street leading to the Close Gate, joined to the upper town only by a series of steep staircases: the Castle Stairs and Long Stairs leading to the Castle Garth and the Tudhill Stairs to the western part of the city. In 1649, The Close contained "many stately houses of merchants and others".[23] To the east stretched a "long and broad Wharf or Key", which was a source of great pride. Built upon land reclaimed from the river over several centuries, it now extended "from Tine-bridge all along the towne-wall" and then beyond it. Brereton called it "the fairest key in England I have mett withal".[24]

Only the axis from New Gate to Sandhill spanned the whole city. Westgate Street, which ran eastwards from the West Gate, was confined to the western sector of the upper town. Gray described it as "a broad street and private; for men that lives [sic] there hath imployment for Town and Country". Perhaps appropriately, this area contained extensive open spaces, the built-up frontage of the streets concealing gardens and orchards that lay between them and the city walls. St John's, "a pretty little Church", lay to the north of the broadest stretch of Westgate Street and the town's grammar school to the south, but thereafter the street divided into a delta of smaller thoroughfares or "chares": Pudding Chare ran up to join the Bigg Market; Denton Chare across to St Nicholas' church; the Bailiff Gate to the Castle Garth. Only Tudhill Stairs, running straight down the hillside to The Close, connected the area directly to the lower town.[25]

Pilgrim Street, the third major artery, was the site of the wheat and rye markets, and was in Gray's estimation "the longest and fairest street in the Town". It ran straight north to south, from the Pilgrim Gate all the way down the eastern side of the upper town, to end at the "broad and square" mass of Allhallows' (All Saints') church, "seated upon a hill" to the east of The Side, from where it looked across the steep defile to the castle. In its upper reaches, Pilgrim Street, like Westgate Street, cut through a substantial area of open land. On the western side, close to the gate, stood a "princely" mansion built by one of the city's merchant elite from former monastic property and separated from Newgate Street by

6. Castle Garth, photographed from the head of Dog Leap Stairs, c.1894. The roof of the 'Black Gate' to the castle and the lantern tower of St Nicholas' church are visible in the background.

7. The Close at the foot of the Long Stairs, photographed *c.*1879. Both the stairs and the former merchant house to their left still survive.

gardens and the extensive open space known as The Nunns. To the east, the houses fronting the street enjoyed long gardens, beyond which the open land of Carliol Croft extended down between them and the north-east stretch of the city walls. A third of the way down, Upper Dean Bridge Street ran west across the dene of the Lort Burn to join Pilgrim Street to the Bigg Market, and thereafter Pilgrim Street traversed the more heavily built-up central area of the city, descending steeply before curving round to end at Allhallows'. Henry Bourne later considered this area "the most beautiful part of the Street, the houses on each side of it being most of them pretty, neat, and regular".[26]

Beyond Allhallows', however, neatness and regularity ceased. To the south of the church sets of stairs ran down the hill to connect it to two narrow streets. Butcher's Bank, "where most Butchers dwell", led west, by a "great Descent", to the junction of The Side and Sandhill. Dog Bank curved round Allhallows' hill and down into the district of Pandon, the south-east corner of the walled city. Below both lay "many Chaires or Lanes that goeth down to the Key side". Bourne, who as the curate of Allhallows' knew the area well, said that most of the houses there were in poor order; they were later described as "narrow, ill-ventilated, and ill-drained passages". In many of them a man could touch both outer walls with outstretched arms, "Broad Chare" deriving its name from the fact that it was wide enough to admit a cart.[27]

Pandon, to the east of Allhallows', was another area of steep inclines, descending into the dene of the Pandon Burn, beyond which lay Pandon Gate, and then rising sharply to the Wall Knoll, crowned by a "high and strong Tower". Originally a separate township, incorporated into the city in the thirteenth century, Pandon was regarded as a district of particular antiquity, containing "many ancient buildings, houses and streets". As it descended towards the wall and the quay, however, it too became a maze of "many narrow Streets or Chaires".[28] These ended at the Sand Gate, at the south-east corner of the walls, close to the quay. But the city did not end there. Beyond the gate lay the long street also called Sandgate and "a vast number of narrow lanes on each Side of it, which are crouded with Houses". This, by far the largest of the suburban settlements that had grown up outside the principal gates of the city, stretched "all along the water side, where Shipwrights, Sea-men, and Keel-men most live, that are imployed about Ships and Keels".[29]

8. Dog Bank, beneath Allhallows' church, photographed *c.*1890.

No one considered either the quayside chares or the Sandgate "faire", and it was perhaps these areas that one visitor was recalling when he observed of Newcastle that "we found the People and Streets much alike, neither sweet, nor cleane".[30] But everyone knew that it was the activities of the inhabitants of these teeming riparian districts that made Newcastle rich. Brereton noted that the city "hath great revenewes belonging unto itt (as I was informed) att least 5,000*l.* or 6,000*l.* per annum". The chamberlains' accounts for the year of his visit show that he was very well informed, and also confirm what he and others knew – that Newcastle's buoyant revenues depended above all on the dues derived from the coal trade.[31] William Camden commented on "the abundance of sea-cole vented there, unto which a great part of England and the Low Countries of Germanie are beholden for their good fires". John Speed noted the same, and that "by means of this and the intercourse and Traffick which it hath, the place is grown exceeding rich and populous".[32] Gray declared roundly that "most of the people that liveth in these parts, lives by the benefit of Coales". He knew that the coal trade was of relatively recent prominence, having taken off "not past fourscore yeares since" (i.e. in the 1570s) in response to the growing fuel needs of "London and other Cities and Towns growing populous". But he also knew that this "had made the trade for Coale increase yearely", so that soon "there was more Coales vented in one yeare, then was in seven yeares, forty yeares by-past". Moreover, "this great trade hath made this part to flourish in all trades".[33]

This was true of the ancillary industries spawned by the coal trade – the building of "many great ships of burthen"; the salt pans of Shields where brine was evaporated using cheap "coales brought by water from Newcastle pitts"; the glass houses located east of Sandgate beyond the Ouseburn.[34] It was true of the trade with the Baltic and Scandinavia for grain, timber, and shipping supplies, and the coastal trade in grain, malt, and other provisions from East Anglia.[35] And it underpinned the general vitality and diversity of an urban economy that was rendered distinctive by the coal trade, but also included the myriad commercial and manufacturing activities to be expected in a major port and regional centre.[36] Gray observed that the reason Newcastle's markets were so thronged was not simply because of the populousness of the city, but because of "the people in the Country (within ten miles of the Town) who

9. An old street in Pandon, photographed c.1910. Pandon was known as a district of "many narrow Streets or Chaires".

10. Sellar's Entry, photographed *c.*1895. One of Sandgate's "vast number of narrow lanes . . . crouded with houses".

makes their provision there, as likewise all that lives by Coale-trade, for working and conveying coales to the water; as also the shipping which comes into this River for Coales, there being some-times three hundred sayles of ships". Brereton compared the city's influence as a provincial capital to that of London: "This towne, unto this countrye, serves in steade of London: by meanes whereof the countrye is supplied with money." And much of that money was in turn spent in Newcastle; on the provisions that flowed into its markets, and on the goods and services supplied by its citizens.[37]

All this had made the city "populous". "Many thousand people are imployed in this trade of coales," wrote Gray, "many live by working of them in the Pits; many live by conveying them in Waggons and Waines to the River Tine; many men are imployed in conveying the Coales in Keels from the Staithes aboard the Ships: one Coale Merchant imployeth five hundred or a thousand in his works of Coale."[38] He was clearly thinking of Tyneside in general; of the urban-industrial belt coming into being along the river from Ryton and Benwell to Shields. But the city lay at the heart of all this, and it grew accordingly. It is unlikely that its population in the early sixteenth century had been more than five thousand.[39] By 1665, it stood at roughly twelve thousand, making Newcastle England's fourth largest provincial city. Most of that growth had probably taken place in the final third of the sixteenth century and the first third of the seventeenth century, as the coal trade boomed, and before the severe dislocations of the Civil Wars. It therefore seems reasonable to assume that the population of 1636 was also in the region of twelve thousand.[40]

That population was far from evenly distributed across the city. Only a third of the households lived in the eleven wards of the upper town to the north of St Nicholas' church, most of them in the heavily built-up area between Pilgrim Street, the Bigg Market, and St John's church on Westgate Street. Two-thirds lived in the thirteen wards of the lower town close to the river. Looked at from another perspective, the eleven wards along the central axis of the city from the New Gate to Sandhill contained just over 25 per cent of all households. The upper town on either side of that corridor was relatively thinly populated outside the ribbons of houses along upper Pilgrim Street and Westgate Street, and the same could be said of the western part of the lower town in the Closegate ward. The five wards of the lower town to the east, however, were densely packed: 45 per cent of all listed households lived there. The chares and alleys of Sandgate ward alone contained a quarter of the city's households. The easternmost wards of Sandgate and Wall Knoll taken together accounted for over 34 per cent.[41]

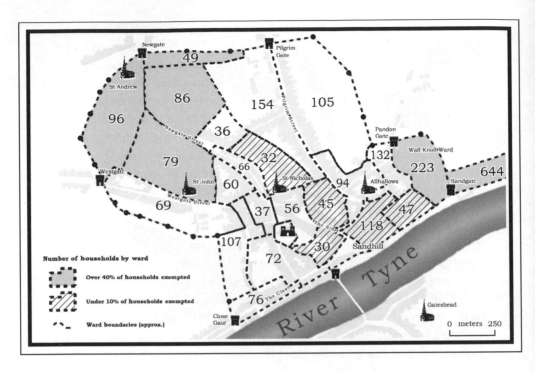

Map 2. Newcastle-upon-Tyne: households by ward, 1665.

The geographical distribution of households also implies something about the social topography of the mid-seventeenth-century city, and the Hearth Tax returns of 1665 provide further illumination. In terms of the average numbers of hearths per household (an indication of the size and quality of houses), the wealthiest wards, with an average of three or more, lay in a strip from the central market area down to Sandhill and the inner quayside, to which can be added The Close. Pink Ward directly above Sandhill averaged almost seven hearths per household, in marked contrast to most of the peripheral wards, with an average of less than two. Four-fifths of the households in Wall Knoll and Sandgate wards had only one hearth. Again, the tax returns listed householders exempted on the grounds of "poverty or smallness of estate". This did not usually mean indigence, but it certainly implied a fairly bare living: commonly the households of those whom contemporaries called the "labouring poor". As Map 2 indicates, wards with exemption levels of less than 10 per cent lay in the same central strip of the town, and exemption levels climbed in the wards between it and the walls.

Those with exemption levels of over 40 per cent lay at opposite ends of the city: in the north-west, between the New Gate and St John's church, and in the south-east, in Wall Knoll and Sandgate wards. Ficket Tower ward to the east of the New Gate, along High Friar Chare, and Ever Tower ward between the New Gate and Low Friar Chare both had exemption rates of over 60 per cent. In the teeming Sandgate ward, 79 per cent of householders were exempt.[42]

This, then, was the city towards which the merchant John Fenwick rode alone in May 1636, returning from a prolonged visit to the country. "About a mile from the towne," he recalled in 1643, he had become troubled with "many sad thoughts", "assuring my selfe to heare ill newes". "And when I lookt up, and see *Newcastle* before mee, my heart burst out with grief." Like Christ before Jerusalem, he wept.[43]

CHAPTER THREE

Wildfire

W HEN JOHN FENWICK ENTERED THE CITY, HE "HEARD PRESENTLY OF
the increase of the plague, and that the night before some six
and thirty died of it". "From thence," he continued, "it daily
increased to foure hundred a weeke, till it had swept away about
seven thousand at least, in seven or eight moneths time."[1]
Fenwick may have exaggerated in retrospect the sheer scale of
the overall mortality. Robert Jenison, in a marginal note to the
Preface to his *Newcastle's Call* dated 2 January 1636[7], stated:
"From *May* 6. Till *Decemb* 31 1636, there have died of the plague
within liberties 5027. Without, some 500."[2] They were at one,
however, in their sense of the rapid progress of the epidemic.
Jenison twice compared its spread to "wildfire", supporting his
conviction that "this plague . . . makes greater speed then ordinarily" by comparison with the bills of mortality for the London
outbreak of 1625. Had not more perished in Newcastle "this first
fortnight since it began or was discovered amongst us, then either
formerly with us, or yet with the great and mother-citie of *London*,
in the first three moneths after it began with them some 11 yeres
agoe"? The point seemed to him to deserve re-emphasis: "I say
there died not so many there in the first three moneths (by their
bils) as with us in our foure parishes, within the space of fourteene
or fifteene dayes, and that only within liberties."[3]
It is impossible, in fact, to trace the spread of the disease
across the city as fully as one might wish. The burial register of
Allhallows', the most densely inhabited of Newcastle's four parishes,
containing over half the population, breaks off in March 1636 and
does not resume until the spring of 1637. That of St Andrew's

commences only in late July 1636. Those of St Nicholas' and St John's are extant, but St John's has no entries between 27 June and 10 August 1636.[4] All this is frustrating. Nevertheless, we are unusually fortunate in having two surviving sets of weekly figures for burials in Newcastle as a whole during the epidemic, and these, as we shall see, can go some way towards compensating for the deficiencies of the parish register record.

The first set of figures was provided by Robert Jenison as an appendix to his *Newcastle's Call*, and was presumably compiled by him in early January 1637. It consists of two lists of weekly burial totals. The first list is headed "The number of those that died at *New-castle*, within the liberties, from the 7. of *May*, till *December*, 31 of the *Plague*" and consists of eighteen weekly totals up to 11 September, followed by a single total for the period from 11 September to 31 December. Next is a list headed "Buried in *Garth-side* in *New-castle* this present yeare, 1636", which gives twenty weekly totals from 30 May to 17 October.[5] The second set of figures was entered into his family Bible by William Coulson of Jesmond (a leading citizen who had witnessed the epidemic) at an uncertain date between the events described and c.1658. It is headed "A true list of the weakly Buerials of such as Deyd of the Plague begune ye 14th of May, 1636, onely within the Corperation of Newcastle upon Tyne", and consists of numbered weekly totals: "The first week 59"; "The 2 week 55", and so on for thirty-three weeks, ending on Christmas Eve 1636.[6]

Of the figures given in the first eighteen weeks of Coulson's list, twelve (including weeks one and two) are identical to those provided by Jenison for Newcastle "within the liberties". Where the weekly totals differ, the differences are usually minor, with the exception of weeks sixteen and seventeen (though even then if we add the two weeks together, Jenison's provide a total of 766 burials, and Coulson's a total of 784). These minor differences, together with the fact that Coulson was able to go on with weekly totals for fifteen weeks longer than Jenison, make it clear that Coulson did not merely copy figures from Jenison's book into his own family Bible. Presumably both men, as significant public figures in the city, had access to weekly "bills of mortality" compiled on the orders of the city's magistrates.[7]

Because Coulson claims to begin on 14 May, but in fact records for his first week the same figure reported by Jenison for 7–14 May, it seems reasonable to assume that the corporation received the first such report on 14 May, and that it included burials that had taken place in the week 7–13 May. This surmise also fits with Jenison's habitual use of overlapping dates for his weekly totals: 7–14, 14–21, 21–28, etc. Presumably he reproduced figures reported on the 14th, 21st, 28th, and so on, which actually covered burials in the weeks ending the previous day: i.e. 7th–13th, 14th–20th, 21st–27th, etc. On these assumptions, we can proceed to create standardized weeks which bring the Jenison and Coulson figures into alignment with one another and also permit comparison with the incomplete, but nonetheless valuable, evidence of parish burial registration. This has been done in the Table opposite.

Here the first column reproduces the figures reported by Jenison and Coulson for the eighteen weeks from 7 May to 10 September. As has been noted, in most weeks they were identical. Where there are minor differences, the higher figure has been preferred except for weeks sixteen and seventeen, for which I have used Coulson's more plausible figures.[8] From 11 September, the weekly totals reported are those of Coulson.[9] These overall figures for burials in the city "within the liberties" or "corporation" can be compared with the registered burials in St Nicholas', St John's, and St Andrew's presented in columns 2–4. This in turn makes possible a simple calculation of the burials "missing" in the parish registration: i.e. the Jenison/Coulson figures minus the registered burials (column 6). As will be evident, most of the "missing" burials in May and June would have occurred in the parishes of St Andrew's and Allhallows'. In July, they would have occurred in these two parishes and St John's. After 7 August, from which date we have unbroken registration for the other three parishes, all the "missing" burials can be attributed to Allhallows' as estimated burials for that parish (column 5). Finally, the Table also includes (in column 7) Jenison's weekly totals for "Garth-side" from 30 May to 16 October – an issue to which we will return.

The figures presented in the Table opposite, together with the evidence provided by the parish of residence of plague victims whose wills have survived, enable us to trace the progress of the epidemic with some confidence. As we know, the city authorities were aware that the plague had broken out by the end of the first week of May. The Jenison/Coulson figures make it clear that significantly elevated levels of burials were being reported in

Table   Progress of the plague in Newcastle, 1636 (burials)

Week	Jen/ Coul	St Nich	St John	St And	[?Allhall]	"Missing"	"Garth- side"
May 1–6	–	1	2	–	–	–	
7–13	59	2	4	–	–	53	
14–20	55	1	6	–	–	48	
21–27	99	4	4	–	–	91	
28–3	122	0	5	–	–	117	30–5: 10
June 4–10	99	0	7	–	–	92	6–12: 24
11–17	162	2	6	–	–	154	13–19: 19
18–24	133	1	4	–	–	128	20–26: 34
25–1	172	8	1	–	–	163	27–3: 40
July 2–8	184	4	–	–	–	180	4–10: 75
9–15	212	7	–	–	–	205	11–17: 66
16–22	270	7	–	7	–	256	18–24: 60
23–29	366	14	–	–	–	352	25–31: 60
Aug 30–6*	337	23	–	40	–	274	1–7: 29
7–13	422	28	32	62	[300]	300	8–14: 17
14–20	346	32	41	47	[226]	226	15–21: 18
21–27	398	44	41	55	[258]	258	22–28: 13
28–3	386	41	47	61	[237]	237	29–4: 14
Sept 4–10	325	36	52	56	[181]	181	5–11: 11
11–17	202	30	35	43	[94]	94	12–18: 7
18–24	197	38	31	34	[94]	94	19–25: 4
25–1	122	17	24	30	[51]	51	26–2: 6
Oct 2–8	197	8	22	20	[147]	147	3–9: 2
9–15	65	7	14	18	[26]	26	10–16: 2
16–22	37	3	7	13	[14]	14	Oct 17: 4
23–29	28	4	3	13	[8]	8	
Nov 30–5	39	6	7	6	[20]	20	
6–12	17	2	7	2	[6]	6	
13–19	22	6	3	3	[10]	10	
20–26	13	1	4	2	[6]	6	
27–3	10	0	10	2	–	–2	
Dec 4–10	12	2	1	2	[7]	7	
11–17	3	0	0	4	–	–1	
18–24	5	1	0	2	[2]	2	
25–31	–	1	0	2	–	–	

Notes:
* = One extra day in order to match Jenison/Coulson figures
– = No registered burials (break in parish registration)
St Nicholas', St John's and St Andrew's figures are from parish burial registers
"Missing" burials = Jenison/Coulson figures minus registered burials
Allhallows' figures in square brackets are estimates: the Jenison/Coulson totals
minus the registered burials in all other parishes

the remainder of that month.[10] They continued to climb in June and July and peaked in the seven weeks between 23 July and 10 September – each of which saw well over three hundred burials – before subsiding slowly in September and more markedly from mid-October.[11]

That was the general pattern. But there is also a more specific story to be told. As the Table on page 31 indicates, there is no evidence of exceptionally severe mortality in St Nicholas' or St John's parishes in May and June 1636. St Nicholas', in fact, usually saw around eight or nine burials a month in normal years in the early 1630s, and St John's around ten. The St John's figures for May and June 1636 are certainly somewhat elevated, but not yet drastically so. As for St Andrew's, we simply do not know. Nevertheless, it seems reasonable to suppose that in May and June, and possibly for much of July, the escalating burials reported by Jenison and Coulson came principally from the parish of Allhallows'.[12] This is consistent with the surviving wills that indicate death from the plague. With the single exception of the will of a man who lived in Castle Garth and was buried in nearby St Nicholas' churchyard on 29 June, the plague wills of May and June come from inhabitants of Allhallows', and more specifically the Sandgate area.[13] John Reay, for example, was a Sandgate miller. Thomas Dodds was "of Sandgate, keleman". William Grame, "skipper", was another keelman who, being "visited with the plague of pestilence", declared his will on 31 May 1636. It was written by Ralph Tailor; the earliest appearance of the young scrivener in the records of the plague.[14]

Sandgate, as we have seen, was the most populous ward of the city's most populous parish, containing a quarter of Newcastle's households in 1665. It was also the poorest ward, a district inhabited principally by the families of keelmen, mariners, labouring men, and the craftsmen and tradesmen who supplied them and the shipping industry; all packed closely together in its narrow chares. One of the city's great middens, or public dunghills, was located there – just outside the Sand Gate itself, with another close by near Pandon Gate.[15] If the optimum conditions for plague, as Paul Slack observes, involved "a large number of people in close proximity to one another, to dirt, and to rats", then Sandgate and its neighbouring wards in the riverfront areas of Allhallows' fitted the bill.[16] Nor was there anything new about that. In the late summer and early autumn of 1603 and 1604, Allhallows' had witnessed unusu-

ally high numbers of burials, many of which were explicitly attributed to "plague", though no such waves of burials occurred in the
registers of St Nicholas' or St John's. Allhallows' was the established
epicentre of infection in Newcastle.

In 1636, however, the epidemic spread.[17] In St Nicholas' parish –
which included the riverside west of Sandhill, the western half of The
Side, and the central axis of the town up to the Bigg Market – plague
was present as early as May. On the 8th and 12th of that month, the
parish clerk marked individual burials "pl". But it was slow to take
hold. Burials remained relatively few throughout May and early
June, and some weeks saw none at all. In the final week of June, they
began to increase and six of the eight burials recorded were designated "pl". Then, after a further pause, the mortality took off in the
last week of July. Now there were burials every day, and by 6 August
a new form of distinction was being observed when the clerk noted
the burial of Alice Aydon as "not of ye plague". As might be expected,
wills made by plague victims resident in St Nicholas' multiplied in
July and continued to appear in August and September as the disease

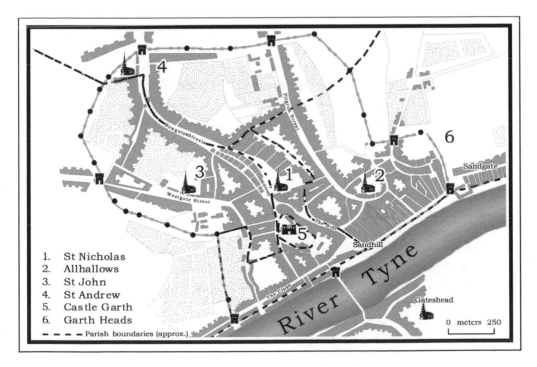

1. St Nicholas
2. Allhallows
3. St John
4. St Andrew
5. Castle Garth
6. Garth Heads
− − − − Parish boundaries (approx.)

Map 3. Newcastle-upon-Tyne: parish boundaries.

raged. The absolute peak in burials came in the two weeks from 21 August to 3 September, which typically saw five to seven burials a day, and occasionally ten or eleven. They began to subside after 25 September, which was the first day without an interment since 25 July, and by October they were down to the levels of late June and early July. Two of the four burials in the final week of October were marked "not of ye plague" – one can sense the relief of the clerk who noted that fact – and by November it was largely, though not wholly, over. The final plague will for the parish was made on 5 November by Robert Mallabar, barber-surgeon, who was buried in St Nicholas' on the 8th. Ralph Tailor was the scribe.[18]

In St John's parish – which included the western sector of the upper town, the suburban strip outside the West Gate, and the nearby settlements of Elswick and Benwell – the first signs of plague came a week later than in St Nicholas' in the form of a cluster of burials on 14–18 May involving the family of Leonard Trumble, blacksmith: first his daughter, then his son, then his wife. But, as in St Nicholas', the mortality was slow to take off. The absence of burial registration for five weeks in July and early August makes it impossible to date the eventual eruption with precision, but by the second week of August the epidemic was raging and from then until September St John's typically saw five to seven burials a day, with as many as seventeen and nineteen on the worst days (1 and 8 September). The first surviving plague will for St John's, that of James Wilson, clockmaker, was made on 12 August. The last, that of Raiph Rowmaine, a tanner who was buried on 2 October, was written by his namesake Ralph Tailor on 29 September. In St John's, however, high mortality continued for two weeks longer than in St Nicholas', and faded more slowly. Few days passed without burials before mid-October, and burial totals remained somewhat elevated even in November. The last gasp of the epidemic came only on 1 December with the burial of "7 poore things out of the Warden Close". Presumably these bodies had just been discovered.[19]

When the plague reached St Andrew's – comprising the northern sector of the upper town, with concentrations of housing in High Friar Chare, the eastern part of Newgate Street, upper Pilgrim Street, and in the Gallowgate suburb beyond the New Gate – cannot be determined. It was present on 8 July, when John Laverrock made his will, and had probably taken hold by 21/22

July, when seven people were buried. By 31 July, from which date there is continuous burial registration, the mortality was heavy, and it continued to be so for nine weeks before gradually diminishing in October. In the worst weeks, St Andrew's saw eight to ten burials a day, and on the very worst days, fifteen or sixteen, and significantly high mortality is evident for four weeks longer than was the case in St Nicholas' and two weeks longer than in St John's. Absolute numbers of burials were also somewhat higher in St Andrew's than in St Nicholas' or St John's – 388 in the nine weeks from 7 August to 1 October, as compared to 266 and 303 respectively – though the populations of the three parishes were roughly the same. When the parish clerk noted "3 day 0" on 3 October, the first day without burials since 31 July, he was clearly looking for signs of hope. He had to wait twelve more days before he could add "none the 15" on 15 October, and a few days more until "19 none & 20"; but while numbers fell thereafter, he could not mark a burial "not of the plage" until 25 November.[20]

Meanwhile, the "missing" burials that can be attributed to Allhallows' – comprising the whole south-eastern sector of the town and suburban Sandgate – suggest that the mortality in that parish probably peaked in August, continued at a diminished but still very severe level in September, and then fell back after the first week of October. That the plague remained present, however, is suggested not only by the figures, but by the fact that more plague wills survive for Allhallows' in October and early November 1636 than for the other three parishes combined. Ralph Tailor prepared several of them.

We have, then, a picture of an epidemic beginning in Sandgate in May, engulfing Allhallows' in June and July, taking off in St Nicholas' in late July, and in St John's and St Andrew's by early August at the latest, and raging generally throughout August and September. From late September and throughout October it gradually retreated, subsiding first in St Nicholas', then in St John's and St Andrews, and finally in Allhallows'. Even then, however, it was not quite over. In October 1637, in the context of petitioning for a reduction of the city's Ship Money assessment for 1636 and an extension of the time permitted for payment, the mayor referred to the inhabitants' sufferings "by reason and occacon of the heavie visitacon of the plague which still remains amongst them". Renewing the pressure five months later, he wrote of "the great visitation . . .

which contynued in a verie grievous and heavie manner both that yeare and alsoe most of the yeare 1637".[21] He exaggerated for the purposes of making his case. The parish registers, available for all four parishes after March 1637, reveal no renewal of heavy mortality in the city. But he was not wholly disingenuous. At an uncertain date in May 1637, Mayor Thomas Liddell had written to his brother-in-law Sir Henry Anderson of his concern that "the plague doth continue amongst us, for the last week there was infected 21 howses and died in the feelds 15 and in the Towne 12".[22] Clearly the authorities were maintaining an anxious watch, and not without reason. In June 1637, the saltmakers of North and South Shields reported of Newcastle "where the sickness hath most bene": "praise bee God the sickness is now almost quite ceased there."[23] Yet the registers of St Andrew's recorded occasional burials (twelve in all) noted as "of the plage" as late as January 1637/8, as well as those of two people "supposed" or "souspected of the plage", and another five who had clearly been regarded with suspicion before being declared "not of the plage".[24] Allhallows' had no burials attributed to the plague between April 1637, when registration resumed, and January 1637/8. Yet on 4 November 1637, William Pringle, a miller of "Ousebarn", outside the city, but within Allhallows' parish, declared his last wishes, being "visited with the plague and haveing a mind and desire to make his will". Ralph Tailor wrote them down.[25] The plague cast a long shadow, and in Newcastle, as in London, "the psychic presence of the plague did not leave the city" even when the mortality abated.[26]

All this, from the early summer surge in mortality and high summer peak to its gradual autumn abatement and subsequent smouldering presence, conforms to the "classic" pattern of an outbreak of bubonic plague. Moreover, it confirms Paul Slack's argument that plague mortality had "a distinct urban topography", being "concentrated in clearly distinguishable areas of each town, in the fringe parishes which were chiefly, though not wholly, inhabited by the labouring poor".[27] In 1636, the plague affected the whole of Newcastle, but, as elsewhere, it was only "superficially indiscriminate".[28] In the period from 7 August to 15 October during which the plague raged throughout the city, and for which we have burials or estimated burials for all parishes, the proportion of all burials registered in St Andrew's (16 per cent) was close to the parish's estimated share of the city's population. St John's, with 13 per cent of burials, was underrepresented, and St Nicholas' (10 per cent of burials) was markedly underrepresented. Allhallows', with 61 per cent of burials, was seriously overrepresented.[29] When we consider that Allhallows' had almost certainly produced most of the burials in the earlier months of the epidemic, it must have been massively overrepresented in the mortality as a whole. That even this may not be the whole story is suggested by further consideration of the weekly figures provided by Jenison for those "Buried in *Garth-side* in *New-castle*" between 30 May and 17 October.

These figures have usually been taken to refer to the town of Gateshead, across the river from Newcastle, to which it was connected by the Tyne Bridge.[30] There are, however, good reasons to question that attribution. In the first place, Jenison refers to "*Garth-side* in *New-castle*". As a local man, Jenison would have known very well that Gateshead was *not* in Newcastle. It was part of the County Palatine of Durham, an entirely separate jurisdiction, and one traditionally hostile to the monopolistic powers claimed by the corporation of Newcastle over the navigation of the Tyne.[31] Second, while Gateshead was often referred to as "Gateside" in this period, it was never, to the best of my knowledge, called "Garth-side". Finally, the parish registers of Gateshead show that the plague did indeed reach the town. Normal burial registration ceased on 22 June and was followed by a list of "The names of those that died in the infection of the plaige & is buried in the Church yard this year: 1636 since the first begyninge being aboute the first of June". The names are numbered, and can be grouped by month, but not by week, since precise dates of burial are not given. Up to 30 September, when normal registration resumed, exactly two hundred names were listed. Jenison, however, gives weekly figures for "Garth-side" totalling 515 burials. Clearly, "Garth-side" was not Gateshead.[32]

Where, then, was "*Garth-side* in *New-castle*"? One possible candidate is the Castle Garth or yard, which was jurisdictionally part of the county of Northumberland, but physically located in Newcastle, on the hilltop south of St Nicholas' church. Bourchier Richardson, writing in 1852, believed that a mass grave had been located there in 1636.[33] However, the timing of the reported burials casts doubt on this possibility. Two-thirds of them took place in June and July before major mortality erupted in the neighbouring parishes of St Nicholas' and St John's. And if the dead came from the riverside sections of

Allhallows' where the mortality was already high, the Castle Garth, some distance away and on top of a steep hill, seems a less than convenient place of burial. Another possibility might be the "Place called the Garth-Heads", a "Place of Pleasure and Recreation", described by Henry Bourne as reachable by a lane to the right beyond Pandon Gate: in other words, to the north of the extramural suburb of Sandgate.[34] A burial ground established there would have been well placed to accommodate the bodies of plague victims from Sandgate in the early months of the outbreak. This seems to me the most likely identification of the "*Garth-side* in *New-castle*". But whatever the case, it seems clear that the 515 burials in Garth-Side must be added to the Jenison/Coulson total of 5,116 burials if we are to appreciate the full scale of the mortality of 1636 in the city and its immediate environs, producing a grand total of 5,631.

That figure gains support from a further estimate of the mortality made by the mayor and aldermen of Newcastle in a letter written in the first week of October to the mayor of Berwick, thanking him for a contribution to the city's relief funds. "The number of the dead is not so manye this last weeke as formerly," they wrote, "being but one hundred twentie two. The great death of people that hath beene, which doth amount to verie neare 6000 persons since the beginning wee feare is cause that there dye fewer now; there being not so many people left in the towne as there was."[35] Whatever the merits of this causal reasoning, they were right about the drastic reduction in the city's population. If at least 5,600 died in all, and that may be an underestimate, then around 47 per cent of the population of the city died in the epidemic of 1636.[36] A third of the population of Norwich had succumbed in the outbreak of 1579. At least 40 per cent of the inhabitants of Colchester were to die in the epidemic of 1665–6. London lost roughly 24 per cent of its people in 1563, 23 per cent in 1603, and almost 18 per cent in 1665. The absolute numbers dying in these metropolitan outbreaks were, of course, far higher than those suffered in Newcastle. In *proportional* terms, however, the Newcastle epidemic of 1636 may have been the most devastating cull experienced by any English city in this period.[37]

Globally, such mortality was catastrophic. But the burden of sickness and death was not evenly distributed. As we have seen, it weighed heavier in particular districts. More, it was most keenly felt by particular families, for, as is well established, plague deaths

tended to cluster in individual households.[38] The progress of the
disease was reported by household. "Doe we not heare morning by
morning," wrote Robert Jenison, "concerning this house and that;
yea those many houses, where not a night or day passeth, but some
one at least or moe are struck dead in it." In time of plague, each
household was in a sense besieged. "I had seen many habitations
laid desolate," remembered John Fenwick, "though I returned
safely to my owne, with all my family, praise to my God, often
strangely preserved from that deadly infection."[39]

Such family clusters of mortality can be inferred from the
surnames recorded in the burial registers. In St Nicholas' parish,
for example, Thomas Wilkinson was buried on 23 July, and both
Grace and Ann Wilkinson on the 24th. Nine Robsons were buried
in the three weeks from 7 to 28 August, six simply designated "Inf.
Robson" (presumably indicating young children), plus James
Robson on the 17th, Thomas on the 24th, and "Widdow Robson" on
the 28th. In St Andrew's parish, "Tho penne and margret penne
James children" were buried on 2 September, and "James penne
swne to James" on the 10th. "Dande Penne", a servant buried on
6 September, may have been a member of the same family. Robert
Toddricke, slater, "the honchback", was buried on 14 August,
William Toddricke on the 17th, Elizabeth on the 25th, and another
William, also a slater, on the 27th. And so one could continue
with depressing frequency. All in all, eighty-five such surname
clusters can be identified in the St Nicholas' register, accounting
for 260 persons, or 68 per cent of all the burials recorded in the
parish between May and December. The St Andrew's register
yields 102 surname clusters, involving 343 people, or 65 per cent of
the burials from July to December. In both cases, the clusters are
concentrated in the peak period of mortality.[40]

These figures are telling, but they are not wholly satisfactory. In
the absence of a full "family reconstitution" analysis, one cannot be
certain that each of these surname clusters did indeed represent a
single household. The nine Robsons, for example, could possibly be
drawn from two or more households of the same surname.[41] In the
case of St John's parish, however, we can be more precise. The parish
clerk of St John's was in the habit of explicitly attributing burials
to the families of individual householders. Married women were
described as, for example, "Judeth Fenwicke wife to Edw: Fen:
tayler" (2 May) or "Robert Cromes wife dyer" (30 August). Children

were registered as "John Sympson son to James Sympson tayler" (12 August), or "one child of William Bells glover" (24 August), and servants and apprentices as "A boy of Roger Swans cordiner" (20 August) or "A wench of Tho Arrowsmyth" (26 August).

This habit of attributing individuals to the heads of the households in which they lived, usually a man, sometimes a widow, is of considerable interest in itself. It may tell us something about the social composition of St John's parish, which was overwhelmingly a parish of small masters, most of whom pursued their crafts in household workshops. Of the 193 men who were given an occupational designation in the St John's burial register in the *whole* of 1636 (not simply the plague months), only a handful were described as "labourer", "workman", or "porter". Fifty-three were given the status designation "yeoman". The rest were almost all given craft or trade designations, the same titles that were used by the guilds to which they doubtless belonged: skinner and glover; cordwainer; weaver; waller; plasterer; tailor; butcher, and so on.[42] In such a context the household to which people belonged may have been even more central to their social identity than was usually the case in seventeenth-century society.

Be that as it may, the idiosyncrasies of burial registration in St John's also permit a closer assessment of the impact of plague mortality upon households in the parish. We cannot know exactly how many households were affected: registration is missing for July and early August. But one can say that we have good evidence that between May and December 1636 at least 256 male-headed households were affected by the mortality in that they suffered at least one death each – sometimes the householder himself, sometimes a wife, child, or servant. This means that close to two-thirds of the households in the parish were affected.[43] The impact of the plague was thus very widespread. At the same time, however, it was also highly concentrated. To adopt a different form of measurement, analysis of the St John's register reveals that at least ninety-two households suffered more than one fatality between May and December 1636, some of them as many as five – and in this parish the details provided by the registration give greater confidence that we are indeed identifying individual households.[44] These hardest-hit families – probably between a fifth and a quarter of the households in the parish – provided a total of 233 burials; some 55 per cent of all burials in the plague months.[45]

The reality behind such figures is even more graphically revealed in the details provided by testamentary records. When William Grame, "skipper", declared his will to Ralph Tailor on 31 May, he had a wife and two children to provide for and his wife was pregnant. His subsequent inventory records the costs of "his beryall and 3 children thear beryalls & funeralls".[46] Clement Curry's wife, "standinge att the dore", conveyed his last wishes to two witnesses gathered "before his dore" in late July, "since which time . . . his wife and one of his children . . . are dead". Robert Walker, weaver, made his will on 27 August "knoweing that his wife and children were lately dead". Three children described as "Inf. Walker" had been buried in St Nicholas' churchyard on 9, 10, and 24 August, and "Ellinor Walker" on 22 August.[47] Matthew Storey of Allhallows', miller, named his wife, Phyllis, as his executor on 18 September. Ralph Tailor wrote the nuncupative will. By the time he returned to write the inventory on 18 November, she too was dead. In the meantime, as we have seen, he had written the will of Raiph Rowmaine, tanner, of "the maltmarket" in St John's parish. Rowmaine distributed his goods among six children, but made no specific provision for his wife, Margaret. Perhaps she was already sick. Rowmaine's inventory lists "funeral expenses for the Testator his wife and a child".[48]

It could be worse still. John Collingwood, a cordwainer, was a late victim of the epidemic, declaring his will on 26 October and being buried at St Nicholas' five days later. His inventory gives "funeral expenses for himself his children and servants beinge 7 in number". The administrator of Ambrose Haddock's estate reported "funeral expenses of the said deceased and of six others of his familie who died all of the plague in his house (besyds Ellysons children who were under his tuicon)". The latter were his nieces, the three daughters of his brother-in-law George Ellison, who had entrusted them (together with their portions) to Ambrose.[49] Both of these cases also serve as reminders that many of the households invaded by the plague were *connected*. John Collingwood was the brother-in-law of the childless merchant Robert Greenwell whose will, made on 22 August, was generous to John's children. Mary Collingwood, John's wife, and Elizabeth their daughter were actually present in the room when Greenwell made his will (and one of the other witnesses was Henry Rowmaine, brother of Raiph). Though the Collingwood household was later overwhelmed by the pestilence in

October, Mary and Elizabeth survived.[50] Again, George Ellison, whose will is not extant, probably granted the tuition of his daughters to Ambrose Haddock at some time in August. George was buried in St Andrew's parish on 3 September. However, one of his daughters, Isobel, was already sick. She made a will on an unspecified date in August, leaving most of her portion to her two sisters and making small bequests to several of her Haddock relatives, including her uncle Ambrose and aunt Ann. She was buried with her father on 3 September. By then the infection had reached the Haddocks themselves. Isobel Haddock, who had witnessed Isobel Ellison's will, was buried on 23 August; the obliteration of Ambrose's family had begun. The plague thus culled not only individual households, but constellations of connected households, thinning the networks of trust and support on which so much depended. By the time Ralph Tailor came to inventory the goods of Isobel Ellison in February 1637, the only survivor of the Ellison and Haddock households was Ambrose's widow, Anne. She was starting again; she had remarried.[51]

CHAPTER FOUR

Diligence and Care of Magistrates

THE CLUSTERING OF MORTALITY AMONG PEOPLE IN CLOSE PROXIMITY was partly attributable to the nature of the disease and its vectors, but it may also, as some contemporaries alleged, have been accentuated by the policies adopted by urban magistrates to combat plague. These, codified as *Orders Thought Meet by Her Majesty and Her Privy Council to Be Executed . . . in Such . . . Places As Are . . . Infected with the Plague*, had first been issued nationally in 1578, were in print by 1579, and received statutory authority in 1604, by which date they were already being enforced in most large English towns.[1]

Newcastle in 1636 was no exception. No minutes of decisions of the city corporation survive for the 1630s, but it is clear that the mayor, Sir Peter Riddell, and the aldermen demonstrated the "diligence and *care of Magistrates*" that Robert Jenison considered vital "outward . . . Preservatives against the Pestilence".[2] "Viewers" or "searchers" were presumably appointed to report plague deaths to parish clerks and enable the weekly monitoring of the progress of the epidemic.[3] Provision was made for the burial of the dead: William Bayles, aged fifty-five, recalled in 1637 that he "amongst others was appointed to be a gravemaker and alsoe a burier [of] the dead in Newcastle . . . by Mr Maior".[4] We do not know whether stray dogs were slaughtered for fear that their hair carried contagion, as had been the case in the outbreak of 1597.[5] But tar barrels were burned in the streets in an effort to dispel infected air.[6] And provision was made "for the reliefe of the poorer sort, of such as are infected or so suspected and the like".[7]

Such extraordinary relief measures were needed not only because of the burden of sickness upon particular families, but also because of the impact of epidemic disease upon the economies of afflicted communities. There can be little doubt that plague often "spelled havoc for normal patterns of behaviour" in economic life.[8] Robert Jenison called it "an enemie of trading and civill commerce".[9] John Fenwick reminded his city in 1643 that the plague "made thee almost desolate, thy streets grown greene with grasse, thy treasure wasted, thy trading departed": the tradition that in 1636 "the Sand hill was in many places Grass-plotts" survived for over a century.[10]

The image of grass growing in the streets, however, was an old trope in narratives of the plague; a powerful symbol of the arresting of everyday traffic. It is not to be taken literally. Indeed, in this respect Newcastle may have been relatively fortunate. Of course, the trade of the city suffered. As early as May 1636, the Privy Council of Scotland prohibited colliers from the Tyne from entering Scottish ports, and by November the bailiffs of Great Yarmouth were petitioning for leave to buy salt from Scottish sources since "the sickness is so at Newcastle and Shields as none dare adventure to fetch any". Again, the "scarcity of Glasse" experienced in London in 1637 was attributed to "the mortallity that fell amongst the workemen at Newcastle this late Visitacon, and now for want of Shipping".[11] But, in implying that trade was at a standstill, Fenwick greatly exaggerated.[12] The accounts of the city chamberlains, kept at the Town House on Sandhill, reveal that almost fourteen hundred ships entered the Tyne and paid harbour duties between the third week of May and the second week of October 1636. In fact, shipping never ceased. Rather, it diminished markedly at the height of the epidemic. In the three months from July to September 1636, the chamberlains' receipts fell by approximately 40 per cent as compared with the same three months in 1635. In October, after which the surviving accounts break off, both shipping and receipts were recovering. For the whole of the contemporary accounting year, 6 October 1635–3 October 1636, the total regular revenues of the city recorded by the chamberlains, most of it derived from shipping dues, fell by only 14 per cent as compared with the previous year.[13]

For Newcastle's maritime trade, then, the plague produced a sharp but temporary slump rather than a total stoppage, and the reason for this is obvious enough: the coal trade was simply too important to the many towns (above all, London) that depended upon fuel supplies from the Tyne for it to be abandoned. Most of the vessels that entered the Tyne in the summer of 1636 came from home ports in East Anglia, with Lynn, Ipswich, and Yarmouth being particularly prominent: the ports most involved in the coastal trade between the Tyne and London. Some of them turn up repeatedly in the chamberlains' accounts making round trips: the *Mayflower* of Ipswich, the *Transportation* of Lynn, and the *Willingmind* of Yarmouth, for example. Others came from ports on the south coast between Dover and Plymouth. A few came each week from ports in Germany, Scandinavia, or the Netherlands: Hamburg, Danzig, Lübeck, Frederickstadt, Christiana, Rotterdam. The great majority arrived in ballast and departed with cargoes of coal, or more occasionally salt. The chamberlains' accounts amply confirm the contention of the Corporation of Saltmakers of North and South Shields, in response to Yarmouth's petition for leave to import foreign salt, that Yarmouth "did willfully neglect the fetching of salt", since, "feare of the sickness" notwithstanding, "the said towne hath bene supplied with Coles from the Shields and also from the very towne of Newcastle where the sicknes hath most bene, and therefore no cause to feare fetching salt more then coles. Nor have the shipping of other ports forborne to fetch salt from the Shields in all this tyme."[14]

All this meant not only a continuing, albeit temporarily diminished, flow of revenue to the city, but also the continued availability of work for at least some of the "shovelmen" and keelmen who loaded the colliers, others engaged in trades dependent on shipping, and those of "the poore" who were routinely paid by the city for "conveying" of ballast at four or five pence a ton to the ballast hills below Sandgate. And there was a further vital dimension to the continuance of trade. Some ships came in loaded with provisions. In August and September, for example, each week saw the landing of malt, "corne", or "freemens rye": the malt from Lynn or Yarmouth; the grain from Lübeck, Essinge, Ornesom, and Burnham. The final week of September even brought "vii barrels aples" from Hamburg. The city was fed.[15]

If Newcastle's coal and salt trades suffered less dislocation than might be imagined, however, a reduction of activity of some 40 per cent between July and September must have spelt privation for many of those customarily employed on the river and about the quay, above all the inhabitants of Allhallows'. And other sectors of the city's economy may have been worse affected. Some trade in provisions must have continued. Bread must have been baked. Beer must have been brewed. The inventory of the baker and brewer Gilbert Hall of Allhallows', who died in early September, included numerous debts owing to him for bowls or bushels of rye, or "for bread", while that of Oswald Fayrealis of St John's parish lists debts he owed for rye and beans bought from five different suppliers.[16] But wider resort to the city's markets presumably dried up as the epidemic spread. There would have been no crowded Saturday markets on Sandhill like the one at which Mark Maslegen heard two fellow glovers quarrelling, or "jarring together", but was uncertain whether the "much moore people" nearby "gave any regard thereunto".[17] There must have been some custom still for the many small master craftsmen of the city – a few were employed about repairs to the Trinity House in late July and early August, for example.[18] But their business would have been hit hard as households retrenched their living costs to essential spending and rural customers ceased to appear. The temporary suspension of entries in the minute and order books of the Shipwrights', Glovers', Saddlers', Cordwainers', Coopers', Goldsmiths', Plumbers', and Glaziers' Guilds might be held to symbolize a general dormancy, if not cessation, of economic activity.[19] The masons' book described them as "disperst in the time of the greate sicknesse". The curriers, feltmakers, and armourers held no meeting after 6 May 1636. And many of these men, and members of their households, were of course rendered economically inactive by sickness and death.[20] It was perhaps such realities that the mayor had most in mind when he later sought relief from the city's Ship Money assessments of 1636 and 1637 on the grounds that the inhabitants' "meanes" were "soe much wasted and decayed by reason and occacon of the heavie visitacon of the plague", and that the "townsmen" were "much impoverished by decay of Trade both in the time of the said sicknes and ever since and thereby disabled to pay the said moneys".[21]

There was, then, more than enough distress to be relieved. The loss of most of the records of city government means that the details of the measures taken in response remain unknown. We do not know whether shipping was confined to areas outside the city itself – though this seems likely, since colliers had always congregated at the mouth of the river where they awaited loading from the keels. We do not know what steps were taken to provision and control the markets, or to distribute the food that is known to have been landed. We do not know whether public assemblies were prohibited (though this was usual in time of plague). We do not know whether medical care for the sick was organized in any way. The Barber-Surgeons' Company minutes show that two ill-attended meetings were held at "Alhallow Church" in May and that a further meeting took place on 13 June at the house of a leading member, George Horsley, "because of the sickness". But they provide no further information, and then break off until regular meetings recommenced on 6 December.[22]

Much remains obscure. But it is clear that the city fathers acted vigorously to preserve their community in at least two respects. First, they provided financial relief. Robert Jenison observed that "*Famine* commonly accompanieth this *Pestilence*, as it did of late yeares most grievously in *Cambridge* [margin: Anno 1630]", and continued that

> it should much more have prevailed with multitudes of the poorer sort among us, were it not that by Gods blessing and the care of our Magistrates in disposing the revenues of our Chamber weekly, in great summes for their reliefe; as also by their and other Inhabitants free loanes, and some good help and assistance made freely by kind neighbours, they were competently provided for; not the sick or infected only, but such as are impoverished through want of imployment in their manuall Crafts and Callings.[23]

The chamberlains' accounts bear this out. If the revenues of the city chamber were down by some 14 per cent in 1635–6, as compared to 1634–5, expenditures were up by some 21 per cent. The difference was accounted for by over 250 pounds described as "moneyes given in charity towards the reliefe of the poore and infected people", and by over a thousand pounds in "loane money" advanced in two loans by "Mr Maior the Aldermen and divers others which they lent towards the reliefe of the infected people".[24] Exactly how this relief was implemented is unknown. But such measures were well advised in a city in which, only three years earlier, simmering resentment against the high-handedness of Newcastle's ruling "inner ring" and their contempt for the freemen's guild had resulted in several days of rioting by "prenteses and men in Sandgate", and in which the large population of labouring people was regarded by the Council of the North as "apt to turn everye pretence and colour of grievance into uproar and seditious mutinye".[25]

The second, and more abundantly documented, of the steps taken by the magistrates was far more controversial: the imposition of quarantine or, as Jenison put it, "keeping the unclean from the cleane".[26] According to contemporary theory, the plague originated in a "miasma" of putrefied air which might be occasioned by particular conjunctions of the stars acting in concert with the "noisome stench" arising from filth, squalor, and decay. At the same time, however, it spread by "contagion": close personal contact with the infected.[27] If the former risk could be reduced by keeping the streets free of accumulations of decaying matter, and combated by efforts to exclude or disperse noxious vapours, the latter could be avoided by the isolation of the infected.[28] In consequence, the national plague orders of 1578 laid down that infected houses should be shut up for a period of six weeks, with all members of the affected household – sick and healthy alike – confined together. This was a controversial policy: as early as 1583, the London authorities complained that too strict an isolation of households – "the sound and infected together" – might serve "rather to increase than decrease the infection" among those so confined. But it was retained right through until the last major English epidemic of the 1660s.[29] In addition, some cities, including Newcastle, also adopted the policy of isolating some of the sick in houses, sheds, or "booths" outside the city walls.[30]

In 1636, Newcastle adopted both forms of isolation. From around mid-June, there are references in the deposition evidence to houses being "shutt" or "shutt upp for suspicion of the plague" in the Sandgate and quayside areas. At about that time, Phillip Doncaster, the elderly curate of Allhallows', "his house being infected with the plague removed himself his goods and family out of his then dwelling house in to another house" in Pilgrim Street. But it was a short respite, for he was soon "spared up" in his new dwelling, presumably by having wooden spars nailed across the door. (The churchwardens of Allhallows' even went so far as to order the nailing up of the "great stair door" of their churchyard to seal off the infected houses on the stairs leading down to the quay.)[31] Thereafter, from July through to September, there are frequent descriptions of the circumstances of confined households in Allhallows', St Nicholas', and St John's parishes in the form of the expedients resorted to by dying householders anxious to make their wills. Ambrose Blatteram was able to hear Edward Holmes "speake through the . . . dore" of his house by "lyeing his head nere unto the said dore". Clement Curry's last wishes were relayed "by and from his wives mouth" to witnesses "standing before his dore and his wife near to the same dore". Many others were obliged to "declare their minds", either directly or via an intermediary, "through a case-ment", "speakinge . . . through the window", or "out of a chamber window", to witnesses standing in the street.[32]

How tightly these houses were "shutt upp" is not always clear.[33] One of Edward Holmes' servants later testified that she had seen Thomas Jackson writing down Holmes' will before the witnesses "through the dore of the said house, which she opened and looked att them". Perhaps it was barred, to prevent exit, but could be opened inwards to permit the taking in of provisions. This was the case in a later Newcastle outbreak during which the apprentice Ambrose Barnes, after the flight of his master and the death of two maids, remained "shut up in an empty large house near the Exchange, without any living creature besides himself, but they rapt at the door when they brought him meat, and he himself came and took it in".[34] Margaret Ridley was "shutt upp" in "her house nere the key side", but she was able to get out through "a backe door opening [into] a chaire called Trinity Chaire", which gave her the opportunity to rail at her neighbour Jerard Stevenson "and say that he was the cause of shutting up of her house", adding "that she would have a fore dore and a back dore to goe in and out when he should not have one of his owne". This was reported by Stevenson's servant Margaret Sharp, who, "being att her said Maisters dore replied and said that she did him much wronge".[35]

Others were more closely confined. When Margaret Hyndmers was sent for on 8 September to be the "keeper" of the merchant John Stobbs, "being a widower and havinge noe body in his house", she "knocked att the dore", but he "spoke to her out of a chamber and told her that he was not able to come and open the dore but willed her to goe to a smith and get his helpe to put her in att a window of the same house, which she did accordinglie".[36] Even within quarantine houses, there could be another form of separation. When several members of a household were confined together, efforts seem to have been made to isolate the sick. It is striking that in those depositions that specify the precise location of sick or dying people, they were

11. An old house on Tudhill Stairs, photographed before demolition *c*.1885. The barred door gives a sense of how houses might have appeared when "spar[r]ed up".

most commonly in an upper "chamber", though inventories indicate that beds were to be found in parlours as well as chambers. Ann Mills, for example, was "lyeinge in a high chamber" in a house in Sandgate which also contained her uncle and aunt, John and Margaret Humphrey, and a servant, Isobel Love, who we are told "did goe upp and downe", presumably to attend to Ann.[37] And wills, as we have seen, were often spoken, or relayed, from upper rooms. That is why Ralph Tailor and his companions mounted the city wall on 8 August, the better to hear Thomas Holmes "looking forth at the window" (probably of the "loft" identified in Holmes' inventory) and "speakinge through the same". When Ralph was called eleven days later to write the will of Robert Moore, he found him isolated in an upper chamber.[38] To judge by surviving inventories of rooms, the relatively small two-storey houses occupied by most of the city's households provided little scope for the separation of the "sound" and the "infected"; but where possible, it seems to have been attempted.[39]

Meanwhile, by August at the latest, some of the sick were being isolated in "lodges nere unto the towne". (In fact, they were "on the Towne Moore of Newcastle", to the north of the city.) It is not clear whether those confined there were drawn from particular areas of the city, or whether their removal to the lodges was voluntary or in some way enforced. Nor is there any indication of how many people passed through them, or died in them. But some details at least are recorded. First, the lodges were quite substantial. There were at least ten sick people housed in the lodge where Jane Young died in late September: Jane, Phyllis Wilkinson, who witnessed her will and lived to tell the tale, and "eight other persons then presente in the same lodge". Second, they were staffed by "watchmen" and "clensers", who were presumably employed by the city, and by some privately hired "keepers". One of the watchmen "putt into writeinge" the will of Anthony Robson in early August, and it was then "kept by one of the clensers", before finally being delivered to Anthony's heir by his keeper and another surviving inmate of the lodges "after they were well", upon "ther coming home".[40]

Whether the measures taken by the city authorities can be deemed a success is an open question. On the one hand, the vital coal trade, and with it employment, was sustained, albeit at a temporarily much reduced level. The city was fed. Relief was provided for the "poorer sort", which Jenison clearly regarded as a significant achievement, and there are no reports of breakdowns of order in the city. There is also evidence to suggest that the quarantine measures imposed by the magistrates and by neighbouring authorities may have inhibited the spread of infection into the city's hinterland. Gateshead was badly hit, as we have seen, but principally in June and July, and burials subsided there long before they did so in Newcastle.[41] Of the other immediately neighbouring settlements, Benwell, to the west of the city, was also seriously affected.[42] Beyond that, the epidemic appears to have been contained. Surviving burial registers for parishes upriver to Whickham and Ryton, downriver to Jarrow and Tynemouth, and south to Chester-le-Street provide no indication of unusually elevated mortality in 1636.[43] Testamentary evidence in the form of wills or depositions referring explicitly to plague deaths in 1636, so abundant for Newcastle, is rare elsewhere: two cases from Gateshead and two from South Shields; one each from Tynemouth, Chester-le-Street, Washington, and distant Corbridge and Haltwhistle. More striking is the flurry of cases from central Northumberland a year later in the summer and autumn of 1637.[44] Such evidence, like the burst of plague burials in Bishopwearmouth (Sunderland) in April–May 1637, or the anxiety of the Durham magistrates over plague deaths in Durham and Whickham in 1638, represents the sporadic fall-out of the great Newcastle epidemic of 1636 rather than the engulfing of the Tyneside region to which it might have led.[45]

All this can be deemed evidence of the success of the Newcastle magistrates in meeting the challenge posed by an epidemic of unprecedented ferocity. At the same time, however, the disease and the measures they took to contain it must have transformed their city. A town that stood at the very centre of the economy and society of a large region had become a relatively separated space: access to the city reduced and controlled; the movements of its citizens restricted. It was not "a solitude" of the kind sometimes imagined.[46] Most of the inhabitants of the city still lived and clung to life. But as the infection spread, the normal rhythms and patterns of daily life must have been drastically disrupted and recast into a new routine of survival, marked by anxiety and watchfulness.

The streets cannot have been deserted. People still needed to move around to obtain food and drink, to find work if it was available, or carry out other necessary business. Some tradesmen's shops remained open. People still conversed with one another, however briefly, sought "to acquaint" one another with news, and recalled "hearing that" this or that person was sick. They "sent for" one another and, when called in this way, they responded.[47] But it is likely that the usual bustle of the streets and chares was much reduced, and unlikely that women any longer sat at their doors working, as Elizabeth Veach, Ellen Bates, and Jane Dobson had done one Monday in February 1633, all "spinning at the doore of Elizabeth", while Jane Dodds looked on, "standing att her doore about two houses distant".[48] Thresholds then spelt safety, not danger. The dominant image of the plague depositions, in contrast, is that of people looking out of doors and windows at small knots of anxious friends and neighbours gathered in the street. And if, as we have seen, some two-thirds of the households of St John's parish suffered at least one plague death, and were therefore likely to have been "shutt upp" at one time or another during the summer and autumn of 1636, then it is not difficult to imagine how streets which had been places of resort and engagement, spaces into which the activities of households and workshops spilled, became instead mere passageways through a townscape of enclosure and separation. They must have smelled different, reeking with the acrid stench of burning pitch, and near the churches, the odour of congested graveyards daily reopened in the hot summer sun. They must have sounded different too: quieter, their ambient clamour reduced, save for the more frequent tolling of the church bells, and the crying of the gulls on the river, audible only when the city is still.

CHAPTER FIVE

Sent For to Write

O NE OF THOSE WHO MOVED THROUGH THIS TOWNSCAPE OF confinement and separation in the summer and early autumn of 1636 was Ralph Tailor. Thomas Finlay, a thirty-six-year-old weaver, "beinge standing at his owne dore", saw him coming up the street on the morning of Thursday, 19 August, together with Michael Moore. And "going by him they desired [him] to accompany them" to the house of Michael's father, Robert Moore, "whoe then lay sick of the plague as they told [him]". Thomas did so, without question, and acted as a witness of Robert's will.[1]

All in all, between 31 May and 5 November 1636, Ralph Tailor wrote at least fourteen of the fifty-seven wills of plague victims that survive for the city. By then he had also written a couple of inventories of the goods of people who had died in the epidemic, and in the succeeding months he wrote nine more (a total of eleven out of forty-six surviving "plague" inventories).[2] His hand is visible in almost a quarter of the surviving probate documents generated by the plague, and it is, of course, the very frequency with which his name recurs in these records that draws one's attention to him.[3]

Ralph Tailor's sheer presence in the surviving probate records of the epidemic is striking. No other known writer of wills (several of whom were, like him, professional scriveners) was responsible for more than three.[4] And if we look at the evidence in another way, his activity becomes more remarkable still. Of the fifty-nine plague victims whose wills and/or inventories survive, Tailor was involved in the affairs of twenty (just over a third). Of those who lived in Allhallows' parish, he was involved with exactly half.[5]

As this implies, most of his work was done within the parish of Allhallows', and in particular its Sandgate and Quayside districts, with occasional forays across Sandhill and The Side and up the precipitous stairs leading to St Nicholas' or St John's. Precise locations are rarely given, but to some extent we can track him across the city. He first appears on 31 May, writing the will of William Grame of Allhallows', "skipper", "visited with the plague of pestilence"; the second identifiable plague will to survive.[6] Four weeks later, on 28 June, he wrote the fifth surviving plague will, made "by word of mouth nuncupatively" by Ann Carr, widow, "daughter and heire of Thomas Cooke, carpenter", who owned a house in "Plummer al[ia]s Beverley Chaire", a narrow alley running up from the quay.[7] There then follows a long gap of forty days before Ralph reappears on 8 August, "sent for" by Hugh Ridley, servant of Thomas Holmes and, as we have seen, "going to his house and standinge upon the townes wall of Newcastle adioyning of the key nere the river", together with Hugh Ridley and John Hunter, to make Thomas' will.[8] This dramatic reappearance prefaced one of Ralph's busiest fortnights. The epidemic was now at its peak, having engulfed the whole city, and he wrote four of the twelve wills surviving for the period 8–22 August. He also stepped outside Allhallows', being the probable scribe of the will of a St John's cordwainer on 16 August, and being fetched by Michael Moore three days later, as we have seen, to attend Robert Moore, house carpenter, in St Nicholas' parish. He was back in Allhallows' on the 22nd, writing the nuncupative will of Cuthbert Woodman, weaver, "his house being infected with the plague and being at that time sicke thereof himselfe".[9] A further gap of twenty-six days ensues until, on 18 September, we find a particularly florid example of Ralph's signature at the foot of the will of Matthew Storey, an Allhallows' miller.[10] The epidemic was subsiding now, but Ralph remained busy. He wrote six of the twelve wills surviving for the period from 18 September to 18 October, mostly in Allhallows', but one, that of Ralph Rowmaine, in St John's.[11] On 10 October, he had revisited the house of Thomas Holmes, after its "clenseing", to prepare the inventory of Thomas' goods; from 18 October, most of his recorded activity involved the listing and appraisal of the goods of plague victims, usually in Allhallows', but once each in St John's and St Nicholas' (he was back at Robert Moore's house on 24 November) and on two occasions in St Andrew's.[12] He wrote one more will, however, on 5 November. It was that of Robert Mallabar, a barber-surgeon of St Nicholas' parish, "visited with sore sicknesse" in the final stages of the epidemic. It is the last will to survive from the plague of 1636.[13] But it was not Ralph Tailor's last known plague will. Almost exactly a year later, as we have seen, he wrote the will of a subsequent plague victim, William Pringle of "Ousebarn", accompanied, as it happens, by Jerard Stevenson, Pringle's business partner and the man allegedly responsible for having Margaret Ridley's house shut up in 1636.[14]

Ralph Tailor, then, wrote both the second and the last of the surviving wills occasioned by the epidemic of 1636. He enters the record at the beginning and he was there still at the end. He did more (much more) than any other individual to create that record. And yet, of course, it remains incomplete. Court depositions made during subsequent litigation, for example, describe the making of seven wills that do not survive, and the court records themselves are fragmentary.[15] We can be sure, then, that some of the wills made during the plague of 1636 have been lost. But we have no way of establishing exactly how many. No master source exists that can resolve this problem. There is no register containing copies of wills proved in the Durham courts for the 1630s. The Probate Act Book for the years 1635–8 survives and contains the names of many Newcastle people whose estates entered probate in the aftermath of the plague: 280 in all for the period October 1636 to December 1637 (four-fifths of them initially entered between October 1636 and June 1637). Yet many of these people had not made wills; they included intestates whose next-of-kin were granted the administration of their estates. And of those who might be presumed to have done so from the terminology of the entries, we cannot be sure how many were actually plague victims. Many must have been. Others were definitely not, for there is evidence of their survival into 1637. Without the independent evidence provided by a will, inventory, administrator's account, court deposition, or parish register entry, one cannot be certain, and all of these sources are deficient. Moreover, the record provided by the Act Book is itself incomplete. Though there are no significant gaps in the foliation between September 1636 and March 1637/8, there are eight known plague victims for whom wills and/or inventories survive whose names do not appear in the book, and in addition probate bonds entered into by those responsible for the administration of estates survive for a dozen people who are also absent from its pages. These missing cases were presumably dealt with elsewhere on an *ad hoc* basis and never entered up in the Act Book of the probate court. In sum, we have no way of knowing just how many wills were made during the plague of 1636, what proportion of the documents created has been lost, or what Ralph Tailor's role may have been in their creation.[16]

What we do have, however, is the record of Ralph Tailor's exceptional level of activity as set down in the many documents that *do* survive, and this can scarcely be illusory. To be sure, it contains some mysteries, notably that of the gaps in his recorded presence. Some of these may be occasioned simply by accidents of survival. He produced three to five surviving documents a month from the second week of August through to November, and the relatively brief hiatus in late August and early September is perhaps unlikely to have been significant. But where was he in the six weeks between 28 June and 8 August? Had he left the city temporarily as the scale and violence of the epidemic became apparent? Perhaps; but if so, why would he return when it was at its very peak? Does he appear more frequently after 8 August simply because in that week John Carr, the principal notary public of Allhallows' parish, fell sick and died? Undoubtedly, this may have increased the need for Ralph's services, but he had already been almost as active as Carr, and he was never the sole scrivener available in the parish.[17] A third possibility is that during this period he was himself sick, or at least shut up in an infected house, and that he survived and returned to work in the second week of August. The period of forty days' absence from the record makes this an intriguing possibility. But all this is speculation. What the record tells us is that for a period of almost six months Ralph Tailor frequently attended the dying to write their wills, usually in Allhallows' parish, where he probably lived, sometimes elsewhere: that he went where the infection was raging, to houses that were shut up and where inhabitants not yet afflicted lived in the shadow of fear.

Robert Jenison was to write vividly of how "the noysomnesse and contagion" of the plague "makes a man a stranger to his own house, to his dearest friends; yea, as it were an enemie to them, and an instrument of death to wife, children, friends; and it deprives a man of comforters in his greatest agonie and need".[18] There is certainly evidence of that. People feared contagion and acted accordingly. Witnesses of nuncupative wills conventionally recalled how they came "as nigh unto his doore as the[y] durst adventure", "as near to her house as he durst", or "as neare as he durst he then lyeing sicke of the plague". Thomas Hayton's will, delivered from a window on 8 July, remained unsigned "because [William Haynes] and thother witnesses durst not goe into the house to him". Some testators clearly understood this. John Stobbs sent for Robert Jopling to "desire him to bring two or three neighbors and come soe nere to his house as they durst" to hear "a true particular of his goods". Edward Holmes asked only that William Jackson "come as neer his house as he durst". Robert Walker, "sitting in his chayre", relayed his wishes via an intermediary at the window to the scribe outside, "being not able to speake unto him through the window without the danger of his health".[19]

Ralph Tailor must have known such fear, but clearly it did not prevent him from hearing and recording the nuncupative wills of dying plague victims far more frequently than any other identifiable scribe. No doubt he too usually kept a prudent distance from the infected, as with Thomas Holmes. But on at least one occasion he was willing to brave an infected house. On 19 August, called to attend to Robert Moore, he and Thomas Finlay entered the house, while Michael Moore apparently remained outside, and went "into the next roomthe where [Robert] then lay", "they standing then in one chamber and the said Testator then lyeing in the next chamber". Then, as Ralph later described it, "after he heard this examinant speake, well knoweing his voice, [Robert] desired this examinant to comitt that to writeinge which he then delivered to hym by worde of mouth through a wall [deleted] partition of dales" (deals: fir or pine boards). He was as certain of Robert's identity as Robert was of his, "well knowinge his voice and tonnge, although he did not then see him"; and "perceiving him to be of perfect mynde and memory", he took down his wishes. It is not difficult to imagine this scene. It was ten o'clock on a Thursday morning. Robert lay in what his inventory called the "upper hall", probably in the great bedstead that dominated the room and surrounded by the best furniture in the house: a wainscot table and chair, two other chairs, a dresser, and a "carpitt cloth". Ralph and Thomas were in "the Chamber" next door, which contained a small bedstead, several "trundle" beds, a "spyning wheele", and a miscellany of other goods. There was a stool and a chest close by it; perhaps Ralph sat down there to write the thirty-six lines of the will. They stayed until the will was written and read back through the wooden partition to Robert, "the which they heard him acknowledge well knowinge his voice". Then Thomas made his mark, Ralph signed his name, and they departed.[20] How long would all this have taken? Medical opinion held that a person might stay in an infected house for half an hour at most, but only if he was not afraid, since fear undermined the body's resistance to infection. Thomas and Ralph both lived to tell their story. Perhaps, as the physicians advised, they had learned to control their fear.[21]

Many did not. Fear was a legitimate response to plague, and the most effective way of avoiding contagion was to shun the sick or – better still – to flee the infected city. Robert Jenison acknowledged that "the common rule of the world, as also of *Physicians* in case of Pestilence, is to flee, or to withdraw a mans selfe *quickly* from places infected". He argued, like many other authors of plague tracts, that to flee the plague could be "lawfull, yea necessary, where and so far as mens callings, especially publicke, will permit them". How far "Ministers who take themselves charged with cure of soules . . . may withdraw themselves in case of grievous and raging Pestilence" he left "to casuists and their owne consciences to determin". He was notably open-minded on the question of "How far a minister being merely a lecturer may flee": "how farr such an one having otherwise no pastorall charge, may both with faith and a good conscience, during apparent hazard to his person, withdraw himself, and so reserve himselfe to better times, meerely out of respect to their good, who for the present seeme a while neglected." But as a lecturer himself, he left this to others' judgment, "least in mine owne case I may seeme too partial" – adding, however, that on this issue his own behaviour had "been as much, if not more guided by the judgement, yea importunitie also of many godly and unpartial Christians (and so, I take, by direction from God) then by mine owne, either judgement, or will at the first".[22]

The implication of this masterpiece of self-serving cant is clearly that Jenison had in fact fled the city and "reserve[d] himselfe to better times".[23] How far others did so is less clear. Of the other clergy, nothing is known of the whereabouts of Jenison's great rival, Yeldard Alvey, the vicar of St Nicholas'.[24] Philip Doncaster, curate of Allhallows', removed to another house within the city, as we have seen, but was soon "spared up" there and died about Michaelmas.[25]

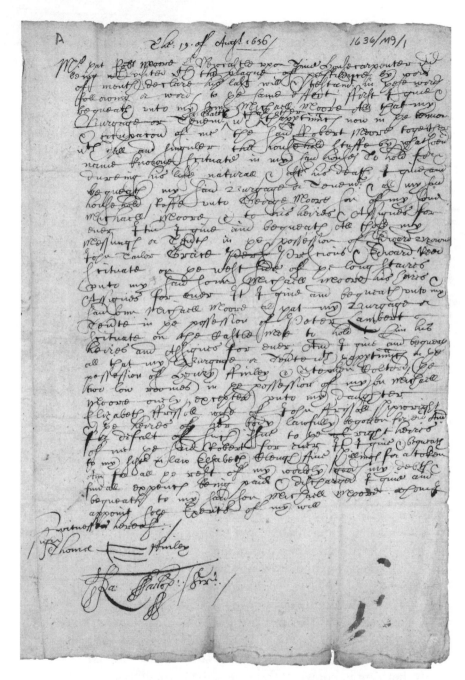

12. The will of Robert Moore, dictated by Moore to Ralph Tailor "by worde of mouth" through a wooden partition on 19 August 1636. Ralph remembered "well knowinge his voice and tonnge, although he did not then see him".

Christopher Foster, curate of St Nicholas', stayed, signing the pages of the burial register, and on two occasions witnessing the wills of sick parishioners. He survived. The baptismal register of St Andrew's for April to July 1636 contains a note by the parish clerk that the entries were added from "notes in my hand after the dethe of the prest wich I did find", suggesting that the curate of St Andrew's may have died in the epidemic, or just before it.[26] The city's magistrates clearly remained at their posts, but some of Newcastle's dominant "inner ring" already lived outside the city and therefore had nearby places of retreat, and it is possible that some of the city's leaders were able to discharge their duties by periodic visits rather than by remaining within the walls. Not one of them is known to have died.[27] What is certain is that many of the wealthier families withdrew themselves altogether as the epidemic broke out of Sandgate and approached the central districts where they lived. One of the reasons that the mayor later gave for the failure of the city to levy Ship Money in 1636–7 was that "during all [that] time the best sort of the now surviving inhabitants remained with theyre families altogether in the countrie and not in the said Towne".[28] One wonders whether the epidemic had less impact in St Nicholas' because a significant proportion of houses in that parish had been vacated. In a sense, the city may have been socially truncated, becoming, in the absence of "the best sort", a society composed primarily of the "middling" freemen and of the labouring poor. For most people could not flee. They had nowhere to go. They had to make such a living as they still could. And Ralph Tailor also remained. He had not been born in the city, as we will see, but it had become his world. It was where he had a role. He stayed, and when he was sent for, he wrote, as was his calling.

CHAPTER SIX

Liveing a Scrivener in the Same Towne

PEOPLE SEEM TO HAVE KNOWN RALPH TAILOR. THEY RECOGNIZED him in the street. They alluded to him familiarly by name alone, apparently without feeling the need to add further identification. Robert Moore knew his voice well. Many others knew where to send for him. He was trusted and relied upon.

We cannot know him as they did. There is no description of his appearance. (Was he fair or dark, lean or stocky, short or tall?) No one mentioned what he wore. (Did he own more than one suit of clothing? Did he wear a cap or a hat?) We do not even know exactly where he lived. Few details of his life are documented. Yet it is still possible to learn something of him from the "instruments" he wrote and the evidence he gave in 1636–7. By following these clues, and those provided by other records of his career, a sense of both the man and the early experiences that made him can be recovered.

He was young. In February and May 1637, testifying before the Consistory Court of Durham, he gave his age as twenty-six.[1] He later stated that he had been born in the parish of St Margaret's in the suburbs of the city of Durham, thirteen miles to the south of Newcastle.[2] St Margaret's still stands on the hill above Framwellgate Bridge, directly across the river Wear from Durham Castle, and his baptism was indeed recorded there on 13 January 1610/11: "Radulphus Tayler filius Thoma"; Ralph Tayler, son of Thomas. (Variant spellings of surnames – Tayler/Taylor/Tailor, etc. – are of course usual in this period, though in adult life Ralph always spelled his name "Tailor".) In May 1636, then, when the plague broke out in Newcastle, he was twenty-five years and four months old.[3]

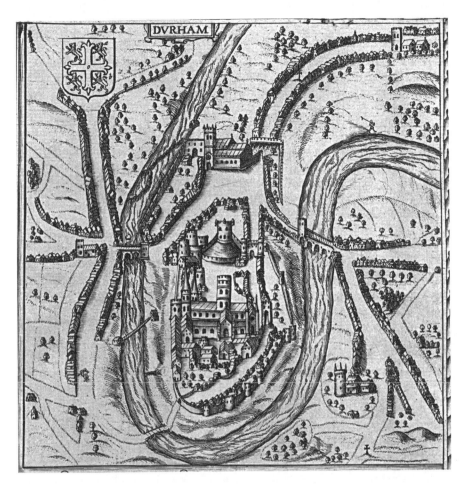

13. The City of Durham, *c.*1610. St Margaret's church, where Ralph Tailor was baptized in 1611, is shown on the left, above the bridge beneath Durham Castle.

Only a little can be discovered of his immediate family. There were many "Taylers" in Durham at the turn of the seventeenth century, with branches well established not only in St Margaret's but also in St Nicholas' parish and in Gilesgate, but I have not been able to connect Ralph's father directly to them. Thomas Tayler does not appear to have been either baptized or married in Durham. Presumably he came to the city as a married man at some time before 1604. His family was demographically unfortunate. A daughter, Isabel, and a son, Edward, were baptized in St Margaret's in 1604 and 1605 respectively, both of whom were also buried in the parish within eighteen months of their baptisms. Two more children, Ann and Thomas, neither of whom was baptized in St Margaret's, were buried there in October and November 1619, and Thomas' wife, Anne, was also buried in November 1619. The reason for this flurry of deaths in Thomas' family remains obscure (there are no signs of an epidemic in the parish in 1619). But whatever the cause, Ralph Tailor lost his mother and two siblings at the age of eight. His father, Thomas, was buried in St Margaret's on 13 September 1627, leaving no will or inventory that might cast further light upon his occupation, his family, or his circumstances. Ralph was by then close to seventeen; but it is likely that by this time he had already left his home city.[4]

In the evidence he gave to the Consistory Court in February and May 1637, Ralph was routinely asked how long he had known the parties to the cases in which he was involved. Those he had known longest were the son and daughter of Robert Moore, both of whom he had been acquainted with for "ten years and more". This would have placed him in Newcastle in 1626–7. In a deposition made in an Exchequer case in January 1650, he stated that he had known the complainants, "the maior and Burgesses of Newcastle upon Tyne", "by the space of twenty fower yeares last past and upwards". This would have put him in Newcastle in 1626, or even 1625.[5] One should not perhaps take such statements too literally, but since Ralph got his own age right on both occasions, one can have some confidence in his estimates. It seems likely, then, that he came to Newcastle in 1626 or thereabouts, at the age of fifteen.

The reason for his coming is obvious enough – to be apprenticed. The precise circumstances of this "advancement", as contemporaries would have put it, remain unknown; but there are grounds for reasoned speculation. He was not the only Ralph Tailor in St Margaret's parish in the 1620s. "Raph Taler" senior, of Crossgate, within St Margaret's, was a tanner of considerable means who had been born in the rural parish of Kirk Merrington to the south of the city and had himself come to Durham (initially to Gilesgate) as an apprentice. In his will of 1634, he honoured the request of his son Miles, who had died young in 1629, to be "loving and assisting" to Miles' two small daughters and his son, Raph junior, who had been born in 1624. Raph senior left each of his grandchildren a portion of a hundred pounds, specifying that in the case of young Raph the money should be "putt forwards . . . for his better advancement" by his uncle John. John was also charged to "have a care of his educacon in a godlie and religious manner until he come to competent yeares and then to putt him apprentice to some trade wherto he shall then stand best affected".[6] If Thomas Tayler was in fact a poorer kinsman, as well as a neighbour, of Raph Taler senior, then it is not unlikely that he named his own son Ralph after him, and that Raph Taler senior was Ralph Tailor's godfather. If so, given the kind of aspirations he had for his own grandson, he might also have helped sponsor Ralph's education and apprenticeship, either financially or by activating his connections.[7]

Alternatively, or additionally, there were Taylers enough in Newcastle, especially in the parish of Allhallows', and some of them were connected to the Talers of Durham. John Tayler senior, a butcher who owned property in Coleman Chare, Allhallows', died in 1617 and left a house in Durham to his younger son, Thomas, sending the boy there to be "brought upp during his minoritye" by his uncle George, a Durham glover. An older son, John, remained in Newcastle. Ralph Tailor was later to have a particular connection to the Butchers' Company of Newcastle, of which one John Tailor was steward in 1637–8. They may possibly have been kinsmen.[8]

Thus we have Taylers in Durham and in Allhallows', Newcastle, who were tanners, butchers, and glovers: connected trades, and perhaps connected families. But Ralph Tailor became a scrivener, a relatively unusual occupation. One more link can be suggested. The will of John Tayler senior was written by William Jackson, a Newcastle notary public who lived in The Side, and who was about forty-four years old in 1617. He was still alive in 1637. William Jackson's professional signature, of which several examples survive, was strikingly similar to that of Ralph Tailor in its employment of swirling loops, slanted slightly to the left, beneath several letters of his name. Indeed, the similarity is so pronounced that it seems to me more than likely that Ralph Tailor learned his trade from William Jackson, and that in this respect at least he adopted the style of his master. Moreover, William Jackson was not only the scribe of John Tayler senior's will; he is also identified within the will as "my cossin".[9] The Taylers of Newcastle and Durham and the notary William Jackson were kin.

In this, or in some similar way, then, Ralph Tailor came to Newcastle, and there he became a scrivener. What did that mean? A scrivener was a "maker of instruments"; an "instrument" being

defined by William West, author of a contemporary guide to the
duties of scriveners and notaries, as "a formall writing, rightlie
ordained and made in paper or parchment comprehending those
things that be covenanted or contracted betweene persons for testimonie or memories sake . . . to the end the things therein comprised
might both more certainlie be kept in memorie and moore easilie to
be prooved".[10] It was an ancient calling, as West pointed out, but one
increasingly necessary in the burgeoning commercial economy of the
period in which greater numbers of transactions were taking place,
and in which they were often conducted over longer distances.[11]
People were increasingly likely to need to employ legal instruments
on a regular basis: bills, bonds, indentures, conveyances, wills, and
the rest. They "lived in a matrix of parchment and paper".[12] This
commercial quickening was a major reason for the growth of popular
literacy in the later sixteenth and seventeenth centuries, especially
among the tradesmen, craftsmen, and commercial farmers who were
most likely to feel the need to be able to read and write. In the diocese
of Durham, for example, literacy among craftsmen and tradesmen, as
measured by their ability to sign their names to court depositions,
improved from just 16 per cent in the 1560s to 50 per cent by the

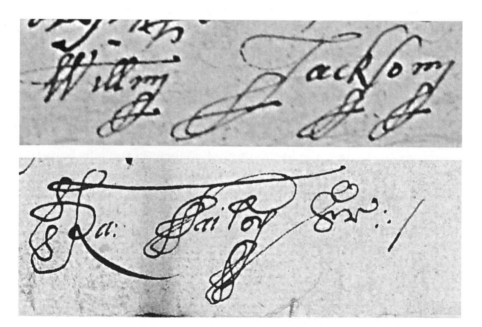

14. The signatures of William Jackson and Ralph Tailor.

1620s.[13] Nevertheless, many such people remained unable to write. Of those who could write, many may have lacked the knowledge and skill needed to draft a legal instrument; and of those who had the necessary knowledge and skill, especially in great trading centres like Newcastle, many were simply too busy to do the job themselves. They needed the services of specialists.

In consequence, most of these documents were prepared by scriveners, and accordingly the numbers of professional penmen grew from the later sixteenth century, though they were rarely sufficiently numerous in provincial cities to be organized in specialist guilds.[14] Whether Ralph Tailor had conceived the ambition to be apprenticed as a scrivener before he left Durham is unknown, but it seems unlikely to have been a random choice. Perhaps he had already shown some aptitude for such a career during his early schooling in Durham. One suspects so. But the final decision may have come later. Scriveners had to serve an apprenticeship for seven years.[15] Yet Ralph was not admitted as a freeman of the city until 1636, which means that his apprenticeship probably began late in 1628.[16] If he had been in the city since 1626 or thereabouts, then he may have spent a year or two acquiring the necessary skills at the town's grammar school (an adequate grounding in Latin was needed for handling documents in that language) and more specifically at the writing school maintained by the freemen "for the training of youth to handle the pen by fairewriting".[17]

At the writing school Ralph would have honed and extended such writing skills as he had already acquired: how to make ink from lamp black ground with "gumme water" and to preserve it in an inkhorn; how to choose a quill and cut a good pen; how best to hold the pen, sitting upright, "your breast from the board", and to guide it with "a sweet command of hand", forming and joining the letters with consistency of size and distance, varying the pressure on the pen, lifting it only at appropriate moments, and avoiding "spatter". He would have become familiar, through the use of "copy book" models, with the formal hands of the period, above all "secretary hand", "the only usuall hand of England, for dispatching of all manner of business". All this constituted "the commendable manner of faire and orderly *writing*, which ought in all businesse to be observed, as well in keeping of Books for Merchants and others, as in all kinds of Engrossments".[18] In his master's house, he would subsequently have gained, by instruction and repeated copying, "perfect knowledge and understanding of all things which are in any sort incident to the making of instruments": the law relating to contracts, covenants, and estates, and "the usuall form of all manner of instruments and the faire and comely writing thereof". (William West provided definitions and examples of trusts, mortgages, leases, surrenders, releases, acquittances, indentures, wills, conditional bonds – including "A Condition to carie coales" – and literally dozens of other instruments that a scrivener might be called upon to prepare.)[19] He would have learned by observation the usual good practice of preparing a "schedule" of the chief points to be included in an instrument, going over them with the parties, engrossing it neatly, having it read (or, if a party was illiterate, reading it aloud), and then seeing it signed, sealed, and delivered (delivery involving the parties' acknowledgment of the transaction by words or symbolic acts).[20]

If he did indeed serve his apprenticeship in the house of a notary public such as William Jackson, Ralph may also have conceived the ambition to rise beyond the role of a mere scrivener. In England, notaries did not have the unique standing accorded them in the legal systems of continental Europe, where they were the only scribes "authorized to produce official records that would be deemed authoritative in a law court", and were required in consequence to maintain registers of their "notarial acts".[21] English common law did not require instruments to be produced by a professional writer: they could be prepared by anyone capable of doing so, and their validity depended on their seals and signatures and the testimony of the witnesses to the transaction recorded.[22] Nevertheless, many legal instruments were in fact prepared by scriveners, as we have seen, and, among scriveners, those appointed notaries public had a more specialized role and enjoyed superior status. Notaries were appointed by the granting of an episcopal faculty (authorization by a bishop), after evidence had been provided of an individual's sobriety of life, training, and competence, and the taking of an oath promising the faithful performance of his duties. Certain officers of the ecclesiastical courts (which employed civil law procedures) were required to be notaries and certain documents used in these courts needed a notary's authentication. Moreover, notaries virtually monopolized the preparation of instruments exhibited in another important jurisdiction: that of the Admiralty Courts, which dealt with ships and shipping matters and also used civil law forms. (Such a court met every Monday afternoon in Newcastle's Guildhall.)[23]

The latter privilege meant that while scriveners (and notaries) were deeply involved in the facilitation of domestic trade, notaries had a peculiarly important role in providing documents used in shipping and in international trade. They wrote bills of lading, agreements to charter ships, "bills of bottomry" (by which shipmasters could borrow against the success of their next voyage), "protests" recording failures to pay, "bills of exchange" facilitating payment at a distance, memoranda of verbal agreements, and other instruments. Moreover, they acted as brokers between English and foreign merchants, and (like some scriveners) they also engaged in moneylending.[24] Notaries, then, had a greater range of business than mere scriveners, and greater opportunities to diversify their activities and to prosper accordingly. The inventory of the notary public John Carr of Pandon in Allhallows' parish, who died in August 1636, provides a flavour of this. At the time of his death he was owed almost 180 pounds by over forty individuals. Some of these debts were "for writings" or "for drawing writings", but most were simply listed as due "by bill" for unspecified services, or (in the case of larger sums) "by bond". He was also owed rents, and had been dealing in fish and in "brick tiles".[25] The role of a notary could open many doors.

Ralph Tailor knew John Carr's business activities, as we will see, and in the course of his apprenticeship he would have encountered other Newcastle scriveners and notaries active at the time: Anthony Norman, who had been John Carr's master; Thomas Clarke, who had succeeded Carr as Norman's apprentice, and later moved to South Shields;[26] Lactantius Sands, aged thirty-five in 1633, who was often employed by the merchant Mr Ralph Brandling "in drawing bonds, dedds, and other writings and was verie often tymes present and did see him write his name to divers bonds and other writings and namelie to tenn bonds at once", and so could verify the signature on Brandling's will; Francis Slinger, ten years older and a notary, who wrote Brandling's will before his departure "to travall in forraine countries . . . in caise it should please god to dispose so of him that he should not returne againe".[27] The young apprentice may have observed their conduct, admired their successes, and learned from their mistakes. Did he know that in 1627 Francis Slinger had been accused of omitting a legacy from a will that he had written; an accusation that Slinger firmly denied, though to his embarrassment he was forced to admit in court that "he doth not now remember the contents thereof"?[28] And if he learned most by constructive or cautionary example, he may also have imbibed, from the works of reference that he studied, the elements of an occupational culture.

Authors of books setting out the forms of legal instruments tended to stress how they contributed to harmony and peace. William West went so far as to compare covenants and obligations to the blood of living creatures which "by the helpe of vaines and artires is conveied and spread abroad through the whole bodie giving life and narishment to everie speciall part and member thereof". The men who prepared them had been deemed "honest and honorable" by the ancients: "whereupon I thinke our scrivener ought to be . . . prudente and just", exhibiting "memorie, understanding and foresight", and "a constant and perpetual wil to render unto everie man his own right". He need not be morally perfect, but if he was "skilfull, diligent, moderate and secret" he would succeed in the "wise, discreet, and sincere executing of his office".[29] This was a particular variant on the set of values that should ideally be inculcated in all apprentices, and that served as an introduction to the distinctive civic culture of the freemen of England's "city commonwealths", with its stress on skill, diligence, honesty, civility, and discretion, the fostering of fellowship and sociability, the maintenance of Christian charity among "brethren" and their families, and the "widespread conviction that persons needed to earn, deserve, and fit themselves to their place" within the civic community.[30]

Ralph Tailor formally assumed that place and its responsibilities in 1636 when he was admitted as a freeman of the city on completion of his apprenticeship. No precise date is given for his admission, but since apprentices were admitted only after being "called" at three successive meetings of the Guild (the general assembly of the burgesses) and since the Guild met in January, April, and October, he had either recently received his freedom when the plague began, or did so close to its conclusion.[31] It seems most likely that he was in fact admitted in January, since on 10 March he wrote his first surviving instrument under his own name and in the following month he drew up two inventories. Both of his clients were widows, one of whom, Margaret Ayre, left her entire estate to "my loveing son John Tailor" and named him her executor.[32] Ralph was getting started and it looks as though a kinsman was putting some business his way.

When the plague came to Newcastle, then, Ralph Tailor was at the very beginning of his independent professional career. In the months that followed he pursued it vigorously, as we have seen, and the resulting documents provide a sense of his personality.

He seems to have been anxious to impress. The will of Margaret Ayre is clearly the product of considerable effort. It is beautifully written in an elegant secretary hand, using black ink and a finely cut pen. The lines and words are evenly spaced and sized. There are pronounced flourishes on the capital letters of the first line, and throughout the document final "d"s and "y"s are swept up to curve over the word concerned before the pen is lifted. It begins with the notarial phrase "In the name of God Amen", and it ends not only with the date, but also with the unusual addition of the regnal year of Charles I and the king's titles – "by the grace of God king of England Scotland France and Ireland defender of the faith etc." – which took up three whole lines. (In the inventory prepared later, he also used unusual Latinate words when describing the contents of Margaret's house: "utensils", "implements".)[33] The young scrivener was laying claim to the professional authority that came with knowledge of forms and calligraphic skill.[34] But he was still somewhat inexperienced and perhaps trying too hard. In his concentration on the presentation of his work, he made mistakes. He repeated one phrase of the preamble without noticing. Coming to the disposition of Margaret's goods, he wrote "I give" too soon and had to delete it before adding "as well moveable and unmoveable". Worst of all, in specifying her place of burial he first wrote "within the parish church of All Saints", no doubt because that was the parish he was most used to naming. It was a mistake, and when his attention was called to it, he had to correct it, erasing the word "church" and inserting "church of St Nicholas" in the small space provided in glaringly smaller script. But he had forgotten to erase "of All Saints", so he simply struck the words through. One senses that by now he was a little flustered.

This was a mixed start. In the months that followed, however, he was to have ample opportunity both to gain experience and to grow in self-confidence. Indeed, in his nuncupative wills he developed a distinctive style, quite unlike that of other scribes active during the plague. For the most part, the form of nuncupative wills provides no clear indication of the circumstances under which they were made, save for the fact that they were unsigned by the testator (or perhaps contained the information that the will was declared "by word of mouth"). For the rest they followed the usual forms, and it is only from depositions that one learns how their terms were actually dictated.[35] Ralph Tailor's nuncupative wills were quite different. He did on occasion write a full formal will – this was appropriate in the case of Elizabeth Harrison, for example, who was still well enough to sign the document.[36] But he quickly adopted an alternative style that might be thought more suited to the urgency of the circumstances and which became his usual form. He wrote memoranda. Centred at the top of the small sheets of paper that he used, he wrote the date, like a heading: "The 19 of Augs 1636"; "The Eighteenth day of September 1636".[37] On two occasions he then opened with a formal "In the Name of God amen", but usually his first word was simply "Md", an abbreviation for "Memorandum". Then came the simple statement that on the day and date "abovesaid", a given testator, "being visited with the plague of pestilence", "declared" his or her last will "nuncupatively" or "by word of mouth" (or both) "in these words following or words to the like effect", in the presence of witnesses "whose names are hereunder written". Sometimes he added that the person was "of sound and perfect remembrance", but usually he did not. Perhaps he wasn't always sure of that. Then came the bequests and last wishes, sometimes punctuated with "Itm" or "It" to itemize them clearly, and usually tersely expressed. Finally, at the bottom left he wrote "Witnesses" or "Witnesses hereof", and there followed the signatures or marks of those who had accompanied him, before a firmly executed "Ra: Tailor: Scr:". All this was written in the same neat, clear hand, with its characteristic small flourishes on certain letters, and using the same black ink and fine-nibbed pen as for the will of Margaret Ayre. The spacing of words and lines remained regular. But both the lines and words were now much closer together, suggesting a certain briskness of execution.[38]

Vigorous, efficient, reliable, effective, of distinctive qualities: one gets the impression from the depositions that he gave in the spring of 1637 that this is how Ralph Tailor had come to think of himself. He was a good witness; precise and to the point and somewhat authoritative in his tone. In describing his procedures, he presented himself as cool-headed, competent, and of sound judgment, even in the face of horrific circumstances. He came promptly when sent for. He jotted down a "schedule" of the particulars of the will, from which it could be "committed to writeing as now it is". He read it out to the testator, heard it "acknowledged", and saw that it was properly witnessed. And he added telling details. Robert Moore, through the thin wooden partition, "asked this examinate his advise whether he had better nominate one executor or more and this examinate telling him that one executor was sufficient he thereupon named his sonne Michael sole executor". He clearly saw himself as a man of business, one of those penmen who kept the wheels of trade turning in his city. He was "well acquainted" with Robert Moore "in the time of his health . . . haveing done divers businesses for him". Asked to examine the signature on the will the notary John Carr had written for himself on 10 August 1636, he confidently stated that it was "written with his owne proper hand well knoweinge the same". Indeed, "he verilie thinketh the same will was written with the proper hand of . . . John Carr, he this examinate haveinge sene divers other writeings written by him in his lifetime". And yes, John Carr was a notary public in Newcastle, which he knew by virtue of himself "liveinge a scrivener in the same towne".[39]

In that phrase, and through the fact that he attested to John Carr's hand alongside the notary Francis Slinger and the scrivener Thomas Clarke, both much older men, one can detect a sense that Ralph Tailor had secured his place in his professional community.[40] He knew his role well, and he was rather proud of it, as his signature itself seems to demonstrate. It was customary at the time for notaries to employ a complex and distinctive signature on the instruments they prepared, with swirls, loops, and knots; it was a means of authentication to prevent fraud. In confirming the validity of the signature on John Carr's will, for example, Thomas Clarke pointed out that after Carr had become a notary public he had taken to writing the first letter of his name "with a knott", just as in the will.[41] This was not the elaborately drawn "sign" or "device" customarily used by continental notaries to authenticate documents: these were very rarely employed in England.[42] Rather, it was a tangled mass of lines immediately preceding the capital "J".

From the very first example of his signature that survives, Ralph Tailor, a newly admitted scrivener, was employing *three* elaborate, and far more finely executed, sets of loops to decorate his name: before the capital "R", on the capital "T", and below the final "r". He must have worked on that signature carefully and practised it assiduously. It was not a professional requirement as such, but it

15. John Carr's signature.

was surely a statement not only of his aspirations in his calling, but also of his personal identity. It set him apart. And every time he wrote it, large and bold, at the foot of a will during the plague of 1636, he was in a sense not merely witnessing the wishes of his dying clients, but emphatically asserting his own continued life and agency. No wonder that by 1637 there was a little bit of a swagger about Ralph Tailor. He was a canny lad, a survivor, making his way in the world, and his manner proclaimed it.

CHAPTER SEVEN

The Dialect of Heaven

Ralph Tailor would have needed such self-assurance as he negotiated the streets and chares of Allhallows' in the summer of 1636, called, as another witness put it, to "take penn, Inck and paper" to write the last wills of his stricken fellow townsmen and women.[1] If he had come to Newcastle in 1626 it is unlikely that he had ever previously witnessed a plague outbreak, and certainly not one of such severity. But like his contemporaries he must have known a good deal about the plague even before he encountered it face to face. One wonders whether, as he walked the streets, or lay in his lodgings in the long intervals between urgent activity, he ever reflected on the larger meaning of this unprecedented calamity.

Robert Jenison devoted over 250 pages to that subject, arguing, with all the rhetorical passion that made him the most renowned preacher of the region, that the plague "is, and must be taken to be, a fearfull signe of Gods displeasure and wrath". He knew very well that there were "second causes or instruments": "whether it be the *Ayre* which is infected, or any other *Person* or thing, which we occasionally received infected, or by whom, or who it at first was brought to our Towne or place; or whether the *unseasonablenesse of the weather* helpe to continue or increase it", giving "hope that when the dog-dayes end, or cold weather or winter approacheth, then we shall heare no more of it or at least have it to abate". But it must not be attributed "*either* to *Chance* or to *second causes* or instruments". The ultimate cause of the plague was "Gods wrathful displeasure . . . to the Communaltie, to the Kingdome, Citie, Towne or place where it is". "The face of an angrie God may, or ought be seen in it". Ultimately, then, it was "an effect of some great, speciall, spreading and raigning Sins".[2]

Such sins were not difficult to identify. First came "*unthankfulnesse* against God and his Messengers", and "envying, hating, and rising against Gods Ministers and faithful servants". Then "Pride, abuse of God's good creatures, Idlenesse, and abominable Lusts"; "unbeliefe", "irreverence", and "ignorance"; "evill examples and company-keeping"; "our pride, our unfruitfulnessee, our sensualitie, our securitie, our manifold defections from God". "The evils wee doe, and that willingly," thundered Jenison, "are the cause of all the evils we suffer unwillingly."[3] He pointed out the appropriateness of the judgment: "wee infect one another by evill example, communication, Company-keeping, though we call it *good fellowship*, by tempting and inticing one another to sinne, by unprofitablenesse in company, whereby wee edifie not one another in the best things: so by *excesse* and abuse of Gods good creatures; by *Pride* in apparel, and garishnesse, whereby we insnare and tempt others to sinne; so by *covetousnesse* and abuse of trading and such like." Therefore God sent a judgment,

> whereby we infect one another in body, by our breathing, touchimg and accompanying with them, and whereby hee breaketh those cursed knots of good fellowes; so whereby our very clothes in which we pride our selves doe infect our selves and others, to the apparent danger of life it selfe; and whereby, through famine and poverty, which commonly accompany the Plague, our excesse, and abuse, both of Gods good creatures, and of trading by oaths, couse-nage, false wares, at least covetousnesse; and our pride and confidence in regard of our wealth, are justly met withal.[4]

And the remedy was plain: repentance, reformation, amendment of life. Each section of the community had its part to play "according to our severall places and abilities". Magistrates should look to "speedy execution of Gods righteous judgements on the wicked . . . (which if it either had been universally and impartially performed; or yet were so done, we never needed to fear such wrath from God)". "Ministers of the Lord" had their role too. They must "stand in the gap, by a right discovery of sin and danger", "with Prayers and solemne Supplications in the publicke Assemblies, and with godly Instructions, Admonitions and Directions given the people". And the people, "and *generally all*", should respond with "unfained

Humiliation of themselves". None should "so far goe about to justifie our selves as to translate the cause of our sufferings from our selves to *other men*" by seeking scapegoats, be they "superiours" or "inferiors". They should look within and find "*selfe-humbling*". As a radical Protestant, Jenison scorned the "popish manner of pacifying Gods wrath", "as by whipping of themselves, going barefoot, or on bare knees, by wearing of hairy shirts, going on pilgrimages and the like". But he recommended prayer, "*Confession* of sinne found out", "*Contrition*", and, above all, "*Reformation* of our lives". The meaning of the plague was encapsulated in Jenison's "maine lesson": "When God manifests his displeasure against us for our sinnes, whether it be by plague and pestilence or otherwise, we are spedily to use the meanes which hee hath appointed to stay and pacify his wrath." "O sinful towne, citie, or place, will we yet sit still? Will we not run out with intreaty of peace, fall downe before him, and make supplication to our Iudge?"[5]

The puritan merchant John Fenwick, one of Jenison's congregation, agreed. When he had been overcome by his premonition of disaster in May 1636, he had recalled Christ's words before Jerusalem and applied them to his own city: "O Newcastle, Newcastle, would God thou in thy dayes had remembered the things belonging to thy peace." In retrospect, he recalled "how loud God spake to thee in that great plague, *Anno.* 1636". It had been the first "warning" to a city "still hardned, and the cry of thy sinnes like *Sodome* is come up to heaven":

in thee is to be found the blood of the Prophets, the blood of the saints oppressed and banished and hunted to death: in thee is found the blood of thy inhabitants oppressed and impoverished, by unlimited authoritie and arbytrarie government. . . . In thee is found the unclennesse of *Sodome*, Adulteries and Fornications in thy Rulers houses: thy filthinesse in thy skirts, transparent to strangers round about thee: in thee [is] found drunkennesse and excesse, with melodie, to see the Church laid desolate. . . . O *Newcastle*! When wilt thou learne the dialect of heaven, speaking loud in thine ears? O *Newcastle, Newcastle! Wilt thou not be made clean, when shall it once be? Jer.13.27.*[6]

Jenison and Fenwick were conventional in their interpretation of the plague as a divine judgment. Both their vision of a community estranged from God and their call for reconciliation and renewal followed the familiar script of the religious plague tracts of the age. But the urgency and intensity of their response were due not just to the scale of the calamity, but to a perception of its significance coloured by the local manifestations of the national and international religious and political conflicts of their day.

Fenwick wrote in 1643, with the benefit of hindsight. When he accused Newcastle of nurturing "the two grand sins that will sink a whole state, a whole kingdome without repentance and reformation: superstition in worship and oppression in government", he was alluding to the policies of King Charles I in church and state, which by that time had provoked rebellion in Scotland (which he supported), precipitated civil war in England (in which he participated as a parliamentarian officer), and occasioned his own sufferings at the hands of Newcastle's royalist elite. In retrospect, the plague of 1636 had become the first unheeded warning of the troubles that were to engulf Charles' three kingdoms.[7]

Jenison, in contrast, wrote in the very thick of the conflicts that culminated in those events. By the 1630s, the optimism of his early ministry in Newcastle, when he had enjoyed the support and patronage of its rulers, had long since faded. Even then, while acknowledging how much the city had been blessed with prosperity, good government, and the preaching of sound religion, he had warned in 1621 of the consequences "if at any time vice, superstition, profanesse etc. be allowed to take root and spread among us". Where religion was allowed to decay, "Gods just judgements usually break in", and "where sensualitie, filthy lusts and pollutions, Drunkennesse and Gluttony are suffered without controlment and condigne punishment, there destruction and vengeance hangs over the head of such a Citie". Therefore magistrates should use "severitie, so farre as your authoritie stretcheth", for "foolish pitty mars the city, and will lay it open to God's judgements".[8] But at that time such a possibility may have seemed remote, and Jenison's "chiefe care, in my Ministerie" was simply "to preach Christ soundly to my hearers".[9]

By 1629, however, times had changed. In that year he found himself censured, and his doctrine called into question, for preaching against the rising tide of anti-Calvinist and ceremonialist Arminianism in the Church of England, a trend prominently represented in Newcastle's vicar, Thomas Jackson.[10] In 1630, now thoroughly embattled, he saw "evill to be verie neere unto our Nation and Cities" in "these dangerous times". In a series of sermons preached in

Newcastle but dedicated to the mayor and aldermen of London, he expounded the duty of magistrates, ministers, and people generally to promote righteousness, and indicted, like Ezekiel, those who would "stop the mouths of Gods faithfull Messengers", "set up Idols in their hearts, either the Pope and Popish Idols, or the world . . . and . . . worldy vanities", "break their more speciall covenants with God of a more holy walking with him", and "[return] to the mire and vomit of their old sins". Without repentance and reformation, he warned, "our doome and destruction cannot be farre off", specifically instancing how "God hath already plagued, not once, but often, most of the best of our Cities and Townes by the fire especially of *Pestilence*".[11] If "God dealt somewhat gently with us here" in 1625, the extraordinary ferocity of the Newcastle outbreak of 1636 seemed the realization of his worst fears.[12] And if Newcastle's sins were evident enough, the message of *Newcastle's Call* was directed not just to his own city but to the nation generally. He wrote too late for his admonitions to affect the fate of Newcastle; by the time he dated his preface there in January 1637, the "visitation" was all but over. Rather, he took the role of "the *Interpreter of New-castles* good meaning" to the entire kingdom, repeatedly linking the fates of "this place and nation", "this place, yea and Nation". "God hath begun with us here" that others might "be warned in time by that bitter cup of ours". This was the greater task for which he had chosen, on the advice of "many godly and unpartial Christians (and so . . . by direction from God)", to "reserve himselfe".[13]

In this way the dystopian vision of the plague served to lay bare and dramatize some of the deepest anxieties and bitterest conflicts of the time. For Jenison and Fenwick, these extended to the fate of the Reformation, the integrity of the Church of England, and the legitimacy of the regime of Charles I. Nor were they alone. One of the most remarkable indications of how some of their fellow puritans in Newcastle perceived and interpreted the plague of 1636 is to be found not in the records of the city and diocese, but in the small leather-bound notebook in which the "confessions" of would-be church members were recorded by Thomas Shepard, minister of the New England settlement of Cambridge, Massachusetts. Shepard took down abstracts of fifty-one such confessions between 1638 and 1645, of which eight were from people who had previously lived in Newcastle, in Heddon, seven miles to the west, or in both. These are accounts of spiritual awakening and struggle rather than autobiographies. They are punctuated by significant biblical texts, rather than precise dates, and the autobiographical fragments that they contain cannot always be coherently ordered. Nevertheless, they tell a story. Most of the people concerned allude to the influence on their spiritual development of Robert Jenison, Cornelius Glover, who had preached in Heddon in *c.*1628–34, or Thomas Shepard himself, who had lived in Heddon in 1632–4 and preached, despite episcopal efforts to silence him, "about and in Newcastle", then "up and down in the country and at last privately in Mr Fenwick's house", before emigrating to New England in 1635. Only one of the Newcastle people who sought to join his congregation had crossed the Atlantic before 1636, and six arrived there between 1636 and 1638.[14]

Inevitably one wonders whether the trauma of 1636 had influenced their decisions to abandon a city and a land hardened in sin and seek comfort in a community of the godly, and in three cases the connection is explicit in the notes jotted down by Shepard. Jane Palfrey testified that although "it pleased the Lord to let me see sin of ignorance", she had still "used a form of prayer" in Newcastle. But "there being a great sickness and all to go from their families, I was cast in a place where Mr Glover lived at Heddon. And there was cast down and brought low inwardly." Returning to Newcastle "convinced of such sins as I durst not commit afterward", she still suffered many doubts. Her husband died. She sought counsel from Dr Jenison. "And then I had a mind for New England and I thought I should know more of my own heart."[15] Elizabeth Cutter had been "born in a sinful place where no sermon [was] preached", but came to Newcastle as a servant "placed in a godly family as I think". She became "convinced" of the need to "fear God, keep His commandments – two of which third and fourth I saw I broke".[16] After some years she "went to another family where people were carnal . . . and after followed with Satan and afraid he would have me away", but she was reclaimed by a Mr Rodwell, "an instrument of much good to me". There are no details of her later life – she was apparently close to sixty years old in 1636 – but one thing is clearly stated: "And I desired to come this way in sickness time and the Lord brought us through many sad troubles by sea and when I was here the Lord rejoiced my heart."[17] Robert Holmes, aged only twenty-two in 1636, recalled a youth when "in days of ignorance I contented [myself] with common prayer and homilies and sometime went to word but lived above twenty years in disobedience to parents and subject in my will to every lust". Coming to Newcastle, he was at first "much given to work and covetousness". But at last he saw that "all things here were empty vanities", and became "terrified about my estate doubting of a sin I lived in", though he could find no repentance until, after hearing a sermon by Jenison, his "heart melted and I had joy". He continued: "And though plague was great yet I went to the word. And seeing one that had the plague, I asked what promise I had to live on and Isaiah 26 – stayed on thee. In my heart I purposed [and] at last came to New England."[18]

These were extraordinary people: acutely anxious about their own spiritual integrity; convinced that most of humankind were predestined to damnation; oppressed by the uncertainty that such a doctrine entailed; and yearning for assurance of their own salvation. Converted, but still rubbed raw by doubt and fear, they lived lives centred on spiritual struggle, in which every significant experience was to be examined for evidence of God's providential purposes. And they were already alienated from both the "vanities" of a "rude" and "carnal" world, and a national Church that stopped the mouths of God's messengers and offered only empty forms: what Holmes called the "sin of common prayer".[19] What the plague meant to them is evident and important. But their heightened perception of its significance cannot provide a reliable guide to what it may have meant to the thousands who were not part of Newcastle's embattled puritan minority.

That the plague came ultimately from God and that, like war and famine, it was a general judgment upon a sinful world, was perhaps widely, even universally, acknowledged. Thus Mayor Thomas Liddell, having expressed his anxiety at a possible resurgence of the sickness in May 1637, concluded conventionally (and no doubt sincerely) with the supplication: "Almightie God in his mercy stay it and give us grace to repent our sins which is the cause of this Judgement."[20] That did not necessarily mean, however, that the plague should be given an interpretation specific to the immediate circumstances of either the kingdom of England, the city of Newcastle, or its individual inhabitants. Sin was, after all, a hardy perennial. Reformation was as elusive as a puritan's assurance of Grace. Pestilence was a recurrent phenomenon and its characteristics were increasingly well known. At the public level it was met, as we have seen, by practical measures taken to contain its spread.

But there is no clear evidence that in a city already chronically underserved with clergy, the most prominent of whom apparently absented themselves, there were public services of prayer and supplication.[21] Such gatherings were usually discouraged. At the private level, and particularly among those shut up in quarantined houses, the acute risk of premature death meant that people exposed to infection were well advised to put both their spiritual and their temporal affairs in order. The testamentary evidence bears witness to how they did so. It reveals a variety of responses, but it does not suggest that the religious interpretation of the plague's meaning was usually at the forefront of their minds.

Two of the surviving wills do indeed refer explicitly to the doctrine of judgments. In a remarkable preamble to his will, dictated in early September, John Heslop, of "Puding Chare" in St John's parish, claimed to be "in good health and perfect memory, thanks be unto god the Author garder and protector of all things as well celestiall as terrestiall for the good of his creaturs". But he continued that he made his will "being att this present visitted by his holy hand with the infecion of Pestilence the rod and scourge of his wrath against offenders for there great and grievous sinnes against his maiestie committed I being on[e] of the greattest and not certaine to remaine hear in this earthly tabernacle the least moment, especiallie now in theise sad and lamentable tymes". He then went on:

> First I give and bequeth my soule to the almightie and alseinge [all-seeing] Providence by whome and through whom I had my first breath and being and to his sonne Jesus Christ that Immaculate Lambe by whose precious death and blood shedding I faithfully and assuredly louke for the Remission and forgiveness of all my offences weere they in number numberlesse And to the holy ghost my comforter and Inspirer and breather of my hart & soule with the inspiracon of his holy spirit, together with the illumination and undarstanding of his holy word and doctrine.

By the time he had bequeathed his "corruptible body" to "its mother earth", "being assured instead there of to put on incorruption", and turned to "other temporall things", Heslop's eloquent testament of faith had filled twenty of the fifty-two lines of his will.[22] More simply, but no less movingly, Robert Wright, mariner, "some tyme of Newcastle upon Tyne but now Resident in Wapping", described himself as "at present under the hand of god visited with that uncomfortable disease called the plague" and ready to make his will "consideringe with myselfe the mortallitye of this world, not knowing how it may please god to deale with me".[23]

These striking statements, however, are wholly exceptional. For the most part, the religious content of wills extended no further than the conventional bequest of the testator's soul to God, the customary first clause of a formal will. One of these, like that of John Heslop, was unusually intense. Timothy Cooke, a wealthy draper, wrote his own will on 7 July: "being sicke in body but perfecte in minde blessed be my gracious god in and through Jesus Christe my lord and onely saviour by and through whose merittes of his bitter death and passion wch he suffered upon the crosse I hope and looke for the remission of and full pardon of all my sinnes and into whose gracious keepinge I commend and comitte my poore faintinge soule."[24] Most, however, were simple bequests of the soul, couched in a conventional Protestant idiom. Some expressed, like Timothy Cooke, the testator's hope through Christ's "meritts", "death and passion", or "pretious death and bloodshedding", to have "full forgiveness of all my sinnes", "to be saved", or "be made partaker of life everlasting".[25] Most simply bequeathed their souls to "almighty god my maker and redeemer", or "almighty god my maker and Jesus Christ my saviour and redeemer", the two commonest forms of words.[26] A number were almost perfunctory, resigning the testator's soul "into the hands of God", or "to God that gave it", or simply beginning "my soule to god".[27]

The formulaic nature of these laconic clauses should not surprise us. It is well known that the terms in which people bequeathed their souls to God in this period rarely provide a direct expression of personal religious commitment. Rather, they usually reflect the preferred forms of words customarily employed by the scribes who wrote the wills.[28] Nevertheless, they can tell us something. If testators rarely chose the words themselves, they did at least approve them when they acknowledged the terms of the will. And it is revealing that, of the six Newcastle plague victims who actually wrote their own wills, all save one (Timothy Cooke) used the same conventional formulae. To this extent, then, these short and simple bequests of the soul, with their echoes of the language of the prayer book rejected by the church's puritan critics, can be said to reveal the basic religious assumptions of people who had internalized the belief system in which they had been raised, but were neither engaged in the theological and ecclesiological controversies of their day nor disposed to ponder deeply the mysteries of salvation or the providential purposes of God.

The testamentary evidence, then, supports Paul Slack's observation that "the diverse religious behaviour of early modern Englishmen seems not to have been radically affected by outbreaks of plague".[29] Rather, it was thrown into higher relief. Some who already knew what Fenwick called "the dialect of heaven" spoke it the more fervently. Some, like perhaps Jane Palfrey and Robert Holmes, may have fully learned it in the trial of the plague. Others simply endured, and when "called", as they sometimes put it, they were content to resign themselves into the hands of God, trusting in the "sure and certain hope of the Resurrection to eternal life" promised them in the burial service of the Book of Common Prayer.

Even this, however, might risk exaggerating the extent to which the people of Newcastle reflected on the religious significance of their ordeal. A further striking feature of the testamentary evidence is that a third of the surviving wills actually contain no bequest of the soul at all. Moreover, many of those that do contain a "soul clause" are in fact nuncupative wills in which it is probable that the bequest of the soul was added by the scribe in an attempt to impose an appearance of normality on an utterly abnormal situation. This is not mere supposition. For instance, the depositions describe how William Robson's will was actually written "after his death aboute two monthes", by William Gilmer, acting on the "directions and instructions" of a former servant and Robson's "keeper". His bequest of his soul "to Almighty God my Creator and to Jesus Christ my Redeemer" was purely scribal convention.[30] Even more explicit is the case of Mabel Walker. Some time after her death, William Preston copied out a paper schedule of bequests "then showed [to him] by one [Michael] Moore", who had taken it down at Mabel's door on the instructions of her servant. And "there being no preamble in the said former will or notes", Preston "added the preamble to the same" – including the simple bequest of Mabel's soul "to Almighty God my creator" – before getting the witnesses to make their marks.[31] Other nuncupative wills are described as having been written on the spot, but in conditions that literally placed a greater than usual distance between the dying testators and the scribes who recorded their wishes. Robert Greenwell told his "keeper", Elizabeth Browne, "how he would dispose of his estate" and she related the details out of the window to John Netherwood, who prepared a will, no doubt hurriedly adding an appropriate "first my soule to god".[32] Robert Walker's wishes were similarly relayed to a neighbour and put down in a will that began with the terse bequest of his soul "to almightie god".[33] John Carr took down Thomas Hayton's directions standing before Thomas' door and then wrote a will with a fairly full, though conventional, bequest of Thomas' soul. But the words are identical to the clause Carr included a day later in the will of Thomas' widow. It was John Carr's usual form of words.[34] Whoever wrote the will of Gilbert Hall on 5 September did it so hurriedly that, in attempting to write "to almighty god my maker", he actually left out the word "god".[35] One should not make too much of that, perhaps, but it is at least possible that, for many testators, the state of their souls was not their principal concern. Indeed, of the many surviving accounts of the making of wills, not one includes a reference to forms of religious consolation in the face of death.[36]

Paul Slack has argued that, in the seventeenth century, religious and secular explanations of the plague, Jenison's first and second causes, coexisted in a kind of compromise. They were not incompatible. But the balance was gradually tipping towards a focus on secular explanation and practical response.[37] This may have been as true of individual as of public responses to the disease. And in this context the wills prepared by Ralph Tailor may provide a clue to his attitudes. It is reasonable to assume that he held the conventional religious beliefs of his day. In all likelihood he had heard Robert Jenison preach, though there is no reason to suppose that he was one of Jenison's followers. When writing a formal will, he followed the usual practice of beginning with the bequest of the soul, and he had a favourite, fairly elaborate form of words when doing so, reflecting his understanding of the doctrine of redemption: "into the hands of Almightie God my maker and to his son Jesus Christ my onely saviour and Redeemer by and through whose precious death and passion I hope assuredly for the full remission pardon and forgivenesse of all my sinns". He used it when he wrote Margaret Ayre's will before the plague and when writing the wills of Ralph Emerson and Richard Browne afterwards.[38] Of the fourteen plague wills that he wrote, however, only three contain bequests of the soul, and in a more truncated manner. These may reflect the testators' spoken desire to include this element.[39] The remainder of his wills followed a distinctive memorandum form, as we have seen.

He usually opened with a statement that on a given date the testator was "visited with the plague of pestilence", which certainly implies a providential view of events, but does not necessarily suggest acknowledgment of the plague as judgment. He twice used providential language when describing the possibility of death: "if it please God to call my said wife and children"; "in case it please God to call her" (which may again record the words actually spoken).[40] For the rest, he wrote witnessed memoranda of what was said "or words to the like effect", and these did *not* include bequests of the soul. They were entirely focused on the business of swiftly and succinctly recording bequests of property and the appointment of executors. Whatever Ralph Tailor may have considered the primary or secondary *causes* of pestilence, his job in the face of the here-and-now reality of death by plague was to help mitigate its human *consequences*. There at least lay certainty. Though made in quite extraordinary circumstances, the wills that he wrote reflected in their contents what has been called "the iron grip of the ordinary".[41] And in the decisions that he and others recorded, and the human responses to which those decisions bore witness, we may perhaps discern both the essential priorities of the people he served and the subtler ways in which the teachings of their religion informed their values and their conduct.

CHAPTER EIGHT

Bequests and Legacies

PEOPLE FEARED INFECTION; BUT THEY KNEW THAT IT MIGHT REACH them, and that knowledge bred a myriad of anxieties concerning their responsibilities in the face of the social disturbance that would be occasioned by their deaths.

Some looked ahead. The physician Robert Henryson made a precautionary will on 4 June, though in fact he survived the epidemic. Two days later John Stobbs of Pilgrim Street called together three of his neighbours to witness the will he had prepared, and when one asked "why he would make his will, he being then in perfect health", answered "that the times were dangerous which moved him thereunto".[1] "Aboute a forthnight before his death", the chapman William Robson "gott his goods inven[t]ared", fearing that in the event of his death "the clensers should deceive him or his".[2] As the plague took off in St Nicholas' parish, Jane Glasenby, spinster, wrote down her wishes on 22 July, while still "[w]hole of body", and sent them to her brother-in-law in Riding Mill, Northumberland – adding on the outside of the folded and sealed will the poignant instruction: "Brother Georges I pray yw lay this safelye up and be carfull that it be not brockene up tell yw heare further from me."[3]

Most people, however, ignored the conventional clerical advice that they should make their wills in the time of their health, so that "having set all in good order, you may more freely depart in peace". They believed, like John Stobbs' neighbours, that the time to make a will was, as an earlier Newcastle testator put it, when "he doubted he should not continew longe".[4] In fact, comparison between the dates of wills and the burial dates of testators (when available) reveals that three-quarters made their wills less than a week before they were buried, and the remainder within eight to fourteen days before burial. This suggests that wills were made only when the plague actually struck individuals, when a house was found to be infected and "shut up", or even when a person actually fell sick. Ann Milborne, for example, was already sick and quarantined when she determined "to sett her house in order". Many delayed until a few days before death, by which time their anxieties were all the more pressing. Despite his earlier prudence, William Robson almost left it too late. Ten days after his goods had been inventoried, both he and his wife Alice were sick, and William was deeply troubled, "saying he was much indebted and would have his wife to pay all his debts", but he was aware that "all he had was to[o] little for his wife", and concerned also about which of his "friends" would discharge his obligations "in caise that both he and his wife should then dye". We know this from the testimony of his former servant and his "keeper", since "noe Clarke [clerk] could be gott to write the same", and he "declared his mind" to them "by worde of mouth for want of a Clarke".[5]

Ralph Tailor was just such a clerk and the role played by the young scrivener and others like him in easing such anxieties is not to be underestimated. Ralph knew the expedients that could be adopted in conditions of pestilence in order to prepare a nuncupative will: hearing the will declared and taking notes; clarifying details (Which Bible? "The said Thomas his wif hir best Byble"); advising when required on procedures (as with Robert Moore's question regarding executors); setting the whole thing down in proper form; reading it back; having it acknowledged and witnessed and hopefully made legally watertight.[6] Such things mattered. To be sure, his services were hardly needed by the poor of Sandgate who had nothing to leave their dependants that needed to pass probate. They were not required by John Carr, Jane Glasenby, Timothy Cooke, or the cooper Robert Harrison, all of whom had the skill to write their own wills. But he was needed by Robert's widow, Elizabeth, to whom Robert had left all his goods "to dispose the same as she thinketh best". Elizabeth could not write.[7] Nor, indeed, could Robert Moore and many of the small master craftsmen and tradesmen of the city who had modest amounts of property to bequeath to their families and kinsfolk.[8] They could find reassurance in the service he provided, and for the most part these were the people he served: a skipper, a keelman, a master mariner, a house carpenter, a tanner, a weaver, a chapman, a miller, a cordwainer, a cooper's widow, and so on.

Most of Ralph's clients, like testators more generally, had gross inventoried estates of less than one hundred pounds and their net worth (all debts paid) was often much lower.[9] Nevertheless, for many of these people the disposition of their limited resources was a matter of acute concern. The legal and cultural expectations regarding inheritance were perhaps clear enough, and by and large they were adhered to. Married men focused on providing for their widows and children; widowed people for their children. Those who were unmarried or childless directed their legacies to close kin, usually siblings or nephews and nieces (with a distinct tendency for women to favour their female kin). Married men usually named their wives as executors. The widowed chose adult children (usually sons), and if their children were too young, they might name siblings (usually brothers) or, if necessary, more distant kin or trusted friends.[10] The conditions created by the epidemic, however, surrounded the achievement of these objectives with an exceptional level of uncertainty.

The will of William Grame, skipper, Ralph Tailor's first plague will, provides an apt illustration. He left everything he had to his wife, Margaret, his son, Edward, and his daughter, Hester. But he continued that "if it please God to call my said wife and children", then his goods were to be divided equally between his brother, an uncle, and a cousin. He also added that "whereas my said wife is now with child my will is that iff it please God shee be safely delivered of a child that the same shall have a full proportionable part of my said goods".[11] Grame was preparing for all eventualities, and in considering his responsibility to his unborn child he was not alone. William Cooke's wife was also sick when he made his will, but he included the provision that "if the child that my wife is with come forward I give it 20 li". And when James Hall, an unmarried man, dictated his will to Ralph Tailor on 13 October, he left ten pounds to his brother's wife, "and the child that it is hoped she is with. And in case it please God to call her and the same child", then the money should be divided between his existing nephew and niece.[12]

Such possibilities were on many minds. Philip Doncaster, confined to his house but able to talk to Edward Wood at the back gate, told him, "Ned if my sonne and daughter dye . . . then I name thee and thy children." John Carr, whose wife was lately dead, made elaborate provision for his two daughters. If either died, the other was to be her heir, and if both died, then his brother, Robert, and if Robert died, then his three sisters. Matthew Waddell, a baker and brewer and another widower, similarly divided his estate between his two unmarried daughters and, "in case that the said daughters should both die", named his brother-in-law John Bell as his next heir. He also nominated John and another friend "to be dooers for his children", i.e. appointed them as tutors for the girls. William Cooke made similar provision for his children "failing my wife", and Cuthbert Woodman, who had named his wife as executor, appointed two reserves "in case she die".[13]

The naming of residual heirs or the appointment of tutors for minor children were not unusual provisions in the more elaborate wills that were made in normal times. What makes the wills declared in 1636 distinctive is the frequency with which such decisions were recorded in clear, often explicit, anticipation of the possible, even imminent, deaths of members of the testators' households and families. And there were some also whose families had already been obliterated by the plague. Robert Walker, "knoweinge that his wife and children were lately dead", left "the small quantitie of goods that it hath pleased god to blesse me withal" (some furniture, his "working loomes", and a good deal of wool and yarn to a total value of less than fourteen pounds) to his fellow weavers the brothers Henry and Thomas Finlay. Henry, who had sheltered Robert in his sickness, was himself dead within days. Thomas, the same Thomas Finlay who had accompanied Ralph Tailor to Robert Moore's house, survived.[14]

Most of these decisions are recorded with a plain, matter-of-fact stoicism that rarely gives expression to either the emotional distress that must often have accompanied them, or the powerful sense of attachment that guided them. Only occasionally does one detect a hint of the latter. Thomas Clark, his wife dead and knowing that his debts far exceeded the likely value of his goods, instructed his brother-in-law to sell his house in Pilgrim Street, to use the residue, once his debts were paid, for "raiseing A portion to his daughter Margarett", and to look to the child's interests. It was all he could do for her now, and he did the best he could. Gilbert Hall remembered a long absent son "if he be living", in case "it shall please god that he cometh home from Travell". Ann Carr, widowed and with no other heir, got Ralph Tailor to record her desire to leave her house and goods to Robert Starkey, waterman, "in consideration of the Love I have and beare unto [him] . . . and the respect and charges which he hath shewed and bene att unto me for these many yeares last past".[15]

Across the river in Gateshead, Thomas Swan was unusually explicit. On 26 September, being "visited and infected with the plague" and close to death, he remade his will, "by reason his children were all dead but one, and that he was greatly indebted and knew not which way it should be paid but that he was likely to leave his wife in much care and trouble". Like Thomas Clarke, he ordered his house to be sold, and after his debts were paid "there should be as much taken forth as would binde [his son] apprentice and the rest of his part to be put into some honest mens hands to be put forward for his use . . . at such tyme as his said sonne should be forth of his apprentishipp". What remained was to go to his wife Katherine, but with a remarkable proviso. "All such goods as were his owne" were to be appraised as part of his estate, but "none of the goods which were his wives and which she brought to him at their intermarriage should be any way diminished but that they should wholly be and remaine to her sole and proper use, saying further that he would be sorie to leave her in worse estate then he found her".[16]

Swan's statement is a stunning expression of a plain man's sense of marital obligation. For the most part, however, the language of the emotions was muted. If they used it at all, most people (or their scribes) tended to fall back on, or perhaps cling to, the conventional formulae of their culture. They referred to "beloved", "welbeloved" and "loveing" wives; "kinde", "loveing", "faithfull", and "trustie" friends; their expectations of a "loveing and carefull mother", and so on.[17] Perhaps they lacked the words to articulate distinctively the feelings that they experienced, or to perceive their relationships in other than stereotypical ways. That is not an unfamiliar reality, and it may be that in their time anything more was deemed inappropriate. But there were two other forms of expression that they could and did employ to convey their emotional attachments, both of which were essentially symbolic. One was the language of "tokens" and the other was the language of place.

Tokens were a familiar, though by no means universal, feature of wills in this period: the bequest of small sums of money or goods "for a token" to individuals for whom the testator had no primary obligation to provide a legacy. Five of the fourteen wills made by Newcastle testators in 1635, for example, included such bequests.[18]

What is striking about the plague wills made in Newcastle in 1636 is not that such tokens were sometimes bequeathed, but that the practice was so prevalent, even under the exceptional conditions created by the plague. It was particularly evident among women. Twelve of the thirteen female testators left tokens, sometimes in considerable numbers. But it was also pronounced among men, two-thirds of whom distributed tokens in their wills. It was not a matter of tokens being more common among people who did not have the primary responsibility for the transmission of a family's property to the next generation (i.e. widows or unmarried men), for while some men focused their attention entirely on their spouses and children, most who had such responsibilities also left tokens. And it was to be found among the relatively rich and the relatively poor alike, though most commonly among those of modest prosperity.[19] The impression given is that people facing death in relative isolation felt a particularly powerful impulse to recall and recognize those close to them in affection, to acknowledge wider ties of obligation or gratitude, and to implant their memory in the continuing lives of others.

They did so with tokens, clearly giving careful thought to who should be included and the nature of the bequest, and then dictating lists to the scribes of their wills, sometimes through doors and out of windows (their accents sometimes audible in the phonetic spelling of names and items). Some remembered kin elsewhere. William Grame's last bequest was "to Margarett Grame in the country one petticott a hatt and a se[e]ing glasse". Then, after further thought, he added a gift to his sister Mary Grame of "a Gowne and a petticote". (This clearly disconcerted Ralph Tailor, who had to squeeze the last item into the space he had left blank above the word "Witnesses".)[20] Ann Milborne left tokens of goods, clothing, or money to her sister-in-law, two nieces, two female cousins, the two daughters of a male cousin, and her two brothers-in-law (one of whom she forgave a small debt).[21] James Wilson recalled his godchildren, leaving twelve pence each to twenty "children known to my wife for whome I have bene surety at the font".[22] Then there were friends. Robert Walker left the skipper George Simson the useful gift of "eleaven herren [herring] barrels". Like many others, he also remembered his servant: Thomas Crosby got a loom, five shillings, and some linen.[23] Neighbours were frequently acknowledged, especially by women. Margaret Hutcheson listed ten women, two of them her sisters, the rest apparently unrelated: to Margaret Smith "a waste cote"; to Jane Elger "a lynn aperne", and "to her daughter Allice a seeing glasse and one sewed cushion"; to Barbary Hodgshon "one coife, one tack band and one crossecloth". Her estate was so small that there was scarcely reason to make a will other than to acknowledge these women among whom she had lived. Mabel Walker, after leaving her house and most of her goods to her children, similarly listed twelve people (seven of them women) with ten different surnames, to whom she left sums of money as small as one shilling or items of clothing ("on[e] brown safegard"; "on[e] brown wastcot") "for a tokin". These legacies were dictated through the dying woman's door to witnesses in the street.[24] Alongside his brothers and sister, Thomas Clark included William Robinson and his wife, Mabel Chandler and her brother ("one paire of jarsey stockins" to each), and "blind Phyllis", who must have been known to all his neighbours. She got "one waistcote and one paire of shoes".[25] Some men also recalled close business associates, like John Mayne, skipper, who left ten shillings each to four men living in Bishop Wearmouth, Monkwearmouth, Tynemouth and "the sheeles" (North and/or South Shields).[26]

Most of these small gifts represented emotional bonds formed over years of interaction in and between households, in the streets and markets, in workshops, on the river, and along the quay. Some had been established or confirmed by the experience of plague itself. Ann Milborne thanked Jane Foster, the "keeper" who had nursed her, with twenty shillings and some linen. John Laverrock similarly gave five shillings to Ann Bell "for her paynes" in nursing him, and Robert Walker left "on[e] Pittecote and a smo[c]ke" to Ann Quarne.[27] Thomas Clark singled out "his Man Edward" (Edward Fletcher, a journeyman tailor) as recipient of "one cloth suit and twenty shillings in lew of his Mother's love in entertaineing [my] daughter Margarett att Table". (The inventory reveals that the child had been sent for safety to Edward's mother in Rothbury, Northumberland.)[28] John Heslop, an armourer, rewarded the friends and near neighbours who had answered his call to hear his will with tokens in the form of weaponry: "a little partesan" to Edward Wood, "a musket" to William Cocke, "a partesan" to Lionel Fetherstonhaugh, and "a pike and a musket and bandelers" to Lionel's brother George, who did the writing.[29]

In the will of George Robson, "musitian" or "minstrel", of St Andrew's parish, all of these elements came together. He was a widower, though whether his wife had died in the plague or earlier is not clear. The epidemic had, however, claimed his children, buried on 2 September as "3 Robsones Gorges the fiddler".[30] On 7 October, the day of his own death and burial, he made his will by word of mouth to two women, presumably his nurses. He had left it late, but he was prepared, for he declared it "accordeing to some notes of his owne writeing formerly sett downe". It consisted almost entirely of tokens. Ten shillings and all his apparel to his brother. Ten shillings' worth of household goods to both his landlord and his landlady. "My best tribble viol" to William Rawe (George owned "tow trible violes" and "tow ould lutes"). "One recorder and a flute" to Robert Browne. Ten shillings to Mary Haddock, two shillings each to Margaret Curd and Catherine Dawson, and a shilling to Alice Browne. Then came the two witnesses: "one waistcoate and one chist" to Margaret Grey and "one linen apronn" to Anne Rawe. The remainder went to "my elected wife" and "deare supposed friend", Jane Browne, including "all the goods I have in the forehouse" and "all my wifes apparell if it were six times as much and my blesseng".[31] George Robson's goods were worth only a little over seven pounds. He was one of the poorest of Newcastle's testators. Nevertheless, he deployed what little he had with deliberation, to acknowledge the relationships that still sustained a life battered by the plague and to express the hopes he had entertained of rebuilding it. His words enable us to recapture his affection for Jane Browne vividly. The other relationships remain largely obscure: articulated only through the tokens he left. But he knew what they meant, and so presumably did those who received them.

The language of tokens thus expressed the emotional significance of the constellations of relationships that defined the personal and social identities of testators. The language of place represented a different, though connected, form of attachment. It is evident from the many references to places that occur throughout the testamentary and deposition evidence, both before and during the plague, that people had both a broad sense of the topography of what was still a relatively small city and an intimate knowledge of the neighbourhoods in which they lived. Properties or events might be placed with reference to the city's principal buildings, streets, or public spaces: "nere unto the new gate", "att a place called the Castle Moate", "neere unto the church yard of St Andrewes", "without the Westgate", "at all hallow banck", "nere the Cale Crosse", "in Sandgate", "in the Close", "in the Pullen market", "next unto St Nicholas churche", "on the west side of the long stairs", "at the head of the Syde", "nere the kay side". Or they might be given a specificity intelligible only to locals: "at William Bewick's house", "over against [Robert Jopling's] shop", "in the house of Margaret Pringle", "at their owne doores", "two houses from him", or by "the house of . . . Anne Shovell her husband".[32] Between these two poles of their sense of place, people also had an awareness of belonging to larger sub-units within the city. The twenty-four wards are rarely alluded to, with the significant exceptions of Pandon and Sandgate. The four parishes, however, clearly had an important place in many people's sense of identity.[33]

All this is reflected in the plague wills. Every testator was identified as "of Newcastle upon Tine", as was expected in documents of this kind. Some could be highly specific in describing locations: "att the foote of the Mannor Chaire"; "near the pudding chayre end and the meale market"; "att the foot of the Syde neare the crosse".[34] Of particular interest here, however, is the fact that some three-fifths of the testators made reference to their parish of residence, and that almost half of them specifically requested that their bodies be buried in their parish churchyards. This, of course, could be merely a matter of convention. It was most likely to be found in those wills that conformed to the standard forms of will-making, and was omitted in others which adopted more abbreviated forms. (Ralph Tailor's crisp memoranda rarely included the name of the testator's parish or burial instructions.)[35] Nevertheless, it was a significant convention at any time, and all the more so when it was adhered to even in the conditions attending the plague.

We cannot know how assiduously any of these people had attended services in their parish churches during their lifetimes, or whether they listened attentively to the sermons preached in them. But the parish registers do bear witness to the place of their parish churches in framing their lives with the rituals of baptism, marriage, and burial. Indeed, for most people the laconic entries recording those events are the only record they left behind of their passage through life. Some may have been relatively indifferent to where they would lie in death, or simply took it for granted. The fuller and dyer Rowland Hedley of St John's parish, after a terse bequest of his soul, left his body "to be buried where it pleased his wife or the rest of his friends".[36] But to others it does appear to have been a matter of real concern. The miller James Dune actually began his nuncupative will, "First I do geve and bequeath my bodye" to be buried in "the churche yard of Alhalowes our parishe Churche", omitting the bequest of his soul altogether in favour of the specification of burial in a space that he regarded as belonging to himself and his neighbours. One might speculate that his sense of membership of his parish community took precedence over his anxiety about the state of his soul. But that would be to press a false distinction. Perhaps for most people their religion was less the daily struggle for sanctification and assurance found among those who made their confessions of faith to Thomas Shepard than a set of assumptions woven into their lives by such rituals: a series of participatory acts that marked the stages of the life course, and ultimately its end.

To specify one's place of burial was to evoke symbolic membership of such a community. Perhaps in a time of plague, when churchyards were congested with dozens of burials each week and mass burial was resorted to, it was particularly important to some testators not to be excluded from places associated with family and neighbour-hood life.[37] Who, one wonders, was tumbled into the pits at "Garth Heads"? For some people the desire to be buried in meaningful places was even more specific. John Carr asked to be buried "so neare unto my late wife Ellinor as possibly I maie or can". Thomas Hayton simply requested burial in Allhallows' churchyard, but his widow, Katherine, who died the next day, added "so neare unto my said late husband as possibly I may or can". Elizabeth Harrison's will, written by Ralph Tailor, asked for burial "so neare unto my late husband as conveniently may be", and Ann Milborne wanted to lie in St Nicholas' churchyard, "soe neere unto my mother and sisters as conveniently may be".[38] Such detailed burial instructions were not unknown in normal times, though comparatively rare. That they persisted in time of plague, when interments must often have been perfunctory, if not chaotic, is striking. They give a sense of what may have gone through dying people's minds, and serve to remind us that these were not people without landmarks in their lives. Elizabeth Cooke asked to be buried in St Nicholas' churchyard "neare unto the hawthorne tree there".[39] What can it have meant to her?

Wills are not usually considered exciting documents. They can seem dry and formal legal instruments. Yet like all such instru-ments they "inscribe relationships".[40] Their itemized provisions reveal the connective tissue of family and community. More, they reflect at one and the same time both the values and priorities of a society and the manner in which particular individuals made choices and expressed agency within the parameters of such social expectations. They are at once generic and unique, with the latter element often finding its clearest expression in those nuncupative wills that retain the flavour of reported speech. All this is true of the Newcastle plague wills of 1636. They involved recognition of obligations and attempts to meet them, acknowledgments of attachments and connections, and attempts to hold and preserve them. They connected what had gone before with what was to come. Scriveners like Ralph Tailor who listened to, noted, and then wrote down these final wishes did more than provide legal assistance in the transmission of family property, vital as that service was. They were the principal professional providers of comfort to the dying. At a time of dreadful uncertainty they helped people to focus their thoughts, to affirm identities about to be extinguished, and to make a "good death" in the face of conditions inimical to the achievement of that powerful cultural ideal. By helping people to declare their minds, they eased them.

CHAPTER NINE

The Attentive Presence of Others

THE SCRIBES OF WILLS WERE NOT THE ONLY ATTENDANTS OF THE SICK and dying. When Robert Jenison declared that pestilence was a force that "scatters us one from another" and "deprives a man of comforters in his greatest agonie and need", he grossly exaggerated.[1] Certainly plague divided people. Fear of the disease *did* breed fear of its victims. Such fear could threaten the abandonment of obligations and the breakdown of social bonds. All this is true. Yet the testamentary evidence that has been largely neglected by historians of plague also reveals repeatedly how such ties could hold firm, and how frequently the victims of plague remained subject to "the attentive presence of others".[2]

The people who hurried through the streets to fetch Ralph Tailor were usually kinsmen of the sick: Hugh Ridley, Thomas Holmes' cousin; Michael Moore, Robert's Moore's son.[3] The witnesses of wills who gathered before doors and beneath windows – usually three or four, sometimes as many as six or seven – were not randomly assembled. They included people identified as kin or "friends": Charles Dods, "brothers sonne" to the keelman Thomas Dods; Ann Straker, sister of Elizabeth Harrison; John Hunter, "somewhat of kindred" to Thomas Holmes' wife; Francis Bainbrigg and Mark Hutchison, the "loveing friends" who witnessed the will Ralph Tailor wrote for Robert Mallabar.[4] There were fellow craftsmen and guild members: John Coxson, first witness to the nuncupative will of John Collingwood, was another cordwainer; Robert Browne was both a mariner like Robert Wright and his "late maister".[5] Above all, there was what has been called "the continuous presence of neighbours". John Watson heard Clement Curry's will, "being [his] neighbor". He had known Clement's family for twenty years. Mary Finlay, "neighbor to Mabel Walker att the tyme of her death" for nine years, "did voluntarily goe to the dore of [Mabel's] house . . . being a neighbour to heare her said will".[6]

Some of these people subsequently died of plague themselves. Most lived to tell the tale. They clearly knew that they were at risk; but the evidence is that on the whole they controlled their fear and doggedly followed whatever moral compass they had acquired in life by precept or example. Such values and expectations are implicit in the way that they described their actions and those of others. There is nothing whatever to suggest that they shared in the "extreme moralization of disease", which could locate blame in its victims and brand them, as Jenison did, as not only sick but also "unclean".[7] They perceived them as simply "sick of the plague", "lyeing sick", "visited" or "infected with the plague".[8] They regarded that condition with sympathy as well as anxiety, and they recognized their obligations towards those afflicted. Many of them are explicitly described as having been "sent for" to hear a will. To have been "sent for", and to have responded immediately ("being his neighbor", "nere neighbor", "next neighbor", "neighbor and gossip", "her frinde and neighbor", or "being his kinsman"), was an absolutely standard means of accounting for a witness' presence at a deathbed in normal times.[9] No other explanation of their response was necessary. It remained so in the plague. Others simply turned up, offering the same explanatory phrases.

People still visited the sick. They should not have done so. True, it was a universally acknowledged duty of Christian neighbourhood to visit and comfort the sick, and earlier accounts of deathbed scenes contain many allusions to this expectation. Emma Wilkinson, a twenty-four-year-old widow of St John's parish, was typical when she introduced her testimony in 1633 with the information that she "was next neighbour to [Elizabeth Elwood] in her life time and att her death and in the tyme of her sicknes did oftentymes goe to visit her".[10] But plague, and the plague orders intended to contain it, posed special difficulties. The London minister Robert Hill, himself a survivor of the metropolitan plague of 1603–4, argued that, to avoid the spread of contagion, visiting those sick of the plague should be confined to "they of a family that are bound to come", "they that will be hired to looke to such persons", and those "honest and aged persons" appointed by the magistrates to inspect the sick. Ministers should not be sent for to attend the dying, since this was to expose them to infection, to risk the spread of the disease, and to hinder their continued ministry among the healthy, as well as suggesting "confidence in the presence of a minister, that he is able to forgive sinnes", which "savours much of Popish Superstition". To those of the sick who cried out, "O but my friendes will not come att me", he offered the comfort that "God will never forsake you", and that "the fewer you have to gaze upon you, the fitter you are to looke up to God". To those of their neighbours who apparently argued that "If I shall die of that disease I cannot flie it by not visiting; if I shall not, I shall not die of it though I visite", he responded that such an argument was "presumptuous", and warned that "if you meane to be freed from the plague, you must use meanes to keepe your self from it".[11]

Despite such strictures, people persisted in recognizing their obligations. John Dove, aged only twenty-four, was a former servant of Clement Curry, and "hearing that he was sicke, did goe to visit him at his house or as neare as he durst". He found John Watson there and together they spoke to Clement's wife at the door, learning from her who Clement wished to act as guardians for his children. On the day after he and three others had heard John Stobbs' wishes relayed to them by his keeper, Robert Jopling (who had known John Stobbs for twenty years) came back and spoke to John himself from outside the house. He must have asked if he needed anything, for the sick man "desired [him] to buy for him some fish as allsoe a pint of wyne with other necessaries". Robert did so, later enquiring after John again from the keeper when he delivered the goods. The three neighbours who visited William Cooke and heard his will "before the dore of his house" were all healthy at the time and "durst not come to [him] after the writeing thereof". But William understood. He "desired them to goe into a neighbours house and there to drinke twoe or three pottes of beere" on his behalf.[12]

Not all visitors were so cautious, for some broke quarantine. Steven Colthard, aged thirty, was "neighbour to Henry Finlay" and was "intrated of" by Henry and his wife to enter their house, where Robert Walker lay sick, to hear Robert's will. He not only did so, but during the next five days that Robert lived, "druw so togeather and had conference togeather divers times" with him. He said that Robert "talked very sensibly of his hearing". Isabel Wiglesworth, "being a neighbor" to Margaret Humphrey, whom she had known for thirty years, "did goe to visitt her at her husbands house in Sandgate", where Margaret's niece Ann Mills lay sick. Also present was Anne Tayte, a family friend of twenty years' standing, who later recalled that "beinge a neighbor . . . and having beene formerly visited and recovered of the playge and hearing that [Ann Mills] lade sicke of the same desease in John Humfreyes house did as a neighbour goe to visit her". She found Ann "lyeing sicke in a chamber", where they had "some speeches". Jane Robinson, a twenty-three-year-old widow, "being a neighbour to [Jane Young] and knoweing that she was visited with the plauge and that she was in a lodge on the towne more of Newcastle did goe to visitt her . . . she . . . having beene former[ly] in the like lodge herself".[13] That simple final clause is eloquent.

To have been sick oneself and to have recovered perhaps gave such courage. (Was that Ralph Tailor's case too?)[14] But there were also healthy people who were willing to shelter the sick when there was no one else to care for them. As we have seen, Henry and Anne Finlay of Castle Garth took in Henry's fellow weaver Robert Walker, and Margaret Humphrey housed her sick niece Ann Mills. Isabel Middleton did not abandon her lodger the waterman Robert Moody when he fell sick, but nursed him until his death. (He left her his goods in recompense and the censorious drew their own conclusions.)[15] Many more, while unwilling to risk direct contact with the sick, took steps to ensure the proper care of those who were confined. Katherine Hayton, who had lost both her husband and son, left her house to her brother Thomas "in respect of his great care costs and paines he took in my and my husbands sicknesse", and a gold ring and linen to her sister-in-law as a token of gratitude for the "care and paines she had of me and my late husband in our sicknesses". Jane Young similarly left all her goods to Thomas Wilkinson and his wife "in recompense of the paynes which they had taken for her in the tyme of her said sickness".[16] John Laverrock prudently made his will before being removed to the lodges on the town moor and gave his cousin Elinor Nycolson "fefty shillings to bestow on me in my secknes and yf I dy to bestow the chardge of my burial". She repaid his trust: her list of "The Charges Laid forth for John Laverrok" shows that she spent all but sixpence of it on such itemized expenses as "keppinge him in the Lodge", "vittel to the keper", "mett and drink for him", and "to Mr Eden for a drink for him iis. vid.", the last item presumably being a medicinal draught.[17] Charges listed in the inventories of other victims of the plague are usually less specific: "for the maintenance of Thomas Eden and his wife and family during the time of their visitation"; "her charges in her sicknes"; "maintenance of her during the tyme of her sicknes"; "to a woman to serve them with watter and meat and drink".[18] The implication, however, is clear. Someone arranged all this.

Such "care costs and paines" frequently included the hiring of a keeper to take care of the sick person.[19] The records provide very few references to medical practitioners attending the sick or dying. There is the medical draught prepared for John Laverrock by Mr Eden, noted above, and on 22 August the barber-surgeon Robert Mallabar was present when Ralph Tailor wrote Cuthbert Woodman's will. (Ralph also wrote Robert's own will two and a half months later.)[20] The rest is silence. But there is much evidence of the role of the women (almost always women) who were hired to tend them.[21] We have already encountered Margaret Hyndmers clambering through the window of John Stobbs' house with the aid of a smith. The rest of her story bears telling. "And when she came to him she found him satt upon the chamber floare not able to gett to his bedd without her helpe, and soone after she helped him to his bedd his leggs failinge him." Once "laid on his bedd", he asked her to send for Robert Jopling and "two or three neighbors" to hear "a true particular of his goods". She did so and, when they came, relayed his wishes "from his mouth to the said Robert", "out of a chamber window". Then she took care of him (with Robert's assistance, as we have seen) until he died the next Saturday morning.[22]

Very little is known of such women, and it is worth recording here the few details that we have for some of them. Ann Pullame was sixty years old. She had been born in Scotland, but had lived in Newcastle for eighteen years. She described herself as "heard of hearinge". Barbara Hall, a widow, aged thirty-five, had been born in Newcastle and had lived there all her life. She had known the family for which she worked for twenty years. She said "her husband is lately dead and left her in debt but howe much she knoweth not". Ann Whaw was also a widow, aged forty-four. Her husband was "lately dead and dyed in debt more than she knoweth of". Elizabeth Browne, yet another widow, aged thirty-five, Jane Foster, a thirty-year-old spinster, and Elizabeth Walker, a married woman also aged thirty, provided no further details of themselves beyond the facts that they had been hired as keepers and had known the parties in whose cases they were called as witnesses for between four and ten years. None of them was able to sign her name.[23]

These women were drawn from the poor of Newcastle, most of them were alone, some of them perhaps recently widowed by the plague, all of them willing to risk their lives for a small wage. Jane Glasenby's keeper earned ten shillings in all, though how long she served is not stated. John Laverrock's keeper got eight shillings for sixteen days, plus "vittell". Sixpence a day was 60 to 75 per cent of a male labourer's daily wage in Newcastle at this time, though somewhat better than the sum the city paid to the poor for shifting a ton of ballast.[24] It must have been attractive enough, for some seem to have hired themselves out as keepers repeatedly. Elizabeth Browne, for example, was Robert Greenwell's keeper on 22 August and witnessed John Collingwood's will on 26 October.[25] Such women do not usually leave their mark in the historical record, beyond their names in parish registers, unless they chanced to commit an offence. In this instance some fragments of their personal histories are preserved because they happened to witness wills.

The keepers were not shut up with their charges for long. People usually died within a few days of making their wills, rarely surviving more than a week.[26] What happened next can be illustrated from the exceptional detail provided by the deponents in the case of Thomas Hayton, a baker and brewer who lived in Pandon. On Thursday 7 July, Thomas had declared his will from a window of his house to the notary John Carr and three neighbours, one of whom was his brother-in-law, and later the same day Elizabeth Walker arrived to serve as keeper, since Thomas' wife, Katherine, was also sick. On Friday 8 July, Luke Courser, aged thirty-four, "being by trade a joyner", came to the house "asking howe he did", and Elizabeth Walker "answered him and told him that they were in hope of his recovery". Luke departed, his services not needed, but that night there was another visitor. William Bayles, who described himself as "appointed to be a grave maker and burier of the dead", and was fifty-five years of age, "hearinge that . . . Thomas Ayton the elder lay sick . . . did call att his house upon Friday att night . . . to know how he did". This time Elizabeth reported that "he was then very sicke". Accordingly, "the next morning being Satterday", William "called at the same house againe and then found him dead". Luke Courser was alerted and sent his twenty-year-old apprentice William Greene "to receave direccons for the length [of the] coffin wherein he was buried". Luke made the coffin and William Greene carried it to the house. William Bayles then buried Thomas Hayton "in the afternoon" in Allhallows' churchyard. By this time Katherine Hayton was also gravely ill; she made her will the same day, asking to be buried beside her husband. But Thomas' body did not go to the grave alone. Elizabeth Walker attended the burial; so did Luke Courser; and so did a neighbour, Grace Shipley, who had watched Thomas declare his will two days before. Perhaps there were others.[27]

William Bayles and Elizabeth Walker both described Thomas' burial as taking place on the "afternoone" of his death. Grace Shipley and Luke Courser said they attended his burial "that night" or the "same night". In all likelihood the interment took place at dusk. Dusk burials had been specified in the plague orders of 1578 as a means of discouraging the large gatherings of kin, friends, neighbours, and fellow guild members that were usual at funerals in this period, and thereby reducing the risk of contagion.[28] That this practice was adopted in Newcastle in 1636 is suggested by William Bayles' initial appearance at night and his subsequent late afternoon burial of Thomas Hayton after ascertaining earlier in the day that a grave needed to be prepared. But no further evidence survives to confirm this. What does seem clear, however, is that even the burials of plague victims of some social substance were relatively simple. The funeral expenses that Ralph Tailor recorded when drawing up the inventory of Margaret Ayre before the plague and that of Jane Mawe in the year following show that between twelve and fourteen pounds were spent on the funerals of these relatively wealthy widows; presumably an appropriate level of expenditure for people of their standing in normal times.[29] It represented the kind of expectation expressed by another Newcastle widow, Elizabeth Elwood of St John's parish, when she specified in 1633 that she wished to be "decentlie" and "honestlie brought forth and buried".[30] In contrast, the funeral expenses of plague victims of comparable wealth and standing were much lower. Cuthbert Woodman's funeral cost eight pounds, the barber-surgeon Robert Mallabar was buried for only six pounds, and the merchant Robert Greenwell for four. The funeral of the tailor Oswald Fayrealis also cost four pounds and that of the widow Ann Milborne, three. The wealthy tanner Ralph Rowmaine's executors paid only five pounds in all for the burials of "the Testator, his wife and a child", while those of the even wealthier cordwainer John Collingwood laid out twenty-seven pounds in total on the funerals of "himself, his children and servants being 7 in number" (an average of less than four pounds each, though it is unlikely that the sum was evenly distributed).[31] Less prosperous people were buried for as little as thirteen or fifteen shillings.[32]

One reason for this marked reduction in the costs of the funerals of Newcastle's citizens was almost certainly the temporary abandonment of the custom whereby the members of the city's guilds were required to attend the funerals of guild brethren or their wives and widows, and to participate both before and after the interment in eating and drinking which could continue for several hours. The average cost of the funerals of seven guildsmen and the widow of an eighth recorded in inventories from 1635, for example, was close to ten pounds, and one of the least expensive of these, that of a paver's widow, involved expenditure on wine mulled with sugar and spices, fish, wheaten bread, butter, cheese and ale.[33] Nevertheless, it would be mistaken to assume that the plague wholly deprived its victims of a "solemne funeral" or "Honourable burial".[34] Moralists might emphasize this deprivation as one of the most distressing aspects of the judgment of pestilence, but the inventories suggest a more complex reality. It is true that the latter are often frustrating in their failure to specify the precise nature of funeral expenses, or in their tendency to lump together funeral expenses with other charges occasioned by a plague death. The joint inventory of Thomas and Katherine Hayton, for example, tells us only that fifteen pounds was "desbursed for thear bearyall and cleansing the house and meat and drinke for the cleansers and coffins and other charges about the same house".[35] But on the rare occasion that further detail is provided it is instructive.

John Laverrock died in the lodges on the town moor, which might lead one to assume a perfunctory burial in a common grave. Yet the itemized expenses submitted by his cousin Elinor show that she paid five shillings for "a linne sheet", six shillings "for a coffin for him", two shillings and sixpence for "iiii men car[ry]ing of him to the church and to the caller" (the "caller" presumably preceding the procession), another two shillings and sixpence "for bred drink to the carriars", and three shillings "to the clark for his burial". In total she spent nineteen shillings (which was 11 per cent of John's modest inventoried wealth of eight pounds, twelve shillings) to provide a funeral of simple dignity.[36] No costs were recorded for food and drink for mourners other than the bearers of the coffin, but other inventories make it clear that such commensality had not been wholly abandoned. Among the debts owing to the baker and brewer Gilbert Hall of Allhallows' parish were nine shillings and sixpence owed "for Emond humble his sons buriall", for which he had presumably provided bread and ale.[37] The funeral of Jane Glasenby of St Nicholas' cost only twenty-four shillings, a modest affair, with a coffin somewhat cheaper than that of John Laverrock. But among the costs were payments for bread, mutton, wine, and beer.[38] Funerals costing three or four times as much as that of Jane must also have included such provision. That of William Hall, whose "funeral expenses and clensing chargs" came to thirty pounds, must have done so on a lavish scale.[39] Hall was exceptional; one of the wealthiest victims of the plague. But the smaller sums spent on others still imply that in Newcastle, as elsewhere in England, funerals often remained, even at the height of the plague, occasions on which at least some kinsfolk, friends, and neighbours gathered to affirm their bonds to the dead and to one another.[40]

The burial registers, at once the most laconic and the most comprehensive of the records of the plague, both confirm those bonds and chronicle the forces that threatened to dissolve them. They can be employed, as we have seen, to trace the contours of the epidemic in time and space, and they also provide insights into the stresses that it imposed upon social structures and social relationships. Each of the extant registers has its idiosyncrasies, expressions of both the registration customs of particular parishes and the perceptions of the individual clerks who kept the registers in 1636. But they also reveal some common themes.

Most of the entries acknowledge the distinctive identity of the individual victims of the plague: they supply a name and a surname, preceded or followed by a date of burial. Many also provide further recognition of the place of these individuals within the social structure of the city, the parish, or the neighbourhood. Superior social rank was indicated by the addition of honorific prefixes: "Mr", "Mrs", "Dame". In St Nicholas' and St Andrew's, the clerks also added marginal pointers to draw attention to certain entries. This was sometimes an indication of rank: "Mrs Isabel Errington", or "Dorete Graye Mr grayes mother", for example. But most often it seems to have indicated personal standing within the parish community. William Robinson, Mabel Walker, Robert Moore, Elizabeth Cooke, and Ambrose Haddock, all people whom we have already encountered, were distinguished in this way.[41] In St Andrew's, some people well known in the neighbourhood were also accorded the intimacy of such designations as "Robert Toddericke . . . which had the honchback", "Gorge the dyer", "Gorge the fiddler" (George Robson), "William Nichollsone to a nickname Mr Mare [i.e. "Mayor"]" (who may have carried himself with a dignity beyond his station in life) and (perhaps less fondly, or just descriptively) "Mistress Grey the papest [i.e. papist]".[42] The clerk of St John's routinely noted the occupations of male household heads, and by implication their membership of a guild and possession of the political rights of a freeman; a practice sometimes, though less systematically, followed elsewhere. And everywhere the importance of the household was underscored by the frequency with which wives, children, servants, and apprentices were attributed to the heads of the households to which they belonged. This practice was systematic in the case of St John's, as we have seen. In St Nicholas' and St Andrew's, it was less usual to describe a woman as "wife of", or "wife to" a named man. But children were usually described as the son, daughter, or child of a named parent, or in St Nicholas' (tersest of the registers) as "Infant" followed by the family surname. And in St John's and St Andrew's, servants, apprentices, and resident journeymen were almost invariably buried under the names of their masters or mistresses rather than their own: "George Kirkhouse his maid"; "Mris Ogles maid"; "one youth of Thomas Chaytor"; "A boy of Cuthbert Stobes"; "pattesones boy"; "John Atcheson his man", and so on.[43]

These general characteristics of burial registration remained in being throughout the epidemic, a significant element of continuity. But as the pressure of the mortality mounted, they were also subject to subtle changes. In St John's, the parish clerk gradually ceased to provide the personal names of wives and children. Entries such as "Alice Bland wife to George Bland cordwiner" gave way by late August to the abbreviated "Henry Fairealis wif skinner and glover", or "Mathew Moores wife slayter". Similarly, while children were initially registered in the form "Tymothy Liddle son to Tymo: Liddle glover", entries providing the child's name were soon far outnumbered by such truncated forms as "A Child of Thomas Watsons sadler", or "2 Children of Thomas Chayters weaver". Regular recording of the personal names of wives and children did not reappear until November.[44] The fact that at the height of the plague the parish clerk deemed the names of wives and children less worthy of record than the trades of their husbands and fathers is striking. It rendered them anonymous, save for their connection to the heads of the stricken households from which they came – a situation that was already the norm for such subordinate household members as servants, apprentices, and resident journeymen. Perhaps it reflected the hurried manner in which the clerk noted down who had been buried each day, or the manner in which their identities were reported to him. But it also carries profound implications both for the manner in which personal and social identities were perceived in the patriarchal, guild-structured society of Newcastle's freemen and for the way in which the plague could harden those perceptions.

In St Andrew's, where the clerk usually provided the names of adults without further attribution, the same practice was being followed in registering the burials of children, and sometimes those of married women, by mid-August. The pressures exerted by a situation in which there were often ten burials a day, and sometimes more than one member of a particular family to inter, are also revealed in a number of particularly poignant entries: "wilkesones wife and child – 2 bur[i]ed in on[e] grave"; "Jo Hall his 2 chilldre bothe in one coffing"; "Margaret Stooke and her chilld both in one chiste"; "Thomas Skolles 30[th] George Skolles 30[th] } in one grave"; "Edward Pigge the 1[st] day Thomas Pigge – in one kofeng"; "dande penne and James Crinstone bothe in one grave servantes".[45] In this parish, however, the element of depersonalization of the dead observable in St John's took more profound forms. In both parishes at the height of the mortality, the relative marginality or low social standing of some individuals meant that they were registered only by surname, or by a surname preceded by the term "one", suggesting that they were imperfectly known to the clerk. Thus we find "Gilles chilld", "Dixsone", "Dawsone", "Symsone", "3 Grenes", "a child of one Maires", "one Milbone and one Dod". This kind of semi-anonymity was much more common in St Andrew's.[46] Moreover, in St Andrew's still other entries – fifty-six in all – were of people who were wholly unidentifiable save for the fact of their poverty: "a powre one"; "a powre child"; "2 powre ones". St Nicholas' had no such entries. St John's had only one – the burial of "7 poore things" discovered in the Warden Close after the epidemic was over.[47] In St Andrew's, the anonymous poor made up more than a tenth of all registered burials.[48]

The burial registers, then, reveal both the intimacy with which some neighbours were known and the limits of that knowledge; the vital importance of the household units to which people belonged, and the existence of people who did not belong to any household of which the clerks were aware; the way that social identities continued to be recognized, albeit sometimes in truncated form, despite the pressure of emergency conditions; and the way in which the plague dramatized the presence of those recognizable only by their poverty. In St Andrew's parish, a relatively poor area of the city, such marginal people constituted a significant minority among the victims of the plague: migrant workers perhaps, as yet without roots in the city; people who belonged to no community beyond the loose connections of the work site or the quayside, the alehouse or the lodging house. Such fragile ties may have been the first to be suspended or severed in time of plague, leaving no one who bore responsibility for reporting their deaths and names, let alone the kin or familiar neighbours who might have supported, identified, and mourned them. And if this was so in St Andrew's, one inevitably wonders what might have been the case in the teeming wards of the riverside districts of Allhallows', where forty or more people may have been buried each day at the height of the plague, but for which no registers survive. How many people in Sandgate went to the grave unidentified and unaccompanied? William Bayles probably knew. Ralph Tailor may have known, though his business was with people of at least small property. We can only ask the question.

Together, the recorded funeral expenses of some of Newcastle's plague victims, and the manner in which the burials of a much larger proportion of the dead were registered, tell a story. In part it is a story of social difference. Death was no true leveller in seventeenth-century England – even in a time of pestilence. It was commemorated and recorded in ways influenced not only by the centrality of such inclusive social institutions as the household and the neighbourhood, but also by their hierarchical structures. Indeed, the plague may have thrown both dimensions of a person's social identity into sharper relief. For some, probably most, burials were attended, conducted in accordance with a person's place in life, and recorded in a form that acknowledged, however briefly, the bonds of family and community. For others, the tenuousness, or even absence, of the recognition that such connections conferred was starkly revealed. But if there was difference, there was also a commonality of experience. The charges recorded in the inventories serve as a reminder that the progress of the plague from the onset of illness to death and burial took place over a matter of days. The clusters of deaths recorded in the burial registers show repeatedly how it could pass through whole households in two or three weeks.

The interspersion of burials in each of the registers – persons of note, members of guildsmen's families, familiar neighbours, inter-lined with the less known and the anonymous "powre ones" – wove together thousands of personal and familial tragedies into a single catastrophic experience in which all had their moment and their place. And while the columns of recorded burials on each page are revealing in their details, they also convey a vivid sense of what Albert Camus called "the slow, deliberate progress of some monstrous thing crushing out all in its path".[49]

Perhaps that is how it was perceived. The city magistrates, collecting the weekly reports of burial totals, may well have appre-hended the entirety of the experience in this way. Robert Jenison, tabulating and publishing the figures they received, gave the plague shape and trajectory; divine purpose also. To others, lacking that sense of weekly progression, it may have seemed more shape-less; "a vast despondency" rather than a measured (and therefore predictable) process of increase, peak, and slow decline.[50] There is some evidence of this in how the plague was recalled. To the administrator of Ambrose Haddock's estate, it was simply "that lamentable tyme", a homogenized period of collective sorrow.[51] For some, memories became blurred. Mary Temple, a servant who had been nineteen at the time, could date an event she had witnessed only as "in thone of the monethes articulate", i.e. the summer of 1636. Margaret Sharp, another servant, said her neighbour's house had been shut up in "some of the monethes [of the plague] a more certaine time she remembreth not". Grace Shipley could date Thomas Hayton's death only as "in the plague time in Newcastle".[52] Others, however, attempted greater specificity, revealing a memory of the plague in which perennial anxiety, and perhaps the monotony of daily endurance, was interrupted by moments of intense experi-ence or urgent activity that were not only vividly recalled but also placed in time.

As might be expected, the precision of such placement varied. Some witnesses could recall events only in relation to the death of a particular testator: it was "aboute a forthnight before his death", "aboute fower or five dayes before his death", "a day or two before her death", "the same day that she departed this life".[53] Others attempted to specify the month but were otherwise uncertain about the exact day: it was "in June last", "in August last", "in July last past".[54] Even so, they could be remarkably specific about the day of the week involved, and even about the time of day – "upon Monday in the forenoone he liveinge till Friday the next after" – as well as about details of the circumstances.[55] Those searching for a date usually referred themselves to the agricultural or ecclesiastical calendar. That might involve considerable approximation. Placing an event "betweene Michaelmas and Martinmas last past" meant between 29 September and 11 November; meaning, in effect, "in the autumn".[56] The description of one will as having been made "about Whitsuntide last past was twelve monethes" was roughly two weeks too early, while the dating of a death as at "Michaelmas then next after or thereabouts" was actually eight days too late.[57] But these are not wide margins of error, and dating by this convention can also prove surprisingly accurate when witness testimony is compared with the evidence of dated wills. Lammas Day (1 August) was the reference point most commonly alluded to, perhaps because it was the traditional date of one of Newcastle's great fairs, and this may have facilitated accuracy.[58] Ann Mills made her will "about a weeke next after Lammas last". It was, in fact, 8 August. Thomas Finlay recalled meeting Ralph Tailor and Michael Moore on their way to make Robert Moore's will "about three weekes next after lammas last past a more certaine time he remembreth not". He did well enough: it was on 19 August, only three days out.[59]

Among those who survived to describe moments within the larger experience of the plague, then, some recalled only a generalized period of distress, but for most their sense of time had not been twisted out of shape. The conventions that they adopted to recover and place events were in keeping with those employed in normal times. Only a few, however, were able to date events with the chronological exactitude of a stated day and month. And one of those who did so was Ralph Tailor. Thomas Holmes' will was declared "upon the eight of August last", and Robert Moore's on "the 19th day of August last past". Yes, he could confirm "that the day of the date of this will exhibited in this cause the plague of pestilence was in the towne of Newcastle articulate of his knowledge".[60] As a writer of legal instruments, he had learned to think this way. Perhaps he also kept a record of his acts, for it was important to have knowledge of such things.[61] What is certain is that he always knew precisely what date to place at the head of the wills he wrote, and that as the plague unfolded he retained a sharp sense of time.

CHAPTER TEN

Houshold Stuffe

RALPH TAILOR WROTE HIS LAST PLAGUE WILL ON 5 NOVEMBER 1636. By then the epidemic was ebbing fast, and the final reckoning had already begun.

First came the task of "cleansing the house and goods", a process frequently accounted for alongside the costs of funerals and other charges incurred by the sick, and occasionally specified in more detail.[1] Whether the clothing and bedding used by the infected were ever burned, as was recommended by the plague orders of 1578, is uncertain. There is no mention of this practice, and it seems likely that people were reluctant to destroy goods of some value even if they had been in contact with the sick.[2] What is clear is that they were commonly washed and aired, and that houses were scrubbed. The administrator of the cooper Richard Rutlidge specifically accounted for eighteen shillings paid to the cleansers of Rutlidge's house "and for coles, candles and sope".[3] This may imply fumigation as well as washing, a further form of disinfection indicated by the payment made by the officers of Trinity House "for pitch and rosin when Peter Mahon's house was cleansed".[4]

Cleansing was another task undertaken by poor women. Ann Bell received five shillings from the executor of John Laverrock "for klensinge his clothes and for her part in klensinge the house", as well as another shilling "paid for hott watter to hir severall tymes" and yet another "for carr[y]ing his cloths afield" for airing.[5] (The open spaces in and around the city must have been festooned with drying clothes and linen as the plague gradually withdrew.) "Tow maid servants" were hired for "clensing the house" of William Grame, and Margaret Henderson got twenty shillings for performing the same service for Thomas Clark's executors.[6] As would be expected, such costs varied with the size of the establishment concerned. The "clenshers" of Jane Glasenby's house got thirty shillings and the woman who scrubbed out Robert Greenwell's house two pounds. Ralph Tailor itemized the expenses for Robert and Elizabeth Harrison's house, which included at least six rooms, as £3. 10s. 4d. "for cleansing the house to three cleansers" and a further two pounds "for their charges during the time they were in cleansing". That would have included not only materials, but also "vitelling the clensers": "mete and drinke to the clensers" could constitute a quarter of the costs.[7] And where infection had recurred, or the mortality had been peculiarly heavy, cleansing might be required more than once. The fact that the connected households of Ambrose Haddock and George Ellison suffered ten deaths over a period of several weeks underlay the payment made by Ambrose's administrator "for cleansing the houses severall times".[8]

Most of these details are provided by the inventories of the goods and debts of the deceased; the next of the plague's "rituals of closure".[9] By law, the making of an inventory was the first step in the settlement of a testator's estate and the execution of his or her will. According to Henry Swinburne, whose *Briefe Treatise of Testaments and Last Willes* was the most authoritative work on the subject, no executor "ought . . . to meddle with the goods of the deceased before he make an Inventory". Such a "true and perfect inventarie" should list "all goods, chattels, wares, merchandizes, moveable and immoveable", owned by the deceased, together with any leases held by the testator, and any unharvested "corne on the ground". Land or houses, however, should not be included. Debts owing to a testator at the time of death should be listed, but the inclusion of debts owed by the testator was optional. All this should be done by the executor, or under his or her direction, "in [the] presence, and by [the] discretions" of at least two witnesses, who might be beneficiaries of a will, or creditors of the deceased, or "other honest persons".[10] Moreover, the testators' goods should not only be listed, but also be "particularly valued and preised by some honest and skilful persons to be the just value thereof in their judgements and consciences, that is to say, at such price as the same may be solde for at that time".[11] This accomplished, one copy of the inventory was to be deposited with the "ordinary" or ecclesiastical judge, one copy would be kept by the executor, and the administration of the estate could commence.

No time limit for the making of an inventory was laid down in law; the matter was discretionary.[12] But clearly it should be accomplished as soon as was reasonably possible. The inventory that Ralph Tailor drew up of the goods of Margaret Ayre in April 1636, for example, was dated almost exactly one month after the will he had written for her. In the year following the plague, he wrote Richard Browne's inventory only three weeks after Browne's will.[13] Such intervals represent normal practice. Of the Newcastle wills proved in 1635, the interval between will and inventory ranged from nine days to ten months, but more than half the inventories were prepared within one month of the will and three-quarters within two months.[14] The circumstances of a plague outbreak, however, could severely disrupt such expectations. At the very least, the inventorying of goods could not proceed until a household was released from quarantine and the house and goods had been cleansed, while such contingencies as the absence of family members who had fled the city, the deaths of named executors, or difficulty in assembling suitable appraisers or compiling lists of debts could occasion further delays.

The evidence bears this out. Of the forty-six surviving inventories of plague victims, only seven (15 per cent) were made within two months of the will or recorded burial of the testator and most of these, perhaps significantly, were of people who died in the later stages of the epidemic. Another twenty-one (46 per cent) were made between two and four months after the testator's will or burial (most of them, in fact, after intervals of three to four months). Thirteen more (28 per cent) were made after gaps of four to six months, and the remaining five (11 per cent) took still longer. Ralph Tailor wrote the inventory of Thomas Hayton the younger, who probably died in July 1636, on 30 April 1637, while the inventory of Robert Mallabar, whose will had been written by Ralph on 5 November, was not prepared until 9 May 1637.[15]

Whatever the precise circumstances occasioning these delays in preparing the inventories of individual testators, the surviving evidence of the inventorying process as a whole conveys a sense of a society slowly stirring, examining its injuries, and heaving itself back onto its feet. The first surviving inventory was made on 14 September: that of the weaver Robert Walker of St Nicholas' parish.[16] Then, after a pause of three weeks, five more survive for October (Ralph Tailor wrote two of them) and eight for November (of which Ralph wrote four). Seventeen were prepared in December and ten in January. By the end of January 1637, the process was largely complete, the remaining five inventories being dated between late February and early May. Robert Mallabar's was the last. In all of this there is no discernible pattern of inventorying starting up as the plague withdrew from particular parishes (though such a sequence might have existed at a more intimate level, as particular streets or districts were judged clear of infection). Rather, the impression is of a process set in motion in October, as the plague subsided throughout the city, and gathering pace thereafter until the job was done.

The spread of the inventorying process over several months and the substantial delays involved in recording the goods of individual testators inevitably raised the possibility that goods might be "meddled with" before they were listed and appraised. As we have seen, William Robson of St Andrew's parish had an inventory of his goods drawn up two weeks before his death, "he fearinge the clensers should deceive him or his". Barbara Havelock had specified in her will of 20 August that her executor Daniel Anderson should have "my Table, Cubbert and butterie and all my woodd furniture for ayre loumes to his house". Yet her inventory of 8 December contained no wooden furniture whatever. Presumably it had already been removed, perhaps by Daniel Anderson, who may have been aware that her debts, funeral expenses, and "charges in her sicknes" far exceeded the value of her goods, and so was anxious to secure his own legacy.[17] Yet most inventories describe fully furnished houses or lodgings, while many list items of particular value, like silver plate, or substantial sums of "ready money". The impression given is that "meddling" of whatever kind was rare. Perhaps many of these houses were still inhabited by survivors of the testators' households. Others may have been securely locked and watched, or guarded by such people as Elizabeth Snow, who was paid ten shillings by Thomas Clark's executor "for keeping the house from [Christ]mas to Shrovetide and coles".[18] Of course, one can never be sure that any inventory was indeed "true and perfect". But once accepted by the ecclesiastical court, it had legal standing. As Swinburne put it, "all such goods and chattels as are contained in the Inventarie, are presumed to have belonged to the testator, and after his death to belong, and to be in the power of the executor. And on the contrary, that no more goods and chattels are presumed to have belonged to the testator, then are contained in the

Inventarie." Anyone alleging that goods had been wrongly included, or omitted, had to prove their case.[19] Drawing up these documents, then, was both a form of closure and a point of departure; an essential stage in the restoration of normality. And to this extent they have a certain liminal quality. They describe houses momentarily frozen in time and bereft of inhabitants (regardless of who may actually have been resident there). They list and count and value and total things standing apparently unused. In their tallies of debts they record relationships suspended. But they also assume resumption, imposing a kind of order and literally taking stock before feet clatter over the floors again, pots hiss, chairs scrape, beds creak, pewter rattles on tables and in washtubs, tools are picked up, and goods are sold.

In all of this Ralph Tailor played a disproportionate role, as we have seen, sometimes as both appraiser and scribe, sometimes simply as the clerk in attendance. He began on 10 October with the inventory of Thomas Holmes, whose will he had written just over two months earlier. He was very busy in November, somewhat less so in December and January, but still called on occasionally to write the inventory of a plague victim until 30 April, when he prepared that of Thomas Hayton the younger. Long before then he was already serving new clients whose deaths were unconnected to the plague.[20]

Preparing an inventory was already a familiar task when he walked into Thomas Holmes' house on 10 October. It was one of the standard jobs that a scrivener might be called upon to perform, and he had certainly done it before.[21] Perhaps he was aware of Swinburne's advice that the best "order" to "observe" in making an inventory was to proceed from "houshold stuffe" to other moveable goods like "corne and cattell", then to "leases of grounds or tenamentes", and finally to "debts due to the testator". Perhaps he just knew from frequent observation that this was indeed the order "for the most part observed at this time here in England".[22] Whatever the case, that is certainly what he did, as indeed did most other scribes of inventories. The form of the resulting documents gives a clear sense of the procedures followed. As one of the four named appraisers, or as the clerk accompanying them, Ralph moved from room to room taking notes. Within each room the contents were grouped into convenient lots, each of which became an 'It[e]m' to be described and then given an overall value. These values were later totalled for the room as a whole. Next came the listing and valuation of the tools of a testator's trade and shop goods, followed by any livestock and grain in store. Then came leases held; then the testator's apparel and any "ready money" in the house. All this was neatly reproduced when the formal inventory was drawn up. Debts owing to the deceased person were then listed, and a total arrived at for the goods appraised and the debts owing. This was usually followed by a list of debts owed by the deceased (which might include funeral expenses, the costs of cleansing, and the like). A net total sometimes followed, preceded by "theare rests cleare", "so there rests cleere", or some similar phrase.

The inventory of Thomas Holmes provides a specific example.[23] It begins with a formal heading, declaring it to be "A true and perfect Inventorie of all such goods And chattels As Thomas Holmes late of the Towne & County of Newcastle upon Tyne yeoman decd. dyed possessed of", stating the date of the appraisal, and naming the appraisers: John Wraugham, John Hunter (who had witnessed Holmes' will), William Ridley, "And Raiph Tailor".

They started "In the hall", the main ground-floor room of the house, and with the fireplace, grouping together the "iron chimney" (a grate for burning coal) and other goods standing or lying near it, including "one paire of tongs", a spit, a "chopping knife", a "brasse ladell", a "frying pann", and a "paire of Tosting Irons": total value sixteen shillings. Then came a "little Table", with a form (a long bench without a back), four chairs, and a stool: six shillings in all. Two large items of wooden furniture came next, a "cubbord" and a "close bedstead": twenty-four shillings. The appraisers then counted and valued fifty-two items of pewter, including dishes, "banqueting dishes", "saucers", many pots, a "hand bayson", a "salt seller", and a "beaker": forty-three shillings' worth altogether, they thought. They turned to the soft furnishings: a dozen items, including bedding, the "courtaines" of the bed, and "one greene rug". Twenty shillings.

Anything else? There were two brushes, perhaps leaning in a corner: ninepence. And then more pots and pans (one of brass, three of iron) and a little kettle: twenty shillings for the lot. Ralph took that down and they moved on to the "kitching", as he always spelled it; in this case an unheated back room containing mostly wooden items for storage or food preparation: a "meale chist", "clothbasketts", a bucket, tubs – among them, three "leaven tubs" – and flour sieves. But there was no oven. Probably Ann Holmes took her prepared dough to the nearest baker. The whole room was valued at only thirteen shillings and fourpence. Then up to the loft, the only

16. Inventory of Thomas Holmes' goods and debts, prepared on 10 October 1636. Note the specification of rooms, the grouping of goods into lots, and the alternation between Roman and Arabic numerals.

other room in the house, and the room where Thomas Holmes had died. It could be heated – there was another "iron chimney" – and it contained a superior table of "wainscot" and "three greene chaires", presumably upholstered. The bedstead was "old". Perhaps the Holmeses usually slept downstairs, but sat, and sometimes ate, upstairs. There was a spinning wheel. And there was a great deal of linen: three "tablecloths" and eighteen "Table Napkins", as well as sheets and pillowcases ("codpillowbers").

That was it for the "houshold stuff". But the appraisers were not yet finished. There was a great deal of grain in the house: "twenty boules of wheat and twenty boules of Rye", which were worth thirteen pounds, and "seaven boules of Meale", worth forty-two shillings.[24] Nearby on the river were Holmes' "foure chalder" keel boat and the "five chalder boote" in which he had a half-share, worth fourteen pounds in all.[25] Then he had "A Lease of A house for certen yeares yet endureinng" (probably this house) worth twenty-five pounds. His apparel, not itemized, was worth four pounds, and he had fourteen pounds "in ready money".

In writing the resulting inventory, Ralph Taylor had proceeded up to this point using Roman numerals, probably employing an abacus or counting board for the difficult task of manipulating sums of money expressed in letters. (In fact, he made a small error in totalling the goods listed as being "In the Loft".) The next item, however, a list of "Debts oweing to the Deceased" by twenty-one men and five women, mostly in sums of less than ten shillings, involved a sudden shift to Arabic numerals. Both the change in numerical notation and the detail involved suggest that Holmes had left some kind of record of those who owed him money. Ralph totalled the debts correctly (in Arabic numerals) as £12. 16s. 10d. Then, returning to Roman numerals, he produced a grand total for "The goods apprized and debts owing the deceased" of £98. 10s. 3d. He then concluded with a list of ten debts owed by Holmes (given in Roman numerals) which he totalled (in Arabic numerals) as £75. 13s. 3d. Almost a third of this sum was accounted for by the debt of twenty-four pounds "for funeral chargs and chargs for there maintenance during the tyme of there visitation & for clensing the house".[26]

Essentially the same procedures were followed in case after case. There were variations in detail, of course. Robert Moore's house had more rooms than Thomas Holmes'. Ralph Tailor must surely have remembered the scene of 19 August when he re-entered the "chamber" next to the "upper hall" just over three months later. None of his fellow appraisers had been there; they hadn't heard Robert's familiar voice through the thin wall. But if he paused to recall those anxious minutes, it cannot have been for long. The house was done, but there was still the carpenter's "workegeare" and "Tymber lying at the Closegate" to appraise, and a "little cow" to view and value.[27]

Goods might be grouped in different convenient configurations. In Thomas Hayton the younger's hall, Ralph described one lot as "Itm. two little potts, two little pans, one paire of belles one dozen of Trenchers one bibell and Three paire of Tempses} xs".[28] Why this collection? Were they piled on Hayton's cupboard? It was different every time; but there was also a generic quality to the process. Rooms; goods; debts; totals; lives gone, tabulated in things owned; lives resuming, starting with a reckoning of things essential to existence; one daily round cut off, another beginning.

There was not a lot of money to be made. Barbara Havelock's executor paid only two shillings for her "will and Invontorie". (There were relatively few goods to list.) Robert Mallabar's paid twenty-one shillings "for the charges of the Apprizers and the clerke for writing this Inventarye & their dinners". (It was a much bigger task.)[29] But the young scrivener probably welcomed whatever fees he could earn, especially if he was commissioned to write two copies, one being a fair copy for the diocesan registry.[30] And each job he was offered, however small, was a sign of trust reposed in him. Cumulatively, his activity built his reputation among his fellow citizens. It also extended his experience, for he was in a sense engaged not only in the listing of goods and the making of an important document, but also in taking the measure of both the material and the commercial cultures of his city. What would he (and others like him) have learned?

As he moved from house to house, he would certainly have become more than ordinarily familiar with the housing stock of the city. Most of the houses described in inventories were probably of two storeys, about half also having a loft and/or cellar, but some were more elaborate buildings. The merchant Thomas Wynn had what appears to have been a three-storey house plus loft and cellar, and when Ralph Tailor and three companions came to inventory the goods of the widow Ann Symons they made their way through a tall narrow house of perhaps four storeys; starting in the "seller" and then proceeding upwards through the "hall", the "chamber over the hall", the "upper chamber", and finally the "upmost chamber". He would have learned that a third of the households inventoried had lived in only two or three rooms (usually a hall or "forehouse", a kitchen, and an upper chamber). Rather more than two-fifths lived in four or five rooms (add another chamber, or a parlour, or a bakehouse or brewhouse), but less than a quarter enjoyed six or more rooms. Ralph inventoried only one house of such size, that of Matthew Waddell, a prosperous baker and brewer. For the most part he dealt with lesser craftsmen and tradesmen. But there were others of such means among the victims of the plague. Thomas Wynn had six chambers. "Mr" Timothy Cooke, a draper, had ten rooms, including two parlours and a study. Ralph might also have observed that half of the houses he inventoried had only one heated room – the hall – while all save one of the rest had fire irons in only two rooms. Matthew Waddell was exceptional again in having four heated rooms. Most people must have felt the chill of northern winters keenly before their fires were laid each morning, but at least they had abundantly available cheap coal to burn.[31]

Inventories, however, were not about houses. They were about goods and chattels, and it was above all a knowledge of such goods that the task of inventorying would have imparted to the young scrivener. As a man at the outset of independent adulthood, it is unlikely that Ralph Tailor yet owned much. His position may have been comparable to that of James Dune of Allhallows' whose inventory was completed on 1 November. Dune was originally from Carlisle. He is described as a miller, but was clearly still working as a journeyman, for almost half the value of his inventory was the two pounds, six shillings owing to him "for waidgis". He lived in lodgings and owned no goods except his bedding and his clothes ("one sute of Apparell, ii waistcotes"; "one course sute of Apparell with 3 shyrtes"; "one horsman cott").[32] But if Ralph was at a similar stage of the life course, he would soon have learned what he might aspire to as a potential member of Newcastle's "middle sort".

"Similarity in living styles," as Keith Thomas observes, "was an important source of social cohesion", and the expected standards of the peer group Ralph Tailor hoped to join are evident enough in the inventories that he and others prepared.[33] In comparison to the rural households of Durham and Northumberland at this time, those of Newcastle's craftsmen and tradesmen were well stocked with domestic goods.[34] Fire irons and sets of cooking pots and pans of brass and iron were virtually universal, as were joined tables and chairs (as well as stools and forms) and cupboards and chests for storage. Many people also owned a dresser. Almost everyone had a proper bedstead (often several) and featherbeds, bolsters, sheets, and pillows to furnish them. Table linen was abundant, as were pewter plates, dishes, drinking pots, "salts", candlesticks, and chamber pots. (The pewter was sometimes weighed rather than counted.) Two-thirds had at least one "carpett cloth" to lay on the best table and cushions to soften unupholstered chairs, and rugs for the floor were common.[35]

Ralph Tailor noted all of this. And the more familiar he became with this generic domestic culture, the more aware he would have become of those items that were less ubiquitous. Around two-fifths of all those inventoried owned small items of silver plate (among Ralph Tailor's clients, Thomas Eden had "one silver beare bowel, Two wyne cupps and Tenn spoones", while the "master and mariner" John Reed had "one silver whissle", perhaps an emblem of his command).[36] A similar proportion owned books, usually a Bible and perhaps a "service booke" where their nature was identified. Ralph recorded Robert Harrison's "one ould bible with divse small books" (ten shillings) and Matthew Waddell's "one Bible and other little books" (four shillings).[37] A quarter owned a set of drinking glasses, usually described as a "glasse caise" or "glasse cage", and a quarter had a "looking glasse" or "seeing glasse".[38] Almost a fifth had weapons in their homes, presumably in order to perform duties of civic defence. Robert Moore had a "musket" and a "halbert". Ralph Emerson had a small armoury: "one musket, one callever a paire of Breudeleries [bandoliers?] one halbert one steele capp", worth twenty shillings in all.[39] Ralph would also have learned to identify and perhaps appreciate goods that were rare and unfamiliar. Clocks were very rare, though Ralph Rowmaine had one, worth thirty shillings. (He also owned another rarity: "a paire of virginalls".) Most others who had any means of measuring time made do with an "houre glasse".[40] Pictures were also rare, though not of great value. The "three paper pictures" in Richard Browne's inventory were worth only sixpence, and Thomas Wynn's "Three old pictures" were valued at two shillings. Then there was Thomas Eden's "pare of playing Tables" and his "skreene", or the "shorte table with drawing leaves" in Elizabeth Franklin's hall; all unusual items of furniture. John Reed was one of only two people who possessed porcelain: "ten cheiney dishes", perhaps acquired on one of his voyages. Elizabeth Franklin had unusual ceramics of a different kind. She had a good deal of "blew waire" (perhaps Delft), including "six broad earthern dooblers of blew warre", worth over three pounds in all, and also "certaine black potts which came from London", worth two pounds. She may in fact have been dealing in such novelties, and in glass. She owed three pounds, nine shillings to "Mr John Dalby of Radcliff" in East London, and her "backhouse" contained several "glasse chists without lids".[41]

These variations in the goods people owned implied distinctions: of status and means, of awareness and access, or simply of personal disposition. We can only speculate as to their social meaning in the specific context of Newcastle's social and commercial milieux, or the social and cultural messages Ralph Tailor may have registered as he listed their presence. He was also, however, learning about another form of distinction: distinctions of quality. He knew an "ordinary dansk chist" when he saw it, and the superior nature of a "wainscott table", a "wainsckott chaire", a "wanded chaire", matching "greene chaires", "fyne chaires", or a "London bedstead". He recognized "Dansk potts" among the pewter, and knew that if cushions were commonplace, those that were "velvett", "needleworke", "sowed", "leather", or "gilt leather" merited identification as such.[42] Conversely, his descriptive language also employed disparaging adjectives. He sometimes used "little" in a manner that seems to imply diminished value as well as small size: "one little form"; "foure little rugs"; "one little wine cup"; a "paire of little racks". But above all he used the term "old": "one old bedstead"; "certaine old furniture"; four "old chaires"; "one old carpitt"; "one old trunk".[43] All this was part of learning to assess goods as a preliminary to applying his knowledge of the local market (no doubt enhanced by the experience of his fellow appraisers) to determine their cash value. He seems to have developed a reliable eye for such matters. Thomas Eden's fairly elaborate furnishings were valued by Ralph and three fellow appraisers on 10 January 1636/7 at just over seventy-three pounds. On 23 March, they were auctioned for a total of just under seventy-two pounds. The appraisers had done a pretty good job.[44]

Nor was Ralph Tailor's practical education confined to domestic goods, for the inventories that he helped to prepare also included "wares", "merchandizes", and "workgeare". More than half the inventories surviving for those who died in 1636, in fact, listed commercial goods and equipment of one kind or another. Ralph

Tailor was not called upon to participate in appraising so elaborate a commercial inventory as that of the merchant Thomas Wynn, who dealt in grain, fish, and wine.[45] He did not attend the three cord-wainers who went through the loft and workshop of their fellow guildsman John Collingwood, valuing the hides and tanned leather, counting up close to two hundred pairs of boots, shoes, "pumpes", and "childrens showes" that were either finished or cut out ready "to make up", and noting his stock of rendered tallow and "his Tubb his lasts his boot trees his liquor potts and other his working gear".[46] He did not count the many bolts of cloth held in store by Timothy Cooke, draper (worth close to nine hundred pounds), or the hundreds of "dailes", "half dailes", "birk spars", and "bumpkins" in the yard of the timber merchant John Susan.[47] In short, he was not employed by the executors of the city's more significant merchants and tradesmen. But he became familiar with the cask staves, hoops, and finished barrels of the cooper Robert Harrison, the brewing vessels and equipment of Matthew Waddell, and the bakehouse of Richard Browne, with its "moulding table", "kneeding chist", and "two rolling pins", as well as Thomas Holmes' keels, Robert Moore's timber and carpentry tools, and Elizabeth Franklin's stock of ceramics. He knew that two-thirds of John Reed's inventoried wealth was vested in his "one eight part of a ship called the John of Newcastle". He may have seen the "barbers basin" and the "web of linen of xviii yardes being much stayned" that were indicative of Robert Mallabar's profession of barber-surgeon. He was aware that a good many tradesmen had stocks of grain sufficiently large to indicate a sideline in corn dealing (John Reed and Thomas Holmes among them). And he cannot have failed to notice that many of them had sums of "ready money" on hand to finance their daily dealings. That was usually a few pounds in the case of Ralph's clients – Robert Moore's £8. 10s. 4d., or Ann Symons' six pounds and six shillings – though one of them, Thomas Eden, had over forty-three pounds, "which was delivered forth of the deceased's house in his life time" to be kept safe until his estate was settled.[48]

As clerk or as appraiser, then, Ralph Tailor would have acquired a sharper awareness of the economic structures of his city. He saw how livings were made and how incomes were spent. He observed the common features of the lifestyles they afforded and also noted the differences between those, like John Collingwood, who lived lavishly, those, like the cooper Robert Harrison, who lived in decent comfort, and those, like the miller William Dixon, who more or less scraped by.[49] Moreover, in drawing up the lists of debts owing to, or owed by, testators, he came face to face with the dynamics of Newcastle's commercial economy. As the debts listed and the deals that lay behind them testified, this was an economy that turned on credit. Households were bound together by "complex strings of interpersonal household credit".[50] Success or failure depended crucially on maintaining a favourable balance between what one owed and what one was owed, and a sound reputation for meeting one's obligations when it came to a "reckoning" was vital if one was to continue to be "trusted". For instance, it was a disagreement over "reckieing or accompting some debts" between Martin Allenson and Elizabeth Almery of Allhallows', he being "not well pleased with her reckening", that led to court action in 1628 to defend her reputation.[51] Death precipitated a comprehensive reckoning for households, sometimes at an inauspicious moment, and in the final act of adding up the value of goods owned by and debts owed to testators, subtracting their unpaid debts and "charges", and figuring out what "remained clear", Ralph Tailor and his fellows would have been alerted both to the relative strength or fragility of particular household economies and to the specific impact upon them of the plague.

It is impossible to be certain of the exact net worth of any testator's estate in this period without the survival of the accounts submitted by executors or administrators to the probate court. These were rarely kept, and very few survive among the probate records of the diocese of Durham for 1636 and 1637.[52] One that does, the account of Margaret Curry's administration of the estate of her deceased husband, John Curry of St John's parish (which predated the plague), gives us a flavour of what is missing. She took responsibility for his goods and debts owing to him (which she collected) to a total value of £130. 3s. 10d. She paid his funeral expenses, the court fees, rent he owed at the time of his death, his servants' wages, and then a variety of other debts, mostly it seems to neighbours in St John's. One was "for cheeses", another "for candles" (both being paid to the wives of the suppliers concerned, who must have handled this side of their family businesses). Two more were debts owed to the cordwainers John Collingwood (twelve shillings) and Thomas Eden (forty-five shillings), both of whom were later to die in the plague. When all was settled, £81. 16s. 6d. remained in her hands (roughly 63 per cent of the gross value).[53]

Such precision is usually beyond us. It is, however, possible to approximate the net personal estate of testators in those cases in which the inventory includes at least the debts owed by the deceased and other "charges" to be set against the gross valuation. These rarely include a note of court fees, and in addition one can never be certain that the executor was able to collect all the debts owing to the deceased (as we will see). For these reasons such estimates are optimistic. Nevertheless, one can at least arrive at an approximate net inventoried estate. This has been done for the thirty plague victims whose inventories provide the necessary details, with the following results. In seven cases (23.3 per cent), the net value was 75 per cent or more of the gross inventoried value. In eight more (26.7 per cent), it was between 50 and 74 per cent of the gross. In six cases (20 per cent), it fell to between 25 and 49 per cent of the gross. In three (10 per cent), it was below 25 per cent of the gross, and in the final six cases (20 per cent), the net value was actually negative. These figures can be interpreted as indicating that in exactly half the cases (those whose net value was more than 50 per cent of the gross) the outcome was reasonably satisfactory by the standards of the time. For some, it was very good. In almost a third of cases, however (those with net values that were positive, but less than 50 per cent of the gross), the estate left to dependants was very seriously impaired, in some cases so badly as to render their position marginal. And in a fifth of cases (those with negative net values), the situation was utterly disastrous.

As might be expected, those with relatively small gross inventory values appear to have been most at risk, though this was not invariably the case. The final reckoning of the inventorying process seems, in fact, to have depended on three principal factors. First, there was the extent to which people had been financially stretched at the time of their illnesses and deaths. John Collingwood was in a strong position. The value of his inventoried estate was high; he had over ninety pounds owing to him, and he owed less than twelve pounds. The chapman William Robson of St Andrew's was less well placed. His goods were few, consisting mostly of his chapman's pack of wares and the value of the lease of his house. He was owed over thirteen pounds, but two-thirds of the debts due to him were described as "desperate debts", unlikely to be paid. He himself owed over thirteen pounds to various creditors.[54] Matthew Storey knew he was in trouble before he died and his will (dictated to

Ralph Tailor) included an entreaty to his two brothers, to whom he owed a total of ten pounds, "to forbeare their money until my other debts be paid and after they are paid then to take and accept of their said moneys by Three pounds every yeare till they be fully paid".[55]

A second, though connected, factor was the extent to which the circumstances of the plague had rendered "desperate" some debts owing to testators that might otherwise have been paid. Margery Holborn's appraisers noted that the debts owing to her totalled over 110 pounds but added pessimistically, "the most part whereof are desperate". The debts owing to the notary John Carr totalled £178. 4s. 2d., mostly in sums of less than five pounds, and often less than one pound, but the appraisers added "whereof a greate part is desperate". Those who drew up the inventory of the baker and brewer William Hall considered the debts owed to him on bills and bonds as good, but when it came to the debts "per booke", described as "triviall debts" (most likely credit advanced to his customers), they considered sixty pounds of the 110-pound total to be "desperate". Indeed, they were so sure of this that they deducted the sixty pounds before arriving at the gross value of Hall's inventoried estate: they entertained no hope whatever that the money could be recovered.[56] Such evidence suggests an exceptionally high level of default on the part of debtors, which severely impacted the estates of some testators. Inevitably one wonders how far this was a consequence of the plague; how far loss of earnings or exceptional expenses had crippled people's ability to meet their obligations; and how many simply died insolvent.[57]

A third factor was the financial impact on households of the costs of sickness and death. Any death, of course, involved expenses, if only those of the deceased's funeral (and in time of plague, as we have seen, funeral charges might be reduced in scale). But as we have also seen, plague might mean that several burials had to be paid for within a short period of time, as well as the charges arising from the maintenance of quarantined households, the employment of keepers, and the cleansing of houses and goods. So far, such outlays have been separately considered, but their cumulative impact could make significant inroads into household resources. The costs of Margery Holborn's "funeral expenses . . . and maintenance of her dureing the time of her sicknes and clensing the house severall tymes" came to more than twenty-one pounds in all.

Robert Eden laid out the same amount "for the mainetinance of Thomas Eden and his wife and family dureing the time of their visitation and their funeral charges of three persons and for cleansing the house and goods". Ambrose Haddock's gross inventoried estate came to almost ninety-two pounds, but thirty pounds (almost a third) had to be deducted by his widow "for the funeral expenses of the said deceased and of six others of his familie who dyed all of the plague in his house (besides Ellysons children who were under his tuicon) and for clensing the houses severall tymes and other necessarie charge".[58]

The evidence does not permit an aggregate assessment of the economic impact of the plague upon the households of the city, but the manner in which these factors interacted to produce a range of outcomes can at least be exemplified in individual cases. For some, the outcome was as satisfactory as could be hoped for in the circumstances. The tanner Ralph Rowmaine's inventoried estate was of considerable value. More than half the debts listed as owing to him when Ralph Tailor wrote his will seem to have been collected by the time his inventory was made over three months later. His own debts were not great, and when the appraisers had deducted them and the charges associated with the deaths of Rowmaine, his wife, and one child, they could confidently state that "theare restes cleare" to his survivors over 114 pounds (around three-quarters of the gross inventoried estate).[59] In contrast, the "skipper" John Mayne was a relatively poor man, most of his goods "old" and of low value. But he was free of debt, and with all his charges paid, the inventory could conclude "soe there resteth good" £8. 15s. 3d., which was around 80 per cent of the gross value.[60] Jane Glasenby was a single woman, possibly a governess. Her personal goods were few, but she had a good deal of "ready money" and no debts owing and few owed. When the costs of her sickness and death were deducted, there remained more than enough to pay the legacies she had left to her nephews in the country and to the four children of "my master Dockter Genisonn".[61]

At the other extreme were those for whom the outcome was disastrous. Thomas Clark, a tailor, knew on his deathbed that his house in Pilgrim Street would need to be sold if there was to be any hope of paying his debts "and raiseing A portion to his daughter Margaret", and his inventory bears out his fears. His debts and the costs of his illness exceeded the value of his relatively comfortable household goods by over seven pounds.[62] William Robinson's gross inventoried estate came to just over ten pounds, but his charges and debts came to more than eighteen.[63] Many of those debts could not have been paid. Nor, perhaps, could those of William Dixon. Ralph Tailor reckoned that he owed over thirty-four pounds to eighteen people (including the overdue rent for his mill), whereas his inventoried goods were worth less than nine pounds.[64] Thomas and Katherine Hayton's inventoried goods came to almost twenty pounds, but against that was set fifteen pounds, "desbursed for thear beariall and cleansing the house and meat and drinke for cleansers and coffins and other charges". Their son Thomas the younger was left a house, but when Ralph Tailor finally drew up his inventory, the value of his modest goods and the debts owed to him, some twelve pounds in all, was exceeded by the sixteen pounds he owed in debts to six creditors and for the charges occasioned by his own plague death.[65]

Finally, there were those for whom the inheritance left to their dependants was seriously diminished, if not wholly blasted, by the nature of their untimely deaths. Ralph Tailor's clients provided examples enough. Matthew Waddell had a substantial inventoried estate of over 178 pounds. But over ninety-six pounds of that was in debts due to him, "the most part whereof is desperate". That would already have reduced his estate by more than half, and in this case we do not know what he himself also owed. Robert and Elizabeth Harrison's plague-occasioned costs wiped more than thirteen pounds off their gross inventoried estate of £22. 13s. 5d. The value of the skipper William Grame's goods (£7. 8s. 0d.) was almost matched by the costs arising from the burials of William and his children and the cleansing of the house (£7. 6s. 8d.). If his wife, the only survivor, managed to collect the ten pounds owing to him, then she might at best have been able to retain the household goods and have a couple of pounds in hand to face the future. Robert Moore was a respected man of modest substance. His gross inventoried estate, including twenty pounds owed to him, was roughly sixty-five pounds. But he owed thirty pounds and in addition there were twenty-four pounds to be paid in "charges for cleansing the house manetince of the sick persons and funeral charges". Even on the optimistic assumption that debts due to him were all collected, the net estate would have been only eleven pounds.[66] Thomas Holmes, as we have seen, had an even more substantial gross inventoried estate of over ninety-eight pounds, including his keel boats (fourteen pounds), the lease of his house (twenty-five pounds), ready money (fourteen pounds), and twenty-seven debts owing to him (£12. 16s. 10d.). But his own debts came to over seventy-five pounds, of which almost a third consisted of the twenty-four pounds owed for "funeral charges and charge for there maintenance dureing the tyme of there visitacon and for clensing the house". And he had bequeathed his half-share in one keel to his cousin Henry and a total of five pounds in legacies to other kin, one of whom was his sister Ann Wilson. Even if his widow, Ann Holmes, was able to collect all the debts owing to him, she would have had to sell the remaining keel, and the lease and some of the household goods, to clear his obligations and pay his legacies. Perhaps she failed to do so. Perhaps that is why Ann Wilson sued her.[67]

CHAPTER ELEVEN

Discords, Variances, and Suites

L ITIGATION WAS THE FINAL FALLOUT OF THE PLAGUE OF 1636, AND there was a good deal of it. Applications from Newcastle for either the probate of wills or grants of administration of the estates of intestates began to reach the courts at Durham in October 1636. The estates of only twelve people entered probate between October and December, then 131 between January and March 1637, and a hundred more between April and July 1637, after which the flood of cases fell to a trickle for the remainder of the year.[1] An unusual number of these applications was contested. The fragmentary deposition books that survive for the first seven months of 1637, covering probably only half of the sessions of the Consistory Court that actually took place in those months, reveal contests over the wills of nineteen testators, while documents filed with three more of the surviving wills indicate that these wills were also subject to question.[2] In all, then, at least twenty-two testamentary "causes" were brought. Seventeen of the fifty-seven surviving wills were disputed (30 per cent), while another five causes were fought over wills that have not survived (if, indeed, they ever existed in written form).[3] In comparison, the complete deposition book for the year ending October 1620 provides evidence of only two testamentary causes from Newcastle, while that covering the four calendar years 1627–30 contains depositions relating to only seven such causes. This suggests that the normal expectation was of around two testamentary disputes a year, a figure that makes the level of litigation known to have taken place in the early months of 1637 even more remarkable.[4]

The frequency with which testamentary disputes arose in 1637 was a direct outcome of the high mortality of the previous year, and more specifically of the swathe that the plague cut through the households of the "middle sort of people" in Newcastle. But if it was in part simply a reflection of the fact that many more people of modest property had died than was usual, it was also a consequence of the peculiar circumstances of epidemic mortality. Contesting a will was not in itself an unusual thing. Such cases inevitably occurred from time to time. What was also at issue here was the manner in which death from the plague, and the preparation of plague wills, threw up reasons to question the terms, and indeed the validity, of the testaments concerned.

Most causes seem to have arisen when an executor took a will to the ecclesiastical court at Durham to "prove" it as the true, whole, and last testament of the deceased person. By then the executor would already have taken charge of the deceased person's goods, having previously had them inventoried. The terms of the wills would have been known among surviving family members, friends, and neighbours, and exceptions to them might be entered at the court by interested parties. Then, as Henry Swinburne described the procedure, "witnesses are received and sworne accordingly, and are examined every one of them secretly, and severally, not only upon the allegations or articles made by the party producing them; but also upon interrogations ministered by the adverse party, and their depositions committed to writing: afterwards the same be published". After reviewing the evidence, the ordinary would pass judgment, and if the will and testament was approved, the executor would enter a bond to account for the administration of the estate.[5]

In nineteen of the causes occasioned by plague wills, the names of the parties at variance can be gleaned from the headings of the depositions taken in the court. On the one hand, there were the executors. Almost two-thirds of them were close relatives of the deceased (the widow, a son or daughter, brother or sister, brother-in-law or aunt). The remainder were friends who were either definitely not kin of the deceased person (a landlady, a fellow weaver, a former apprentice) or whose relationship to the deceased was never specified.[6] On the other hand were those lodging objections. Eight of them can be clearly identified as relatives of the deceased (sons or daughters, brothers or sisters, a "cozen") and another two were definitely non-kinsmen (another former apprentice, for example). But the rest (almost half of those who brought complaints) cannot be precisely identified on the available evidence. One can only surmise that they

were possibly more distant relatives who had emerged to make a
claim on the estate; a suggestion supported by the fact that when
witnesses were questioned as to their length of knowledge of the
parties to the cause, they frequently declared that these plaintiffs
were unknown to them, or that they knew them only "by sight".[7]

If we go on to juxtapose the plaintiffs and defendants in particular
causes, a definite pattern emerges. Where executors were widows or
children of the testator, they were invariably challenged by very
close relatives: a widow by a son, brother, or sister of the deceased,
for example, or a child of the deceased by one of his or her own
siblings. Where the executorship had passed beyond the testator's
widow or children, however, to a brother or brother-in-law, a more
distant kinsman or an unrelated person, there was a strong likelihood that the challenge would be launched by an "unidentified"
plaintiff. Again, one suspects that these were more distant relatives
who believed themselves entitled to a share in the estate, especially
if the devastation of the testator's family meant that his or her goods
were not directly descending to a widow or children. To this extent,
plague mortality may have broadened the pool of parties willing to
assert an interest in the disposition of an estate. But whether those
lodging objections were close family members or more peripheral
claimants, it was the nature of the "exceptions" raised that most
vividly demonstrated the disruptive impact of the circumstances of
plague deaths upon the authority of the last wills and testaments
that the court was called upon to approve.

Henry Swinburne defined a last will as "a lawful disposing of
that which any would have done after death"; "a testifying or
witnessinge of the minde", in which "the will and mind of the
testator doe appeare by two sufficient witnesses".[8] It was transformed into a last will and testament by the naming of an executor
whose essential duties were "to cause an inventarie to be made, to
procure the will to be proved and approved, to pay the testator's
debts and legacies; and finally to make an account".[9] In English law
it did not need to be written down unless "lands, tenements and
hereditaments" (i.e. real estate) were to be bequeathed, though it
was considered "a good and safe course" that it should be committed
to writing if possible. What was crucial was that the testator be
"of perfect mind and memory", that he demonstrate "a mind
and purpose then and thereby to make his testament or last will",
and that the declaration of the will be witnessed.[10] Nor was any

particular form of words required. What mattered was that "the Testators meaning do appeare: which meaning is to be preferred before the propriety of words". As Swinburne wisely opined, "the tongue is the utterer or interpreter of the heart, yet cannot every man utter all that he thinketh, and therefore are his words subject to his meaning". In consequence, he insisted that "the purpose and meaning of the testator is the life and soule (as I may tearme it) of the testament, without the which the testators words are but wind". In his view, "meaning (as a Queen or great Commandresse) doth rule and over-rule . . . in Wills and Testaments". Meaning was "the Queene or Empresse of the Testament", and where there was doubt, it "ought before all things to be sought for diligently; and being found ought in any wise to be observed faithfully".[11]

Eloquent as Swinburne was on the need to determine the testator's meaning, it is perfectly evident that what he termed the "unsolemn" nature of English wills, their relative paucity of formal requirements, left plenty of room for the raising of questions.[12] Moreover, the manner in which wills were made in time of plague greatly exacerbated such uncertainties. In the first place, there was the problem that so many plague wills were actually or effectively nuncupative wills. Strictly speaking, a nuncupative will was one made by word of mouth only: when the testator "doe name his executor, and declare his minde by words of mouth, without writing before witnesses". Even if never committed to writing, it was deemed to be "of as great force and efficacy (except for lands, tenements and hereditaments) as is a written testament".[13] If the terms of a will "made first by word of mouth" were "afterwards put into writing", it remained nuncupative "notwithstanding the reducing thereof into writing". However, if such writing was "brought to the testator and approved", or if he "declares it should be written and it is written during his life", it could be considered a proper written testament, i.e. one committed to writing "at the making thereof".[14] All these circumstances are by now familiar to us from the accounts of the making of the wills of Newcastle's plague victims.

Swinburne disliked nuncupative wills. They were hastily drawn up and raised too many "points as be doubtfull in law".[15] Therefore he strongly advised that while no "precise form of words" was required in such a will, "neither is it material whether the testator do speake properly or unproperly", it was nonetheless essential that "his meaning doe appeare". The testator must speak "plainely", "simply and certainly", and above all "must as much as he can avoide *obscuritie, and ambiguitie*". This was the best means to "avoid long and costly suites".[16] Yet in time of plague, wills made under such conditions, with all their potential consequences, were inevitably even more common than was usual. And they were yet more subject to a second problem that Swinburne discussed at some length: that of ascertaining the purpose, will, and meaning of a testator "being so ex[t]reame sicke that he is wel nigh dead", when it might "not appeare plainely whether he be of perfect minde and memorie", and who might be subject to "the interrogation of some other demanding of him whether he make this or that person his Executor and whether he give such a thing to such a person", or other pressures from those labouring "with tooth and naile to procure the sick person to yeelde to their demaunds".[17]

All of these problems (and others) were evident in the testamentary causes from Newcastle heard in 1637. Some were beset by the "obscuritie and ambiguitie" against which Swinburne warned. Did Mabel Walker name her daughter Barbara her sole executor, or merely imply that it should be so by leaving Barbara "all the residue of her goods"? Barbara's brother William wanted to know.[18] William Cooke had left his dwelling house to his wife, Margaret, "during her widowhead", but added that "after her decease" it should go to his son and executor, William. He also left her "two closes and one garth [i.e. yard] for her widowhead". What, then, were Margaret's rights in these properties: tenancy for life, or just for the duration of her widowhood? What if she remarried?[19] William Robson was "much indebted" and, when asked by a kinsman two hours before his death "if he had left his friends nothing", responded that "all he had was too little for his wife". But in leaving his wife, Alice, everything once his debts were paid, and naming her his executrix, he apparently made a conditional reservation of the lease of his house, "the which he said his sonne should have or some of his in caise any of them did come to Newcastle". One of the Robsons, perhaps the absent son, did indeed come to Newcastle and challenged Alice.[20]

Most objections to wills, however, seem to have been rooted in suspicions that a will exhibited by an executor was "imperfect" by means of what Swinburne termed "some *originall defect* or corruption".[21] Not everyone was disposed to quarrel about such things. Ambrose Haddock's nuncupative will had been witnessed by only one person, but his widow, Anne, was prepared to honour his reported wishes all the same. In her administrator's accounts, submitted on 10 May 1637, she noted that she had paid a total of ten pounds in legacies to his "brethren and sisters . . . according to his mind and direcon upon his death bedd, tho there was but one witness to prove the same". Perhaps her willingness to avoid contention also owed something to the facts that almost forty-eight pounds remained to her and that by the time she rendered her accounts she had remarried and was rebuilding her life.[22]

Not every interested party was so complaisant. Sometimes it seems to have been simply a matter of disappointed kinsfolk seeking to establish whether or not a valid will had actually been made, as in the cases of the nuncupative wills of Ann Milborne and Elizabeth Wiggham, or those of Jane Young and Anthony Robson (both of whom had died in the lodges on the town moor).[23] John Carr's will presented a special case of this nature, since it had been written by Carr himself. It had been witnessed, but none of the witnesses was called to give evidence in court. Perhaps they were dead. Instead the court heard a string of testimonies from men (including Ralph Tailor) who could identify Carr's hand and signature.[24]

Other cases, however, clearly involved specific allegations. One of these was that the will exhibited was incomplete, or, as Swinburne termed it, "imperfect in respect of will", since the testator "hath begun, but cannot finish as he would, being prevented by death, insanitie of minde or other impediments". Suspicion of such a situation underlay the interrogatory put to Ralph Tailor and John Hunter in the case of Thomas Holmes, asking "whether the said testator at the making of his said will before the same was finished did wax soe extreame sicke and imperfect of understanding, That he was forced abruptly to leave off, before he had fully concluded the same". This was why they explained that he had indeed broken off temporarily, but that he had returned to the window, heard the will read, and acknowledged it – though, as noted earlier, Ralph had to admit that he had remarked subsequently that "he was not certaine whether the said testator was of perfect mynde and memory at the making therof yea or noe".[25] Another allegation was the exertion of undue influence upon the dying person. Isabel Middleton was suspected of this in the case of her long-term "tabler and soiorner" the waterman Robert Moody; as were Henry and Thomas Finlay, who cared for Robert Walker after the deaths of Robert's wife and children and were named his heirs and executors.[26] It was acknowledged that Ann Mills (whose will was written up by Ralph Tailor long after her death, allegedly only after Ann's brother George had commenced suit) had declared her will in response to prompting from her aunt Margaret Humphrey, who "asked her what she would doe with her goods". Margaret, who had sheltered and taken care of Ann, was made Ann's principal heir and executor. George accused her of fraudulent practice, one of his claims being that Ann was "altogether insensible" for days before her death, "out regious [outrageous] in her sicknes and knew not what she did". On the other hand, testimony was given by those present that Ann "did not rage in her sicknes but died patientlie"; and that when asked "why she would give her brother no more" than a token of household linen, she had answered "that her brother was an unthrift and would spend all he had". The will stood.[27]

Even more contentious were causes in which it was claimed that more than one will had been made, the second will voiding the first, since in law a testator could alter or revoke a will at any time while he or she lived and "the last and newest is of force".[28] Thus, the merchant John Stobbs, as we have seen, prudently made a will on 3 June, in the early stages of the plague. Being unmarried and childless, he left his house to his nephew John Stobbs junior, and other properties to his "late apprentice" George Lambe, whom he also named as his executor and made heir to the first house if John junior died without issue. His current apprentice, Robert Fenwick, received a legacy of books and cash. However, on 8 September, when he was dying, John Stobbs apparently made a second, nuncupative will via his keeper, through a window, in which, according to three witnesses, he left his houses to John Stobbs junior and to Robert Fenwick. George Lambe was cut out, and when one of the witnesses later asked John's keeper, Margaret Hyndmers, "to put the said testator in mind of . . . George Lambe and to desire him to remember him", she returned John's answer "that he said he had nothing to give neither would he give him anything". Some three weeks later John Stobbs junior also succumbed to the plague, after dictating a will to Ralph Tailor in which he named "my loving friend Alexander Veitch" as his heir and executor. Veitch was later granted the administration of his estate without dispute. When the case of John Stobbs senior's will came to court, it was being fought between George Lambe, as Stobbs' executor, and one John Fenwick, presumably acting in right of Robert's claim.[29]

Even more dramatic was the case of Cuthbert Woodman, a master weaver with a substantial estate, for whom two nuncupative wills survive in the probate records. The first was declared "by word of mouth" on 22 August before six witnesses and written by Ralph Tailor. In it, Cuthbert bequeathed his house to his wife, Isabel, who was also named executor, and generous cash tokens to eight close relatives, one of whom, his brother Anthony, was to have both twenty pounds "for a token" and the forgiveness of a debt of seventeen pounds that he owed Cuthbert. The second, dated 24 August, was apparently written at the behest of Richard Harrison, Cuthbert's keeper. In this will, Cuthbert left his house and all his goods to his brother Anthony, named him executor, and cut out both his wife and six of the relatives who had been left tokens two days before, including his mother and his sister. It stated that his "writeinges" (deeds) were to be found "either in my deske or in my chist but my wife will convey them awaie and not suffer them to be seene without suite", and advised Anthony to consult a Mr Baker and one Henry Hodgson for direction since "they knowe how my writeinge[s] are". All of this was said to have been told to Richard Harrison "whom he charged and required as he would answeare him in an other world that he should write down his said will". He should then "deliver it secretly" to Anthony, "who the daie before menconed was at the said Cuthbert his doore but the said Cuthbert his wife tooke her husband in her armes and would not suffer him to speake or come to his said brother at which time he was much moved and said unto her god forgive the[e] for thou would have me doe my brother and his children wronge".[30]

This extraordinary case certainly came to the attention of the court, and two copies of each will remain on record together with Woodman's inventory. The second will, however, was not signed either by the alleged witness, Richard Harrison, or by whoever wrote it down, and it appears to have been voided.[31] Harrison was apparently called as a witness, but no depositions survive to cast further light on what may have transpired. One can only wonder whether Isabel Woodman did indeed prevent her husband from seeing his brother on 23 August, in the knowledge or expectation that he intended to alter his will and believing Anthony to have been well provided for already. But if she did, it may well have been because she believed her husband's mind had become unhinged.[32] For the final source of testamentary disputes was, of course, the belief by the dissatisfied party that the testator was not, in the phrase used in almost every will, "of perfect mind and memory".

The law laid down that "every person is presumed to be of perfite minde and memorie, unless the contrary be proved" by specific instances of deranged behaviour. Even the chronically sick were deemed to be capable of making a valid will so long as they could communicate by "gestures and sensible speeches", or respond clearly to questions put to them.[33] But the plague provided ample grounds for claiming that testators' dying agonies had deprived them of their reason. Such claims were advanced, as we have seen, in the cases of Thomas Holmes and Ann Mills. They may have had a role in the case of John Stobbs, certainly did in that of Cuthbert Woodman, and are to be found in the interrogatories relating to other causes. Was it true that for three days before his death Thomas Hayton "raged with the violence [of the plague] and was altogether insensible and speechles and not of sane memory"? Had Robert Moore, isolated in his upper chamber, been of unsound mind when he made his will? Elizabeth Frisell, his daughter, who may have felt that she deserved better of her father, or that she should have been made joint executor with her brother Michael, believed he must have been. Ralph Tailor, who had listened to his familiar voice through the wall, and answered his question regarding executorship, knew better.[34]

The aftermath of the plague, then, brought contention: born of antecedent rivalries, disappointed expectations, personal animosities, or simple opportunism, and nurtured by outraged senses of entitlement and festering suspicions. And the resulting litigation, of course, gave Ralph Tailor his final role in the drama of the plague, as a witness deposing before the Consistory Court in the Galilee Chapel of Durham Cathedral. In this, as in his activity as a scribe, his visibility is exceptional. Of the forty-six witnesses whose depositions have survived in cases relating to wills made during the plague, only Ralph Tailor made more than one. In fact, he appeared before the court on at least three occasions between 27 February and an uncertain date in May 1637, giving testimony in the cases of Thomas Holmes, John Carr, and Robert Moore, and he may have been there even more often. It was probably while in attendance at the court somewhat earlier that he wrote up the "schedule" of the bequests made by Ann Mills, at the request of those who had witnessed her final days, and as the scribe of

Cuthbert Woodman's first will he must surely have appeared when that case was heard.[35]

That Ralph was called so frequently to testify to the making of disputed wills he had written does not imply any failure of professional competence on his part. The wills he had made (including those in dispute) were apparently approved by the court, and they remain on record. Indeed, the procedures that he described himself as following (writing them immediately, reading them back, and having them acknowledged and witnessed) gave them a more secure legal standing than many nuncupative wills. As we have seen, he described his performance of his duties confidently, and the confidence others reposed in him was recognized in his being called as an expert witness in the validation of John Carr's hand. Rather, his prominence as a witness reflected his disproportionate role in the creation of the written record of the plague: the wills and inventories that still enable us to trace aspects of its course, its impact, and its consequences.

The depositions that he and others made in Durham elaborated that record and, as we have seen, they provide evidence of a different nature. They told stories of the plague. They were accounts of personal participation in specific events, describing what individuals had seen and heard, and creating from these memories brief narratives.[36] In part, of course, the stories they told were shaped by the need to address issues of particular legal significance and by specific interrogatories put to the witnesses, both arising from the allegations made by the parties to a cause.[37] But the fact that they were framed in this way does not devalue their significance as evidence. Allegations voiced in court were themselves based on stories already told; they arose in the first place because the provisions of a will and the circumstances of its making had already been talked about. They were based on information that had circulated, questions that had been asked, and memories that had already been recalled and expressed; around the fire in the hall, in the streets and markets of the city, in alehouses, taverns, and churches, on the quay, wherever people gathered and talked.

The issues later raised in court must have been generated in such contexts. Clearly people talked about the plague. Perhaps it was one of the ways they dealt with the trauma they had endured; recalling the dramas of death, and the faces and voices of the dead, even as they picked up the threads of their lives and resumed the daily routine of existence. Stories might give grounds for disquiet. The conditions of the plague had imposed what one historian of privacy has termed "interruptions of social knowledge" which could breed anxiety and distrust.[38] The voicing of suspicions, rumours of impending trouble, awareness that objections were being lodged and charges laid, requests to appear as a witness on behalf of one party or another, conversations between witnesses, litigants, and legal advisors, or among witnesses themselves, would all have helped to elaborate these memories. People would have been prompted to think themselves back to specific moments in that "lamentable time", locating them in time and space, and stimulated to recall and clarify details of what they had seen and heard, comparing individual variations of memory, and discovering the "overlap in recall and expression" which is evident in what they later deposed.[39]

The records are rarely explicit about such things – though we know that word was abroad that Ralph Tailor had said he was not sure that Thomas Holmes was of sound mind when he made his will. But they are implicit in the whole process that culminated in the making of depositions. And closer examination of what the witnesses said about their relationships to the parties in dispute helps give a sense of the social milieu from which their stories of the plague emerged. They were conventionally asked how long they had known the parties concerned, and responses to that question are recorded for thirty-eight witnesses (including Ralph Tailor) in relation to a total of eighty-six litigants. Over two-thirds of the litigants had been known by the witnesses concerned for more than two years, and over half for more than five years. Less than a quarter were known only by sight or not at all.[40] Almost three-fifths of the witnesses knew both parties to the conflict, while the remainder knew one but not the other. Many of those involved must also, of course, have known one another. This was the world of regular interaction and intimate personal knowledge through which information percolated and in which memories were retrieved and shared.

Among those who gave evidence, what has been called a "normative memory" of particular events may have been created long before they came to court.[41] Certainly the stories they told were shaped by the key points known to have been at issue and by the supplementary questions put to them. But the events they were asked to describe were not necessarily in themselves controversial. Usually they simply recalled having been present at the making of a will, rather than whether the testator had "raged", or whether particularly significant words had been spoken. There is no reason to suppose that most of them were not describing what they had indeed witnessed as they had come to remember it. Moreover, their testimony included much that was of no particular legal relevance. As we have seen, there were many circumstantial details with no direct bearing on the case: where Thomas Finlay was standing when he saw Ralph Tailor and Michael Moore coming up the street; how Margaret Hyndmers got into John Stobbs' house; who took the measurements for Thomas Hayton's coffin. There were the modes of expression, turns of phrase, and glimpses of conventional attitudes and values that reveal a shared culture, a "commonality of background and experience, outlook and expression".[42] There was no need to say more than "being a near neighbour" or "as a neighbour" to explain a person's presence as a visitor, or willingness to come to bear witness to a will.

In the depositions, then, we can hear the voices of the city; not unmediated, to be sure, but real. And they present a remarkable range of voices. They were male and female (twenty-seven men and nineteen women). They were young and old (the youngest only twenty and the oldest over sixty, with the average age of the men being thirty-five and the average age of the women thirty-four).[43] They came from scriveners, weavers, joiners, cordwainers, a keelman, labourers, and servants, and included both the relatively prosperous and the poor. Indeed, the circumstances of the plague gave to some of the poor – especially poor women, the servants acting as nurses for sick masters and mistresses, and the keepers hired specifically to tend isolated plague victims – an altogether exceptional role. Predictably, their credibility as witnesses was sometimes challenged. Any witness could be objected to by the party against whom he or she was produced on the grounds of "dishonestie in manners", "want of judgement or understanding", or "affection more to the one party then to the other", and the words of the poor were always particularly vulnerable in this respect.[44] That is why many of the keepers who gave evidence were asked to detail their economic circumstances and personal histories, and why Isabel Wiglesworth was questioned about both her relationship to Margaret Humphrey and her personal morality. (She explained that her alleged indebtedness to Margaret was "onely 9d. for beere and ale", that she had been married nineteen years, and that while it was true that her husband was away as a soldier at Harwich and that Thomas Thompson lived in her house as a lodger, Thomas happened to be "lxxx yeares of age".)[45] Nevertheless, the courts did not exclude their testimony.[46] In the case of plague wills, their voices were often crucial. Only they had been present. They had conveyed the vital terms of wills. In a curious reversal of the usual order of things, the plague had empowered them, and their role as witnesses also renders them historically visible and audible.[47]

Litigation, then, released stories of the plague: conventionalized, indeed, but not fictional (unless we are to believe that the judges who listened to and acted upon them were exceptionally gullible).[48] The depositions that contain them related to particular cases and recalled individual experiences, but taken as a whole they reveal the lineaments of a collective memory of the plague that had formed among the people of the city. By the time they were made, Robert Jenison had already taken it upon himself to define the public memory of the plague. In *Newcastle's Call* he provided an account of its origins and statistics that traced its course. But his images of the plague were generic stereotypes, the familiar dystopian vision of the plague tracts, taken down from the shelf to advance the moral agenda of his religious interpretation of the epidemic's significance. The depositions made at Durham had no such larger purpose, and they provide an alternative vision. They are fractured and fragmented, but they vividly record the remembered experiences of the mostly obscure people who had endured the calamity and survived. They created a record that enables us to recapture something of the texture of that experience: how it felt; what it meant. And if they were made in response to the claims and counterclaims of familial conflict, they also reveal, as we have seen, that despite its horror it was less destructive of social obligations than is often imagined.

CHAPTER TWELVE

Ralf Taylor Notarie Publicke

L ET US RETURN TO RALPH TAILOR. THE YOUNG SCRIVENER'S flamboyant signature was our point of entry to the story of Newcastle's great plague, and his frequent recurrence in the records that it generated provides a thread of personal narrative linking together those aspects of that calamity that can be reconstructed. We should, then, take final stock of his role, ask what became of him, and consider the place of the plague year in his subsequent career.

The year 1636–7 was the first of Ralph Tailor's independent professional life. When the plague threatened to overwhelm his city he was one of those who chose to stay and do his job. Perhaps it was the only way to hold on to his emergent adult identity. But by doing so, he became one of those who helped preserve the integrity of the urban community.[1] The record of his activity shows that no one did more to produce the documents that were crucial to the maintenance, preservation, and, when necessary, reconstruction of the social bonds that held together both family and civil society. The making of wills and inventories was always central to those processes. They recognized obligations to family and kin, friends and neighbours. They took stock of family resources, acknowledged debts, and provided for the orderly transmission of property between the generations. Their terms not only conveyed goods, but also embodied values and expressed emotional bonds: to people, to places, to institutions, and to communities. They were both a final expression of the personal agency of testators, exercised within the constellations of relationships that defined them, and a source of comfort to the dying. In the conditions of an epidemic, with the threat that it posed to familial and communal survival, it was all the more vital that all this continue, and the significance of the "instruments" concerned was in a sense magnified.

Ralph Tailor provided many of the instruments that facilitated these processes. To be sure, he did so for a fee. But the fact that this was how he made his living would hardly have been a matter worthy of remark to his neighbours. It does nothing to detract from the significance of the service he provided to the small property owners of the city. And there was a further consequence of direct import to the fledgling scrivener. For his activity during the plague year also served to embed him deeply in Newcastle's freemen community. The extent to which this was so can be revealed by two simple exercises in the reconstruction of social networks.

In the course of writing wills and inventories between March and December 1636, Ralph Tailor had recorded encounters with eighty-one people: seventy-two men and nine women.[2] Fourteen of these people were testators for whom plague wills survive: the thirteen plague victims for whom Ralph wrote wills during these months, and the merchant John Stobbs, whom he met on the eve of the plague while appraising the inventory of Elizabeth Franklin.[3] However, twenty-nine of the people Ralph is known to have encountered in the course of his work also left evidence of direct connection to additional testators during the plague. William Cooke, for example, helped Ralph appraise the inventory of the miller William Dixon. He was the son and executor of the cord-wainer William Cooke senior, and he had also been a witness of the wills of Roland Hedley, a fuller and dyer, and of the armourer John Heslop, and had been left tokens of friendship by both. Thomas Eden, another cordwainer whose will was written by Ralph Tailor in mid-August, happened to owe the notary John Carr twenty pounds at the time of his death. The connections could be still more complex. Robert Robinson, whose occupation is not recorded, and William Robinson, who was a goldsmith, both worked with Ralph Tailor on the inventory of the mariner John Reed, whose will Ralph had written. They were both also witnesses of the will of Barbara Havelock, widow. In addition, William was left a token of esteem by the tailor Thomas Clark. He later appraised the inventory of Robert Mallabar, barber-surgeon, who had been with Ralph Tailor at the making of the weaver Cuthbert Woodman's first will on 22 August and whose own will was written by Ralph on 5 November. Tracing connections of this kind reveals that such known "second-order" linkages (i.e. those established through an intermediary) connected Ralph to an additional eighteen of the testators for whom plague wills survive. The surviving evidence, then, shows that Ralph Tailor either met, or was connected at one remove to, a total of at least thirty-two testators: over half of the people for whom plague wills survive.

Limited as they are by the incomplete nature of the surviving evidence, such findings nevertheless convey a strong sense of the intimately interconnected world through which Ralph Tailor was moving in 1636. And this is only the tip of the iceberg of relationships of kinship, neighbourhood, and exchange that certainly existed between the households of the craftsmen and tradesmen of the city. This can be exemplified by following a particular chain of recorded connections among people most of whom are by now familiar to us.

When Ralph Tailor wrote Margaret Ayre's will on 10 March 1636, it was witnessed by Humphrey Hunter and John Hunter, who were perhaps brothers, and the executor was John Tailor, Margaret's son by an earlier marriage, who may, as has already been observed, have been a kinsman of Ralph. Humphrey Hunter was also present, along with four others, when Ralph Tailor wrote the plague will of Ann Carr on 28 June, but this connection cannot be further pursued. John Hunter, however, remains more visible in the evidence. He was sent for on 8 August, together with Ralph Tailor, to hear the will of the keelman Thomas Holmes, whose family he had known for twenty years. He also helped Ralph make Holmes' inventory two months later, and survived to give testimony in February 1637. Thomas Holmes, in turn, was the "uncle-in-law" of William Grame, "skipper", whose will Ralph had written on 31 May. Perhaps Ralph Tailor was asked to attend both testators because of his existing connection to John Hunter.

John Tailor, Margaret Ayre's son and executor, may have provided Ralph's initial introduction to the household of the carpenter Robert Moore. He himself was a tenant of Moore, living in a house "scituate on the west side of the long staires". Robert Moore's son and executor, Michael, who had known Ralph for ten years and brought him to write his father's will on 19 August, had himself taken notes on the will of Mabel Walker a month earlier, standing outside her door.[4] He was a neighbour and he knew her well: back in 1628, his father, Robert, had witnessed the will of her former husband, Anthony Walker. Michael lived in two rooms of a property in the Castle Garth, parts of which were also occupied by Henry Finlay and Steven Colthard. It was Henry Finlay, a fellow weaver, who took in Robert Walker in his sickness (and later died of the plague himself). Steven Colthard witnessed Robert Walker's will and survived to give evidence, alongside Ann Whaw, Robert's keeper, on how it had been made. As a neighbour, Michael Moore had attended at the door. One of the principal beneficiaries of Robert Walker's will was another weaver, Henry Finlay's brother Thomas, the same Thomas Finlay who accompanied Michael Moore and Ralph Tailor to witness the will of Robert Moore. Thomas' wife, Mary, had been another witness of the will of Mabel Walker, along with Mabel's servant Elizabeth Tailor, and one Ann Tailor, whose relationship to Mabel is not specified.[5]

The entanglement of the Moores and the Walkers (not to mention several Tailors) becomes yet more apparent when we find that Michael Moore later served as an appraiser of the inventory of the widow Margaret Hutcheson. One of her heirs was John Walker, another carpenter, who was probably a kinsman of Mabel Walker, since she left him a token of one shilling in her will. John Walker was also named as the coexecutor of the first will of Cuthbert Woodman, yet another weaver, which was written by Ralph Tailor on 22 August, and he later helped Ralph appraise the inventory of Robert Moore, no doubt at the request of Robert's executor, Michael. We have now come almost full circle. But it can be added that Michael Moore's sister Elizabeth, who later challenged his executorship of their father's will, and had also known Ralph Tailor for ten years, was married to the shipwright John Frisell. John Frisell owed money, both "by his bill" and "for drawing writings", to the notary John Carr. Ralph Tailor, of course, knew John Carr's business writings well enough to attest in court to the validity of the hand and signature of Carr's own will.

This chain of recorded relationships linked at least eighteen households and stretched across the city from the Long Stairs to Sandgate ward, via the Castle Garth, Pandon, and the quay. This was Ralph Tailor's world. The tendrils of connective tissue generated by kinship, neighbourhood, the practice of trades, and the conduct of business gave the society of seventeenth-century Newcastle its cohesion. Ralph Tailor's role in preserving their integrity served to fix his place in that world more firmly. He had conducted himself well, and it is surely not fanciful to suggest that his service in the plague laid the foundation of his subsequent career.

The records provide a very clear indication of the confidence he must have felt about his situation in the months following the plague. On 23 March 1637, a sale was held of the goods of Thomas Eden, cordwainer, of St John's parish, whose will had probably been written by Ralph on 16 August 1636, and whose inventory had been prepared by Ralph and three others on 12 January 1637. Remarkably, the executor kept two itemized lists of the goods sold, their buyers, and the prices paid, which he submitted with his administrator's accounts. At least thirteen men and twenty-six women were present at the sale and were recorded as buyers of goods. Among them was "Raiph Taylor". He bought "one feather bed and a bolster", "A houle doobler" (a large serving dish), "one chist", and "half a dozen of Table Napkins and one chaire", for a total sum of thirty-four shillings and twopence. Even more interesting is the item "sould to Raiph Taylors wife one standing bed two cod pillow bers [pillowcases] & A Towell} xxiiiis". Ralph Tailor had married.[6]

When had he done this? There is no record of his having married in any of the parishes of the city before March 1636.[7] Nor indeed would he have been free to do so while still an apprentice. During the plague months registration ceased altogether in Allhallows', and in the other parishes marriage registration fell to a very low ebb. It was not a propitious time for marriage, nor was Ralph Tailor among the very few whose marriages were recorded in the extant registers. He must therefore have married later, during the surge of marriages that took place between November 1636 and the spring of 1637.[8] He cannot be identified among those marrying in the parishes for which registration survives, and he did not marry by licence. It therefore seems most likely that he married in his home parish of Allhallows' in one of the months before March 1637 during which, as the contemporary clerk noted in the register book, "ye Register . . . is wanting".[9] But it does not really matter. What is clear is that Ralph Tailor had married at some point in the months following the plague, and in March 1637 he and his new wife were at the sale of Thomas Eden's goods together, acquiring the basic furnishings to set up their household.

It was to be a relatively long marriage by the standards of the seventeenth century. The burial of "Grace wife of Ralf Taylor Notarie Publicke" was recorded in the Allhallows' register on 30 March 1662.[10] In the intervening years the couple had prospered. Ralph himself lived until July 1669 and died, at the age of fifty-eight, a man of considerable substance; indeed, an urban gentleman. In the Hearth Tax return for Michaelmas 1665, "Mr Ra. Taylor" was assessed as the occupant of a six-hearth house in Corner Tower Ward, a relatively wealthy ward located below Allhallows' church, comprising the houses "upon the Key-side as their dowirs opin southwards towards the King's Wall". He was one of only 6 per cent of Newcastle's householders who dwelt in a house with six or more hearths. In addition, "Raiph Tailor" was listed as in possession of unassessed houses in Pandon Tower Ward, to the east of Allhallows', and in Austin Tower Ward, which comprised the chares immediately east of Sandhill.[11] Why these two dwellings were not assessed is not clear, but the fact that Ralph Tailor had become the owner of several houses is confirmed by his will of 2 July 1669, which refers to one house located in Cowgate, to the east of Pilgrim Street, and to "severall messuages [houses] in Pandon". The south-eastern wards of the city, close to the river, were still his territory. But he had also reached out towards the sea. He owned several "messuages" in North Shields, and a "key and wharf" newly erected there. No inventory of his goods survives, but clearly Ralph Tailor had done well in the thirty-three years that had passed since the plague of 1636.[12]

Some moments of what had been a flourishing career remain on record. In the course of 1637, as we have seen, he settled down to normal business. By then, the city was already being repeopled by migrants. In April 1638, the mayor reported that many of the inhabitants were not "auncient townsmen", for "the nowe [present] inhabitants (many of them being [such as] did never dwell in the Towne before) beganne to resort thither about the later end of the yeare 1637".[13] Ralph Tailor wrote at least three post-plague wills, five inventories, a set of administrator's accounts, and a lease for a shop in Sandhill that year, and no doubt produced numerous more transient "writings" that have not survived.[14] Whether he took any part in the events of the Bishops' Wars and the English Civil Wars which followed soon afterwards is unknown. He probably witnessed the Scottish occupation of the city in 1640–1 and the siege of 1644. He may have caught a glimpse of Charles I when the defeated king was held in Newcastle in 1646 (in its finest house, near Pilgrim Gate). He almost certainly encountered Robert Jenison again. The great preacher had returned to Newcastle in 1645 after its surrender to parliamentary forces, and as vicar of St Nicholas' proceeded to institute a Presbyterian system of church

government and to promote, with the aid of a sympathetic magis-
tracy, the moral reformation he had long desired. Yet even as the
"acknowledged leader of the church in Newcastle", he remained
embattled.[15] And at the end, aged almost seventy, and suffering
from "the continued and groweinge paine of the strangurie and
stone" in his bladder, he used the preamble of his will of 27 October
1652 to declare himself "the same in old age in matter of Judgment
and doctrine against all the novelties of poperie Arminianisme
Socinianisme Antinomianisme Anabaptisme and other new sects of
this age and of Libertie abused".[16]

Ralph Tailor certainly played no prominent role in the political
and religious upheavals of those turbulent decades.[17] Rather, he
served the city corporation in being under every regime of the
Interregnum and under the restored monarchy of the 1660s.[18] By
1647, now aged thirty-six, he had achieved the dignity of being
appointed a notary public, and it was in that role that he presented
his own apprentice Thomas Thompson to the Guild of Newcastle as
a candidate for the freedom of the city.[19] From 1649, Ralph was
repeatedly named as one of the "River Jurors" charged with the
presentment of nuisances affecting the navigation of the Tyne, and
in that role he was sometimes specifically requested to "view"
potential problems and subscribed the resulting reports.[20] In
January 1650, he was well enough known as a safe pair of hands
to be one of the city's principal expert witnesses in an Exchequer
case involving the breach of its privileges. He gave a deposition
revealing detailed knowledge of the legal rights of the ship carpenters and shipwrights of Newcastle, and he cited chapter and verse
on attempted breaches of their monopoly on shipbuilding and
repairing by specific individuals, "all of them foreigners" (from
Gateshead, South and North Shields, and Sunderland). With the
same confidence he had shown in 1637, he asserted that "this
examinant knoweth the better to depose" on that, since he himself
had been present and borne witness when the people concerned
had entered bonds not to offend in future.[21]

Perhaps he was already diversifying his business activities.
He was closely involved with several of the city's guilds. When he
died he left twenty shillings each "to the poore of the Company
of Butchers" and to similarly distressed members of the Company of
Shipwrights and the Company of Bakers and Brewers. The last of
these charitable bequests was granted "forth of the salary they are

oweing me", perhaps for keeping their records, and it commemorated a relationship that went back at least twenty years. From 1649, the accounts of the Company of Bakers and Brewers periodically recorded money "spent att severall times at Raiph Tailors", probably on the commensality accompanying convivial business meetings of the company's officers at his house.[22] As we have seen, his relationship to the Shipwrights was at least as long-standing, and his shipping interests continued to develop until the eve of his death. By that time the bulk of his income probably came from his various commercial activities and from house rents. In 1663, he advised the city corporation on a wharf and its rental potential, and in 1665 he was admitted as a member of Newcastle's Trinity House, which exercised jurisdiction over the navigation of the Tyne and provided for the safety of coastal shipping far to the south. In 1667, he was one of the two signatories to an advertisement sent by Trinity House for publication in the official *Gazette*, "for the public good", regarding the relocation of a lighthouse and the safest channel into the Tyne. He also remembered "the poore people liveinge in the Trinity House in Newcastle" in his will, leaving them twenty shillings a year. And by then, of course, he had built his own "key and wharf".[23]

Ralph Tailor, then, became firmly implanted in the civic institutions and commercial life of his city; never one of its narrow and notoriously exclusive elite, but certainly an insider who was apparently respected for his ability and who had some clout in his sphere (which, of course, also included his continuing notarial practice).[24] Beyond that, however, his personality remains somewhat enigmatic, and there is an element of ambiguity, or at least ambivalence, attached to some of the fragmentary records of his later life. One might say, for example, that he was a good citizen who served Newcastle well in troubled times, whoever happened to be in charge; or, less charitably, that he was a survivor, even an opportunist, who always knew which side his bread was buttered. His only known letter reveals a confident, busy, and successful legal practitioner exerting his influence with the officers of the probate court in Durham in June 1650. He greeted these "frends" warmly, and excused himself for his absence at a recent meeting of the court, since "my occasions suddainely called me away". He wrote in a good cause, "intreating" the immediate appointment of an administrator of the goods of Thomas Gray of Longbenton, a small farmer who had died of the plague more than five years earlier, to the use of Gray's young daughter. "The childs meanes is not much as you may perceive by the Inventarye," he explained. Worse, "the meanes is in other hands who are likely to be poorer daily (though now low enough) soe as if course be not speedily taken the child may come to lose all". He recommended the appointment of the bearer of his letter, the child's aunt, "who hath hitherto mainteined her of her owne charge". So far so good. But he went on to add, "I pray you question not the matter", and to request that "the administration be antidated sufficiently" to achieve the desired outcome. It seems that, when necessary, he was prepared to cut corners.[25]

A comparable ambivalence is detectable in his own will.[26] He took evident pride in his commercial success, and displayed a certain sensitivity to his public reputation. With reference to the quay and wharf at North Shields, which he told readers of his will "I lately built", he added that the property also included a parcel of ground that "I left unbuilt to preserve that kennel or conduit which conveys away the underwater from my houses and others on the north side of the streat". He went out of his way to present himself as a responsible developer. Yet it is also evident that success could provoke conflict. He complained that one Matthew Hall had "unjustly gained the possession of and deteineth" his houses in Pandon, an accusation somewhat out of keeping with the reconciliation of disputes urged upon will-makers as a means of preparing themselves spiritually for death. In fact, his will contains no dedication of his soul, though he alludes, in the conventional phrase, to the "estate which the Lord hath bene pleased to endow me withall in this world". There is no evidence to suggest that he was in any way heterodox in his beliefs. He did not appear on the long list of dissenting noncommunicants from Allhallows' presented to the Consistory Court in December 1662, and he wished to be buried in the churchyard of his parish.[27] He was probably as good a churchman as most, but he chose to leave his conception of the fate of his soul and his relationship to God unspecified.

If he was a complex man and not easy to read, he may also have been in one respect a disappointed one. He had no children to survive him, and few close kin of his own. The dense kinship network that may have framed his youth had frayed and faded in the course of his adult life. His widow, Margaret, to whom he left his newly developed property at North Shields and the residue of his goods, and appointed his executor, had been his wife for less than eighteen months.[28] The man he called "my sonn" was in fact the husband of Margaret's daughter by a previous marriage. His "brother" Roger Jobling was the husband of Margaret's sister Grace. At least one, and possibly both, of the two women designated "my sister", to whom he left tokens, may have been similarly connected to him by marriage.[29] The use of the language of kinship in such an inclusive manner was not unusual at the time, though it may also reflect a desire on his part for close family who were otherwise absent in his life. For his principal bequests, Margaret apart, went to three people, each of whom was designated "my cosyn", the all-purpose term used by contemporaries to indicate a kinsperson of unspecified proximity.[30] None of them was a Tailor, but one, Peter Wilson, was a scrivener.

Ralph Tailor was no saint. He founded no civic dynasty. Yet his will also bears testimony to the place he had established in the community he was about to leave. His principal bequests made, he left tokens of "a good gold ring", or cash sums, usually ten or twenty shillings, occasionally more, to no fewer than twenty-three named people (and an additional ten shillings each to "my household servants"). Ten of the recipients were recognized as kinsfolk, the marital kin described above and two more people he called "cosyn", one of them a Taylor who lived in Durham. Two were friends, including "my old friend" Mr Matthew of Durham, to whom he had written in 1650. There were at least two godchildren. He also remembered his former apprentice Thomas Thompson, now a professional colleague and a neighbour in Corner Tower Ward, and there were eight others, most of whom can be identified from the Hearth Tax return of 1665 or the admission records of Newcastle's freemen. With the exception of those from Durham, the people acknowledged lived for the most part in the wards of the riverside districts of Allhallows': in Corner Tower, Austin Tower, Pandon, Wall Knoll, and Plummer Tower wards, and, of course, in Sandgate.[31] They dwelt mostly in houses with three to six hearths. Their known occupations are equally predictable: four masters and mariners; four shipwrights; two bakers and brewers; three scriveners; a lawyer, a butcher, a cordwainer, a bricklayer, and a draper.[32] These were the attachments he had formed that were still in being at the time of his death. They embodied the institutions and spaces within which he had lived. He also acknowledged another kind of attachment: to the places that marked the trajectory of his life. He left five pounds, his largest charitable bequest, to the poor of the parish of St Margaret's in Durham, "in which parish I was borne", and he asked to be "decently interred under my Graves stone in Allhallowes Church yard". To have such a gravestone, at a time when permanent church-yard memorials were still a novelty, was itself a mark of the distinc-tion he had achieved, and it may have been in place already because his first wife lay beneath it. On 14 July 1669, "Ralf Taylor Notary Publique" was buried there.

That stone is long gone.[33] So are most of the details of Ralph Tailor's life. One can speculate as to how the documentary shards that remain relate to one another, but there are too many aspects of his life that remain undocumented, too many days that left no record, too many places into which we cannot follow him. We cannot fully know what he became, and it is especially difficult to relate the dying man of 1669 to the young lad of 1636. A whole lifetime lay between. He had lived in interesting times. He had witnessed inva-sion, occupation, and siege. He lived through civil war, regicide, the Commonwealth and the Protectorate, and into the Restoration. He survived several more outbreaks of the plague, though none remotely on the scale of that of 1636. He probably knew about the building of Tyneside's earliest waggonways, the wooden railways invented to transport coal more efficiently to the river, and may have smiled to hear his coal-rich region hailed by William Ellis as England's "Indies": "Correct your Maps: Newcastle is Peru."[34] Yet we know little of how all of this might have affected him; only the laconic fragments of a manifestly successful career. To be sure, he had done well. But to the best of my knowledge he never again left such an imprint on the records from which we make history as in the year from May 1636 to May 1637; and that was a direct outcome of his role in the summer and early autumn of 1636.

The plague year had been his starting year and his testing year. His conduct in "that lamentable time" had established his profes-sional career, intensified his activity as a maker of "instruments", gained him the income and the goodwill that gave him the confidence to marry, and accelerated his transition into independent adulthood. Whatever he had seen, heard, and endured in the summer and autumn of 1636, and whatever mark those experiences had left on him, he had earned his place and he ended the plague year with some optimism about his future. We might best leave him there.

Epilogue

THIS BOOK HAS BEEN ABOUT AN EVENT AND AN URBAN SOCIETY AND culture that have become remote in time. It represents an effort to recover them. It is also a book about historical documents: how they came to be made, who made them, and what we can make of them in attempting to recover and understand the past.

Most of the city that Ralph Tailor knew no longer exists. It has been engulfed in the rebuildings of the nineteenth and twentieth centuries. The bridges of the industrial age fly above and beyond the steep inclines of the old town, carrying rail and road traffic smoothly to the edge of its original confines and on into its modern extensions. Places that were once at the centre of its life have been relegated in significance; areas that were once peripheral, or beyond the walls, have been developed and promoted. Yet traces of an older Newcastle are still there for whoever cares to look. They are most visible in the fabric of the city: in the substantial remains of the castle, where it all began; in the three ancient churches; in the Blackfriars precinct, the Guildhall (beneath its later cladding), and Trinity House. Stretches of the city wall still stand in Bath Lane and Stowell Street, between the former West and New Gates, and to the north of Whitefriars Place, from where it descended in what were called the "Breakneck Steps" to The Close. You can walk the former perimeter of the city between them in little more than an hour, finding along the way surviving towers that seem like exotic islands in the townscape; part of it still, yet strangely out of place. But, perhaps more fundamentally, there is the street plan. It was much altered by the elegant rebuilding of the early nineteenth century, but much of it remains. You can still follow the old central artery from where the New Gate stood by St Andrew's church, down through the Bigg Market, past Pudding Chare, to St Nicholas', and then down The Side into Sandhill. You can descend the Long Stairs from Castle Garth, emerging into The Close beside a late medieval merchant's house (now a bar and dance club) and take your lunch across the road in a converted complex of sixteenth-century warehouses beside the river. You can walk along the broad quayside, ascend to the Carpenters' Tower, and try to imagine the teeming chares of Pandon and Sandgate that once lay below, and a river crowded with ships and keels.

The old city is gone; but it endures, partly in its tangible remains, partly in the imagination. And much the same can be said of the event. All historical events leave echoes, but they do not resonate with equal force or share the same capacity to persist. The historical sociologist Phillip Abrams defined an event as "a happening to which cultural significance has successfully been assigned". William H. Sewell suggests that "historical events should be understood as happenings that transform structures".[1] Such meaningful and transformative events often echo loudly from the start. They are the great events that become accepted as the chronological landmarks and reference points of history as we conventionally understand it: the Norman Conquest; the Reformation; the Civil Wars; the "Glorious Revolution" of 1688; the American and French Revolutions. Other events, however, are assigned no such larger societal meaning and lack such transformative power. They may have been of no less importance to the people who lived them, but they fade, fall into the shadows, become devalued and irrelevant in the grander scheme of things. This makes them more interesting. It is more of a challenge to recover their texture and their meaning.

The Newcastle plague of 1636 was such an event. It was powerfully experienced at the time, and vividly remembered for a few years. Robert Jenison and John Fenwick tried to assign it a particular meaning, as we have seen. But, astonishingly soon, it seems to have been forgotten. It found no place in William Gray's celebratory *Chorographia* (1649) or in Henry Bourne's pioneering *History of Newcastle upon Tyne* (1736). The implication is that it had already ceased to have a place of note in the official memory of the city. Perhaps it had been overshadowed by Newcastle's dramatic role in the national calamities that soon followed, and was diminished in significance by demographic recovery, renewed prosperity, and the disappearance of plague as a threat after 1665.[2] It awaited rediscovery by the antiquarian scholars of the later eighteenth century. James Murray interlined a passage on the plague into his manuscript history of the city, composed in the 1770s; perhaps he had just heard of it. John Brand gave it twenty lines in 1789. Both accounts were largely based on Jenison's tract.[3] Fuller treatment came only with the work of Bourchier Richardson, an early Victorian public health official with a professional interest in the history of epidemic disease. But if the plague of 1636 was no longer ignored, it was neither closely studied nor accorded prominence in the history of the city.[4]

If this event was historically eclipsed, reduced in visibility and in significance, much the same can be said of the urban society and culture that experienced it. Of course, there are continuities; those persisting "family resemblances" in social institutions, in attitudes and values, in language, without which the past would be incomprehensible. Nevertheless, cumulative change has gradually transformed the social and economic structures of the city, its institutional matrixes and forms of government, its available technologies (not least those of medicine and communication), the beliefs and practices, characteristic experiences and expectations of its people, and the material environment that they inhabit. Socially and culturally, no less than physically, the city that experienced the plague has become more distant and less accessible. The context within which that disaster occurred and was understood has ceased to be, and that disconnection encourages and consolidates the historical amnesia of the shallow, present-minded culture that we inhabit.

Like the townscape of the old city, however, both forgotten events and a historically distant culture can be recovered and apprehended, at least in part. Their traces survive not so much in streets and buildings as in libraries and archives. They are preserved and increasingly accessible. They are there to be found, in books like the three copies of Jenison's *Newcastle's Call* that are known to exist, and even more in the host of records that the people of seventeenth-century Newcastle left behind: the court books and parish registers, the chamberlains' accounts and guild minutes, and all those written instruments made "for testimonie or memories sake" which, as William West correctly predicted, have the power to save things from "the consuming canker of oblivion".[5]

By using such records intensively and in combination, "searching and joyninge . . . some of these dismembered members", we can not only recover the details of disregarded events but also use them, separately and in combination, to trace the contours of former states of being.[6] We can reconstruct the course of the plague, assess its impact, and assign it a different kind of meaning: not that which attaches to a transformative historical moment (which it was not), but the meaning that derives from what such an event can tell us about the society and culture in which it took place.[7]

This study has been an exercise in historical rediscovery of that kind. It began accidentally. Neither Ralph Tailor nor the event he did so much to record had been part of my research agenda before I encountered his signature and read the deposition that first aroused my curiosity. That drew me in; but, once begun, the research and the analysis were pursued systematically. I became one of those described by Alice Munro as "driven to find things out" and "put things together": "You see them going about with notebooks, scraping the dirt off gravestones, reading microfilm, just in the hope of seeing this trickle in time, making a connection, rescuing one thing from the rubbish."[8] Yes; but there was more than one "trickle in time" to find and connect; more than one thing to rescue. In putting things together, I started out with the general intention of describing the experience of the plague more fully than had been attempted hitherto. But more and more I found myself compelled to use the evidence it generated to explore a world of intersecting social relationships, the values that informed them, the material environment within which they were conducted, and the conflicts that could disrupt them: finding things out.

In attempting that, I am acutely conscious of the limits of what can be achieved, even in a study of this kind. One can read the surviving records closely, paying attention to the details; ask what can be done with them; analyze them individually and in combination; try to put what they reveal into context; link them thematically; create narratives and construct interpretations. But there are always limitations in the evidence: silences; absent presences. There is so much that I do not know, and cannot know because the evidence fails. The reactions of the city's governors to the crisis can only be sketched. The economic dimensions of the experience of the epidemic cannot be recovered in full detail. The horror of what occurred in Sandgate and the poorer wards of Allhallows' and

St Andrew's can only be imagined. Ralph Tailor probably knew something of what it was like there, but he did not write about it. He had no occasion to do so. He was a scrivener, not a memoirist. He wrote what he was sent for and paid to write, and he spoke when the courts required it. The records that he and his fellows created are inevitably biased socially towards people of small to middling property, the freemen of the city and those they employed. He had no reason to record all that he knew, or that he had heard. And beyond these documentary constraints, there are also the limitations of my own historical imagination that will no doubt rise to haunt me: the questions I did not think to ask; the things I may have misunderstood; those I simply got wrong.

Nevertheless, three things seem clear to me at the end of this exploration of a moment in the past. First, in setting out to write the story of the plague through the recorded activities of one young scrivener, I soon found that there was not one story of the plague, but many. Those stories alerted me again to the variety of human experience in the past. It is all too easy to homogenize past societies and people, sometimes to the point of caricature, for the purpose of constructing neat paradigms to compare and contrast with, and flatter, our own "modernity". But that is a project of narcissism rather than of history. Their lives were as complex as our own, their emotional palettes as rich, and their range of responses as varied. There was no single experience of the plague. As we have seen repeatedly, its events had different outcomes for different people, and they also had different meanings.

Second, the records of the plague contain many voices; some of them speaking directly, most mediated by scribes like Ralph Tailor. In them, we can hear the sober voice of authority; the passion of the preacher who had drunk too deeply on what he took to be the Word of God; the anguish of some; the stoicism of others; voices raised in anger; voices that expressed gratitude, resignation, humour, and compassion. Some of them belonged to people of note; candidates (had they known it) for the *Oxford Dictionary of National Biography*. Most, however, were those of people who were obscure outside their own community, and even within it: mere craftsmen and tradesmen, plebeians, women, servants, poor hirelings, the young. All these voices had something to say about the plague. All of them deserve to be heard. But I cannot deny that the words that seem most compelling to me are those of the common people whose aspirations, decisions, and observations were recorded only because they had the misfortune to be sick of the plague, or because they happened to witness particular moments in its passage through their worlds. They were not self-conscious annalists or diarists, distanced theorists or pre-programmed moralists. They were not unusual in their preoccupations or pretensions. And for that reason their understandings of their obligations, and their descriptions of what they remembered, or cared to remember, have a special authenticity. Insofar as they were scripted, their scripting was implicit, an authentic expression of the innate values of their culture. And then there are the quirks and peculiarities that convey their rich individuality. Listening to those voices is to engage with what Lena C. Orlin calls "under-represented lives".[9] Underrepresented historically, but culturally representative, their voices offer an exceptionally valuable perspective on the event they suffered and witnessed.

Third, recapturing that perspective both extends and corrects our perception of the plague. As Colin Jones observes, the plague treatises of early modern Europe elaborated and perpetuated a myth of dystopia and salvation: "the myth of a personal, religious, and community life inverted, plus the myth of salvation and integrity refound".[10] That myth gave plague a meaning that served the purposes of secular and religious authority. But as has been written of a later epidemic scourge, that of cholera, disease in itself has *no* meaning; it "acquires meaning and significance from its human context, from the ways in which it infiltrates the lives of the people, from the reactions it provokes, and from the manner in which it gives expression to cultural and political values".[11] In the most profound and moving reflection upon the impact of the plague in early modern England, Paul Slack fully recognized "the divisive impact of plague on social ties". But he concluded that "no reliable balance sheet" of good and bad behaviour was possible. Responses depended above all upon the antecedent state of social relations. And he was impressed by the extent to which English cities seemed to have escaped the worst forms of dislocation, panic, scapegoating, and hysteria: "the social fabric . . . appears to have been stable and resilient."[12]

What we know of the response to the plague of 1636 in Newcastle confirms the power and resilience of the associational life of the city; of the bonds of family and civil society among people brought up, as the schoolmaster Richard Mulcaster put it, "not to live alone, but amongst others".[13] When their world was threatened with collapse, the people of the city managed to hold firm; to contain the disintegrating forces that were unleashed among them. Their ability to do that owed much to the actions of their governors. But it also owed at least as much, and perhaps more, to the frequently documented refusal of people who shared a space, knowledge of one another (good and ill), and obligations to one another (reluctant or willing) to renege upon those commitments. Those who stayed and encountered the plague revealed a capacity to confront their fear, if healthy, and their pain and anguish, if sick. They *came*: "being a neighbour", or as kinfolk, fellow guildsmen, friends, employees. If sick, they acknowledged their debts, material and emotional. They envisioned a future for others if not for themselves, even for those unborn, and they helped provide for it as best they could. This was not Jenison's or Fenwick's imagined dystopia, gruesome though the reality must often have been. Those godly men meant well, according to their lights, but the intensity of their engagement with the controversies of their day blinded them to the real and lasting meaning of the plague as it was lived and endured. What it meant in actuality was what Camus' Dr Rieux concluded: that "what we learn in time of pestilence" is simply "that there are more things to admire in men than to despise".[14]

The memory of the plague faded; eclipsed by other traumas, and by the commercial and industrial dynamic that revived and transformed Newcastle in the following two centuries. Even when it was recovered as an event of note in the annals of the city, it might be said of those who had experienced it what William Gray observed in his reflection on the ancient gravestones in the choir of St Nicholas': "Not one word of their good deeds; their generations and names are worne out."[15] But not quite; not yet. The records remain, and with them the city's memory. You can read them for yourself. They contain voices. They tell stories. They name names. If you read the stories, the old city becomes peopled again; alive and spirited even in its distress. If you know the names and have imagined listening to their voices, you can walk the streets on a quiet morning and hear them whispering.

Notes

PREFACE

1 C. Ginzburg and C. Poni, "The Name and the Game: Unequal Exchange and the Historiographical Marketplace", in E. Muir and G. Ruggiero, eds, *Microhistory and the Lost Peoples of Europe*, trans. E. Branch (Baltimore and London, 1991), p. 3.
2 The phrase is David Sabean's, quoted in M.W. Gray, "Microhistory as Universal History", *Central European History*, 34 (2001), p. 427.
3 Ginzburg and Poni, "The Name and the Game", p. 3; G. Levi, "On Microhistory", in P. Burke, ed., *New Perspectives on Historical Writing* (Cambridge, 1991), p. 97.
4 Ginzburg and Poni, "The Name and the Game", p. 8; E. Muir, "Introduction: Observing Trifles", in Muir and Ruggiero, eds, *Microhistory and the Lost Peoples of Europe*, p. viii.
5 E.P. Thompson, "Anthropology and the Discipline of Historical Context", *Midland History*, 1 (1972), p. 45. On contextualization in microhistory, see Levi, "On Microhistory", pp. 106–8.
6 The phrase quoted is borrowed from J. Fentress and C. Wickham, *Social Memory* (Oxford, UK and Cambridge, MA, 1992), p. 53, though they use it in a different context, that of the structure of oral poetry.

PROLOGUE

1 Durham University Library, Archives and Special Collections [hereafter D.U.L.] DDR/EJ/CCD/2, Folder 20.i.1637–6.v.1637, fo. 10v.
2 *Ibid.*, fols 10–10v. According to Henry Bourne, writing a century later, the stretch of the city walls of Newcastle running along the quayside by the river Tyne divided the quay into inside and outside areas. Holmes' house was presumably in the street just inside the wall. H. Bourne, *History of Newcastle-upon-Tyne or The Ancient and Present State of that Town* (Newcastle upon Tyne, 1737), p. 132. Three visitors in 1634 recalled being able to march "all a breast" on the walkway of the wall between the "key" and the town. That is where Ralph Tailor and his companions must have stood. L.G. Wickham Legg, ed., *A Relation of a Short Survey of 26 Counties* (London, 1904), p. 31.
3 D.U.L. DPRI/1/1637/H17/1–4.
4 D.U.L. DDR/EJ/CCD/2, Folder 20.i.1637–6.v.1637, fos 11, 12, 13, 23v; Folder 19.v.1637–17.vi.1637, fo. 85–85v.
5 Wickham Legg, ed., *A Relation of a Short Survey of 26 Counties*, p. 27. Clearly Bede's tomb was still pointed out to visitors, despite the destruction, at the Reformation, of the shrine that had previously occupied the site.
6 D. Pocock, "Place Evocation: The Galilee Chapel in Durham Cathedral", *Transactions of the Institute of British Geographers*, new series, 21 (1996), p. 382.

CHAPTER 1 STORIES OF THE PLAGUE

1 P. Slack, *The Impact of Plague in Tudor and Stuart England* (London, 1985), p. 3.
2 C. Jones, "Plague and its Metaphors in Early Modern France", *Representations*, 53 (1996), p. 97.
3 The literature is now very extensive. Among the most notable contributions, see e.g. J.-N. Biraben, *Les hommes et la peste en France et dans les pays européens et méditerranéens* (Paris, 1975–6); C.M. Cipolla, *Cristofano and the Plague: A Study in the History of Public Health in the Age of Galileo* (London, 1973); C.M. Cipolla, *Faith, Reason, and the Plague in Seventeenth-Century Tuscany*, trans. M. Kittel (New York and London, 1979); G. Calvi, *Histories of a Plague Year: The Social and the Imaginary in Baroque Florence*, trans. D. Biocca and B.T. Ragan Jnr. (Berkeley and Oxford, 1989). For England specifically, see J.F.D. Shrewsbury, *A History of Bubonic Plague in the British Isles* (Cambridge, 1970); *The Plague Reconsidered*, Supplement to *Local Population Studies* (1977); R. Finlay, *Population and Metropolis: The Demography of London, 1580–1650* (Cambridge, 1981); E.A. Wrigley and R.S. Schofield, *The Population History of England, 1541–1871* (London, 1981), esp. Appendix 10; Slack, *Impact of Plague*; J.A.I. Champion, ed., *Epidemic Disease in London* (Centre for Metropolitan History Working Papers Series, No. 1, 1993). Demographic studies have led some scholars to question the identification of some epidemics as bubonic plague, and even to question whether the disease as presently known was responsible for most early modern outbreaks: see e.g. G. Twigg, "Plague in London: Spatial and Temporal Aspects of Mortality", in Champion, ed., *Epidemic Disease in London*, pp. 1–17; and for the most ambitious revisionist work of this nature, S. Scott and C.J. Duncan, *Biology of Plagues: Evidence from Historical Populations* (Cambridge, 2001). These epidemiological issues are, however, beyond the scope of the present study.
4 M. Healey, " 'Seeing' Contagious Bodies in Early Modern London", in D. Grantley and N. Taunton, eds, *The Body in Late Medieval and Early Modern Culture* (Aldershot, 2000), pp. 163, 164, 165. See also her "Discourses of the Plague in Early Modern London", in Champion, ed., *Epidemic Disease in London*, pp. 19–34.
5 Jones, "Plague and its Metaphors", p. 108ff, quoting pp. 108, 112. Each of these "scripts", as Jones shows, also had its recommended remedies: repentance; the adoption of a balanced bodily regimen; good government.
6 I. Munro, "The City and its Double: Plague Time in Early Modern London", *English Literary Renaissance*, 30 (2000), pp. 241–2.
7 Jones, "Plague and its Metaphors", pp. 109, 110, 118.
8 *Ibid.*, pp. 113, 117–18.
9 Slack, *Impact of Plague*, p. 284.
10 J.S. Amelang, "Introduction: Popular Narrative and the Plague", in J.S. Amelang, trans. and ed., *A Journal of the Plague Year: The Diary of the Barcelona Tanner Miquel Parets, 1651* (New York and Oxford, 1991), pp. 4–5; C. Cipolla, *Faith, Reason, and the Plague*, p. ix.
11 *Ibid.*, p. 12–13.
12 *Ibid.*, pp. 10, 15–16, 19, 25. The passage in question is to be found on pp. 68–71 of Parets' text.
13 Amelang, "Introduction", pp. 17, 18, 19. For the similarities of approach in the narratives of other contemporaries, see Amelang's valuable Appendix I, "Other Voices: An Anthology of Popular Plague Texts", especially those by Platter (Zurich, mid-sixteenth century); Casale (Milan, 1576); de Vargas (Malaga, 1649); de la Vega (Seville, 1649); Estriche (Saragossa, 1652).
14 Cipolla, *Faith, Reason, and the Plague*, p. 21.
15 There are many modern editions of what remains a much used text. Among the more recent, see e.g. D. Defoe, *A Journal of the Plague Year*, ed. C. Wall, Penguin Classics edn (London, 2003).
16 Slack, *Impact of Plague*, pp. 19, 20, 287–94. For a more recent exploration of contemporary medical and religious discussions of fear of the plague, and the risk it posed of "the breakdown of religious and social norms", see A. Wear, "Fear, Anxiety, and the Plague in Early Modern England: Religious and Medical Responses", in J.R. Hinnels and R. Porter, eds, *Religion, Health, and Suffering* (London and New York, 1999), quoting p. 339.

17 D.U.L. DPRI/1/1637/H17/1–4.
18 G. Calvi, *Histories of a Plague Year*. See p. 4ff for her methodology.
19 The phrase quoted is from A. Camus, *The Plague*, trans. S. Gilbert, Vintage International edn (New York, 1991), p. 308.

CHAPTER 2 THE DESTROYING ANGELL AND THE EYE OF THE NORTH

1 Finlay, *Population and Metropolis*, p. 111. Slack, *Impact of Plague*, p. 151 and ch. 6, "Metropolitan Crises", *passim*. Slack's figure for the total population in 1636 includes the City of London, the "liberties", and the "outparishes".
2 Slack, *Impact of Plague*, pp. 61, 62, 66. For the severity of the 1588–9 outbreak, see G. Bourchier Richardson, *Plague and Pestilence in the North of England* (Newcastle, 1852), p. 15. Slack stresses that "the importation of a more virulent strain of the plague bacillus from outside appears to have been necessary for a major epidemic", and that the more general English outbreaks of plague tended to be the culmination of broad tides of infection sweeping across Europe and to coincide with outbreaks in Germany and the Low Countries: *Impact of Plague*, p. 68.
3 Bourchier Richardson, *Plague and Pestilence*, pp. 17–26.
4 R. Jenison, *Newcastle's Call, to her Neighbour and Sister Townes and Cities throughout the Land* (London, 1637), p. 23. As a "lecturer" at Allhallows' church from 1622, Jenison was employed by the city to preach sermons, but did not have responsibility for the cure of souls. For a brief account of his career and many publications, see W.J. Sheils, "Jenison, Robert", in *Oxford Dictionary of National Biography* [henceforward *Oxford D.N.B.*], and for a fuller account of his role in the religious and political life of the city, R. Howell Jnr., *Newcastle-upon-Tyne and the Puritan Revolution: A Study of the Civil War in North England* (Oxford, 1967), *passim*.
5 Jenison, *Newcastle's Call*, p. 2.
6 Shrewsbury, *History of Bubonic Plague*, pp. 371–2, 384.
7 Jenison. *Newcastle's Call*, pp. 4–5. North Shields was at this time part of the parish of Tynemouth. The burial register for 1635 does not in fact indicate an upsurge of burials in the latter part of the year, though it may be of significance that, of the seven burials for August to November 1635, six are described as being "of sheles": Northumberland Collections Service [henceforward N.C.S.] EP 52/1A (Tynemouth, Christchurch).
8 Such a pattern of winter dormancy and spring recrudescence is described in Slack, *Impact of Plague*, p. 67, and in Twigg, "Plague in London", pp. 1–5. See also Cipolla, *Cristofano and the Plague*, pp. 19–20 for the case of Milan in 1629–31.
9 *The Diary of John Evelyn*, ed. G. de la Bédoyère (Woodbridge, 1995), p. 25.
10 Jenison, *Newcastle's Call*, pp. 5, 119, 178.
11 R. Jenison, *The Cities Safetie* (London, 1630), Epistle Dedicatory. The phrase "eye of the North" was derived from William Camden's *Britannia* (London, 1607 edn), p. 667. In the English translation, originally published in 1610, it was rendered as "the very eye of all the townes in these parts": W. Camden, *Britain, or A Chorographical Description of the Most Flourishing Kingdomes, England, Scotland, and Ireland*, trans. P. Holland (London, 1637 edn), p. 809.
12 "The Journal of Sir William Brereton, 1635", in J.C. Hodgson, ed., *North Country Diaries (Second Series)*, Surtees Society, 124 (1915), p. 15.
13 Based on a survey of adjectives employed (often repeatedly) in W[illiam] G[ray], *Chorographia, or A Survey of Newcastle upon Tyne* (Newcastle, 1649), *passim*; "Journal of Sir William Brereton", p. 15ff; Camden, *Britain*, trans. Holland, p. 809ff; John Speed, *The Theatre of the Empire of Great Britaine* (London, 1611), p. 89.
14 Gray, *Chorographia*, pp. 5, 6, 7. See also pp. 11, 16, 18, 22. Though there was a Roman fort on the site, there is in fact no evidence of an associated settlement. As an urban place, Newcastle was a Norman foundation. See D.H. Heslop, "Newcastle and Gateshead before A.D. 1080", in A.J. Pollard and D. Newton, eds, *Newcastle and Gateshead before 1700* (Chichester, 2009).
15 Gray, *Chorographia*, pp. 7–12, 31.
16 *Ibid.*, pp. 8, 22, and *passim*. My description and sketch maps of the city are based upon Gray, the comments of visitors in 1634 and 1635, and Bourne's *History of*

Newcastle upon Tyne, published in 1736, together with the detailed map provided by Bourne and the plan of the city in 1610 by William Matthew inset in the map of Northumberland in Speed's *Theatre of the Empire of Great Britaine*.

17 Wickham Legg, ed., *A Relation of a Short Survey of 26 Counties*, p. 31; "Journal of Sir William Brereton", p. 16.

18 Gray, *Chorographia*, pp. 22, 26; Bourne, *History*, pp. 47–51. "Bigg" was the northern term for barley. Bourne commented that in the upper part of Newgate street "The Business and Trade . . . is chiefly that of the Tanners" (p. 48).

19 Gray, *Chorographia*, pp. 13, 26; Bourne, *History*, p. 53.

20 Gray, *Chorographia*, p. 25; Bourne, *History*, p. 122.

21 Bourne, *History*, p. 123; Gray, *Chorographia*, pp. 23–4.

22 Gray, *Chorographia*, p. 12; "Journal of Sir William Brereton", p. 16.

23 Gray, *Chorographia*, pp. 25, 28; Bourne, *History*, p. 126. Writing in 1736, Bourne explained that The Close had formerly housed many of the "principal inhabitants" of the town, as the large and stately rooms of its houses bore witness, but that "Of late years these Houses have been forsaken, and their wealthier Inhabitants have chosen the higher Parts of the Town".

24 Gray, *Chorographia*, p. 18; "Journal of Sir William Brereton", p. 19; Bourne, *History*, p. 132. Bourne commented that in the early seventeenth century the small "water-gates" cut through the city wall to give access to the quay had been locked at night, a few remaining open to permit masters of ships and seamen to pass between the town and their vessels. For the reclamation of the quayside area, see B. Harbottle, "The Medieval Archaeology of Newcastle", in Pollard and Newton, eds, *Newcastle and Gateshead before 1700*, pp. 29–32.

25 Gray, *Chorographia*, pp. 16, 27–8; Bourne, *History*, pp. 22, 51.

26 Gray, *Chorographia*, p. 27; Bourne, *History*, pp. 81, 85, 88, 89, 123. The Lort Burn (sometimes called "Lorkburn" in the early modern period) ran more or less along the line of the present Grey and Dean Streets. Its lower stretch, running under The Side, had been paved over by the seventeenth century. Higher up, it was bridged at Upper and Nether Dean Bridge Streets. Contemporaries almost invariably used the name Allhallows' to refer to the church and parish now known as All Saints'. I am following their usage in preferring the name Allhallows', but it is also a useful way of distinguishing the medieval church from its successor, the superb church of All Saints' erected on the same site in the late eighteenth century.

27 Gray, *Chorographia*, p. 25; Bourne, *History*, pp. 108, 133; Bourchier Richardson, *Plague and Pestilence*, p. xv. The experience of spanning a chare with both arms outstretched, as described by Bourchier Richardson in the early nineteenth century, can still be replicated in Plummer Chare, where the modern buildings follow the old street line.

28 Gray, *Chorographia*, pp. 17–18. The walls at Pandon incorporated part of the Roman Wall, and Gray tells us that "As old as Pandon" was a local proverb.

29 Bourne, *History*, p. 154; Gray, *Chorographia*, p. 12.

30 Wickham Legg, ed., *A Relation of a Short Survey of 26 Counties*, p. 31.

31 "Journal of Sir William Brereton", p. 16. The revenues for October 1634–October 1635 in fact amounted to £5,146. 15s. 2d.: Tyne and Wear Archives [henceforward T.W.A.] 543/26, fo. 93.

32 Camden, *Britain*, trans. Holland, p. 810; Speed, *Theatre of the Empire of Great Britain*, p. 89. Robert Jenison may have been echoing Camden when he wrote of "our mines of coale (by which our Towne hath hitherto beene as the *Hearth* to warme most places of this our Iland . . .)", in *The Height of Israels Heathenish Idolatrie in Sacrificing their Children to the Devill* (London, 1621), Epistle Dedicatory, B3v.

33 Gray, *Chorographia*, pp. 32, 37. For the rise of the British coal industry, and the dominant place of the north-east in its early history, see J. Hatcher, *The History of the British Coal Industry. Vol. 1, Before 1700: Towards the Age of Coal* (Oxford, 1993) and D. Levine and K. Wrightson, *The Making of an Industrial Society: Whickham, 1560–1765* (Oxford, 1991).

34 Gray, *Chorographia*, pp. 37, 40; "Journal of Sir William Brereton", pp. 16–17. As a Cheshire man, familiar with the salt industry of his home county, Brereton was

particularly interested in Tyneside's salt production, the technology used, and the competitive advantage provided by cheap coal.

35 The significance of these trades is evident in the chamberlains' accounts: T.W.A. 543/26, *passim*.

36 As is emphasized in J. Langton, "Residential Patterns in Pre-Industrial Cities: Some Case Studies from Seventeenth-Century Britain", in J. Barry, ed., *The Tudor and Stuart Town: A Reader in English Urban History* (London and New York, 1990), p. 200.

37 Gray, *Chorographia*, p. 26; "Journal of Sir William Brereton", p. 19.

38 Gray, *Chorographia*, p. 34.

39 Newcastle was not included in the Great Subsidy of 1524/5, the tax returns upon which population estimates for the early sixteenth century are usually based. However, in the Poll Tax of 1377, the city had 2,647 taxpayers, a total that should have included all persons above the age of fourteen. If children under fifteen constituted roughly 35 per cent of the population, as has been estimated by Wrigley and Schofield for the 1540s, then this would yield a total population of approximately four thousand in 1377. Given the long demographic stagnation of the late middle ages, it is unlikely to have been significantly larger in the early sixteenth century, and an estimate of five thousand seems, if anything, generous. Estimate based on A. Dyer, "Ranking Lists of English Medieval Towns", in D.M. Palliser, ed., *The Cambridge Urban History of Britain. Vol. I, 600–1540* (Cambridge, 2000), p. 758; Wrigley and Schofield, *Population History of England*, p. 528.

40 The Hearth Tax returns for 1665 list 2,513 *households* for the twenty-four wards of the city. Converting that number into a total population estimate depends upon the estimated number of persons per household used as a "multiplier", and the question of whether or not an allowance should be made for possible omissions. Welford suggested a total of 12,500. Howell arrived at a final estimate of approximately 13,000. Langton has suggested 11,600. I am splitting the difference. Given the sufferings of the city in the plague of 1636, and during the Civil Wars of the 1640s – which involved siege, two occupations by Scottish armies, and a temporary pause in the expansion of the coal trade – it seems to me unlikely that the population had grown significantly between 1636 and 1665. In the early sixteenth century, Newcastle was probably England's eighth largest provincial city. By the early seventeenth century, it had moved up the urban hierarchy decisively, and in the late seventeenth century it was to overtake York. See R. Welford, "Newcastle Householders in 1665", *Archaeologia Aeliana*, 3rd series, 7 (1911), p. 56; Howell, *Newcastle-upon-Tyne and the Puritan Revolution*, p. 8 and Appendix, Tables I–III; J. Langton, "Urban Growth and Economic Change: From the Late Seventeenth Century to 1841", in P. Clark, ed., *The Cambridge Urban History of Britain. Vol. II, 1540–1840* (Cambridge, 2000), p. 473. For the rank order of urban populations, see E.A. Wrigley, "Urban Growth and Agricultural Change: England and the Continent in the Early Modern Period", *Journal of Interdisciplinary History*, 15 (1985), Table 7.1.

41 Based on the figures provided in Howell, *Newcastle-upon-Tyne and the Puritan Revolution*, pp. 350–1, Appendix, Tables I–II, and Welford, "Newcastle Householders in 1665". Welford provides details of the ward boundaries from a contemporary description. The precise figures are as follows:

New Gate – Sandhill corridor (11 wards)	: 638 households (25.4%)
Western upper town (3 wards)	: 244 households (9.7%)
Eastern upper town (3 wards)	: 308 households (12.3%)
Western lower town (2 wards)	: 183 households (7.3%)
Eastern lower town (5 wards)	: 1,140 households (45.3%)
Total	2,513 households (100%)

42 Based on the figures provided in Howell, *Newcastle-upon-Tyne and the Puritan Revolution*, pp. 350–2, Appendix, Tables I–III. The exemption rate for the entire city was 41.3 per cent. For further spatial analysis of the city's social and occupational structure in 1665, see Langton, "Residential Patterns in Pre-Industrial Cities", pp. 182–91, esp. pp. 188–91.

43 J. Fenwicke, *Christ Ruling in Midst of his Enemies* (London, 1643), Epistle
    Dedicatory, A4. Fenwick was a cloth merchant and the son of a Stamfordham gentry
    family. If he had been visiting them, he was probably approaching the city from the
    west at the time of his premonition of disaster – perhaps cresting Westgate Hill. For
    his life and career, see A.J. Hopper, "Fenwick (Fenwicke), John", *Oxford D.N.B.*

CHAPTER 3 WILDFIRE

1 Fenwicke, *Christ Ruling in Midst of his Enemies*, Epistle Dedicatory, A3v.
2 Jenison, *Newcastle's Call*, Preface. The note and date are on the final page of
   the Preface. Jenison used the old style of dating, under which the year began on
   24 March. His 2 January 1636 is therefore 1637 under the modern system of dating.
3 Jenison, *Newcastle's Call*, pp. 5, 177–8.
4 Technically, Newcastle had only one parish, St Nicholas', the vicar of which was
   appointed by the bishop of Carlisle. The other three were parochial chapelries,
   served by curates. Nevertheless, it was already conventional to refer to them as
   parishes, and that convention is followed here. The original parish registers are
   held at the N.C.S.: EP 86/1 (St Nicholas'); EP 9/2–3 (All Saints [Allhallows']); EP
   13/1–2 (St Andrew's); EP 73/3 (St John's). Microfilms are also available there and at
   the T.W.A. Since the boundaries of the four parishes did not coincide exactly with
   those of the wards of the city used for taxation purposes, one cannot be precise about
   the numbers of households living in each at the time of the 1665 Hearth Tax assessment. However, grouping the wards falling principally into particular parishes
   provides the following rough estimates of the proportion of households living in each
   parish: Allhallows' 52 per cent; St Nicholas', St Andrew's, and St John's, roughly 16
   per cent each.
5 Jenison, *Newcastle's Call*, pp. 250–2.
6 Coulson's figures were published by F.W. Dendy as a note on "The Plague
   in Newcastle" in *Proceedings of the Society of Antiquaries of Newcastle-upon-Tyne*, 3rd
   series, 1 (1905), p. 48. Dendy points out that Coulson purchased his estate at
   Jesmond, a prestigious satellite parish just to the north of the city, in 1658. Since he
   signed the list "Wm. Coulson of Jesmond", this implies that "he either did not make
   or did not sign the entry until that year".
7 Though London's bills of mortality are the most famous, other cities also required
   the reporting of vital events, above all as a means of gaining early warning of
   worrying rises in burials. See Slack, *Impact of Plague*, pp. 128–9, 239.
8 For these weeks Jenison gives figures of 246 and 520, while Coulson gives totals of
   398 and 386. The sudden fall indicated by the first of Jenison's figures, followed by
   an even more sudden leap in the second, seems to me less plausible than the
   plateauing suggested by Coulson's figures.
9 As can be seen, Coulson's weekly totals for the period after 11 September come to a
   grand total of 969 burials, as compared to Jenison's grand total for the same period
   of 908 burials. Thus, using the Coulson figures not only provides weekly specificity,
   but is also consistent with the general interpretative preference for the higher
   figure reported.
10 Comparison with pre-plague burial registration suggests that Newcastle's four
    parishes usually witnessed a total of around fifty burials a month in the early
    1630s, which suggests a fairly high crude death rate as a normal reality. From the
    second week of May more than fifty burials a *week* were being reported.
11 The absolute peak, in the week of 7–13 August, saw over four hundred burials, just
    as John Fenwick claimed. Perhaps he too had seen the figures, or at least read
    Jenison's book (though, as we have seen, his overall estimate of losses was much
    higher than Jenison's).
12 Allhallows' usually saw around twenty-five burials a month in "normal" years. If the
    "missing" burials came mostly from Allhallows', then it was already witnessing ten
    times that level in May and over twenty times that level in June.
13 The exception was William Robinson. He had made his will earlier, but the inventory
    indicates that he and his wife died of the plague. The parish clerk also noted "pl" beside
    his burial entry. Though not a wealthy man, he was one of some distinction. His will

describes him as a "painter and Deputy Herald" by profession. Henry Bourne, alluding to an early seventeenth-century manuscript known to him, mentions that William Robinson lived in a house in Castle Garth and "was Deputy Herrald under Norroy, *King at Arms*. This Man wrote in a Book the Arms of all the Mayors of this Towne . . . until his Time". This may have been one of the "6 books of Armes" mentioned in his inventory. D.U.L. DPRI/1/1636/R9/1–2; Bourne, *History*, p. 121.

14 D.U.L. DPRI/1/1636/R2/1–2; DPRI/1/1636/D3/103; DPRI/1/1636/G8/1–2.

15 There were also middens at the West Gate and the Close Gate, and a vast one, which served the upper town, by the castle wall. Excavations indicate that in the course of the sixteenth century some four metres of rubbish was deposited in the castle ditch. Bourchier Richardson, *Plague and Pestilence*, p. xv; B. Harbottle, M. Ellison, et al., "An Excavation in the Castle Ditch, Newcastle-upon-Tyne, 1974–6", *Archaeologia Aeliana*, 5th series, 9 (1981), pp. 88, 93–4.

16 Slack, *Impact of Plague*, p. 159.

17 The accompanying sketch map of parish boundaries is based upon T.W.A. D/NCP/3/1, "Plan of the Ancient Boundaries of the Town and County of Newcastle-upon-Tyne" by Thomas Oliver (1852) and D/NCP/3/23, "Parishes of Newcastle *c*.1900". The boundaries are inevitably approximate, given the nineteenth-century changes to the street plan of the city.

18 N.C.S. EP 86/1 (St Nicholas'). For Mallabar's will, see D.U.L. DPRI/1/1637/M2/1.

19 N.C.S. EP 73/3 (St John's); D.U.L. DPRI/1/1637/W9/1 (James Wilson), DPRI/1/1636/R12/1–2 (Raiph Rowmaine). The Warden Close was near a postern north of the West Gate, near the present junction of Bath Lane and Rutherford Street, and was listed by Gray among the suburban districts of the city: Gray, *Chorographia*, p. 40. Perhaps the bodies of these anonymous victims had been found during a post-plague search of the area.

20 N.C.S. EP 13/1–2 (St Andrew's); D.U.L. DPRI/ 1/1637/L4/1 (John Laverrock). Five more plague wills survive for St Andrew's up to 7 October.

21 The National Archives [henceforward T.N.A.] SP 16/370/81; SP 16/386/78.

22 T.N.A. SP 16/376/35.

23 T.N.A. SP 16/362/90.

24 N.C.S. EP 13/1–2 (St Andrew's). Most of these burials were of anonymous people: "a salore"; "powre ones"; or simply entered as "burialles of the plage" without a name. There were several more in November 1638, and a final case in March 1638/9, all save one being described as a "powre one".

25 N.C.S. EP 9/3 (All Saints' [Allhallows']). For Pringle, see D.U.L. DPRI/1/1637/P9/1. He was not buried in Allhallows'. The only subsequent Allhallows' plague burial was that entered as "Henry Smithes man/ plague" on 8 February 1637/8.

26 Munro, "The City and its Double", p. 242.

27 Slack, *Impact of Plague*, pp. 143, 153.

28 *Ibid.*, p. 192.

29 Using population distribution derived from the 1665 Hearth Tax: Allhallows' 52 per cent; St Andrew's, St Nicholas', and St John's, 16 per cent each.

30 See e.g. J. Brand, *The History and Antiquities of the Town and County of Newcastle upon Tyne*, 2 vols (London, 1789), vol. II, p. 456; R. Welford, ed., *History of Newcastle and Gateshead. Vol. III, Sixteenth and Seventeenth Centuries* (London, 1887), p. 337; Shrewsbury, *History of Bubonic Plague*, p. 382; Howell, *Newcastle-upon-Tyne and the Puritan Revolution*, p. 7.

31 See A.C. King and A.J. Pollard, " 'Northumbria' in the Later Middle Ages", in R. Colls, ed., *Northumbria: History and Identity, c. 547–2000* (Chichester, 2007), p. 79; R. Britnell, "Medieval Gateshead", and P. Rushton. "Gateshead 1550–1700 – Independence against All the Odds?", both in Pollard and Newton, eds, *Newcastle and Gateshead before 1700.*

32 T.W.A. Microfilm 1139 (Registers of Gateshead, St Mary's), fo. 163ff; Jenison, *Newcastle's Call*, pp. 251–2.

33 That belief, however, seems to have been based solely upon inference from Jenison, coupled with Bourchier Richardson's own experience of seeing "vast numbers of skeletons" uncovered during railway excavations in the area: Bourchier Richardson, *Plague and Pestilence*, pp. 28–9. It is now thought that these were most likely from a

major Anglo-Saxon cemetery in the area, for which see D.H. Heslop, "Newcastle and Gateshead before A.D. 1080", in Pollard and Newton, eds, *Newcastle and Gateshead before 1700*, p. 20.

34 Bourne, *History*, p. 153. Garth Heads is clearly marked on Charles Hutton's map of the city, drawn in 1770 – lying between the Carpenters' Tower and the Keelmen's Hospital. John Brand's *History and Antiquities*, p. 449 also identifies "the Garth-Heads, behind Sand-Gate".

35 J. Raine, "A Letter from the Corporation of Newcastle upon Tyne", *Archaeologia Aeliana*, 2 (1832), pp. 366–7. The letter is undated, but the number of burials reported the previous week is identical to that given by Coulson for 25 September to 1 October. The letter must therefore have been written in the week following. This also serves to confirm the source of Coulson's figures.

36 The likelihood of an underestimate is suggested by the fact that the testamentary records reveal plague deaths in the parishes for which registration survives but in which no matching burial entry was recorded.

37 Slack, *Impact of Plague*, pp. 16, 107, 150–1. Slack (p. 107) describes Colchester's experience in 1665–6 as "the highest death rate so far discovered in any major urban centre in the period". If it equalled or even exceeded that of Newcastle, however, it remains the case that no English city is known to have lost such a high proportion of its people to the plague prior to 1665–6. The Newcastle outbreak was "undoubtedly one of the most disastrous visitations by bubonic plague ever sustained by any town of comparable size in the British Isles": Shrewsbury, *History of Bubonic Plague*, p. 384.

38 Slack, *Impact of Plague*, p. 177. For an example of such clustering in the mining parish of Whickham, four miles upriver from Newcastle, see K. Wrightson and D. Levine, "Death in Whickham", in J. Walter and R. Schofield, eds, *Famine, Disease, and the Social Order in Early Modern Society* (Cambridge, 1989), p. 141.

39 Jenison, *Newcastle's Call*, pp. 119–20; Fenwick, *Christ Ruling in Midst of his Enemies*, Epistle Dedicatory, A3v.

40 N.C.S. EP 86/1 (St Nicholas'); EP 13/1–2 (St Andrew's); EP 73/3 (St John's).

41 Efforts were made to minimize this problem by counting as separate surname clusters people of the same surname whose burials were widely separated in time. Nevertheless, it remains possible that people of the same name dying at much the same time were from different households.

42 An additional ninety-six men were given no occupational designation. One can speculate that they were unskilled or semi-skilled, or at any rate not independent masters. The fact that they constituted only one-third of the men buried, whereas men with what might be deemed "classic" trade designations made up almost two-thirds, contrasts strongly with the occupational structure of Allhallows', where in 1631 only a third of the men buried belonged to guild-organized trades (the largest groups being shipwrights and mariners) while most of the rest were ascribed labouring occupations (notably "keelman", "shovelman", and "labourer"): N.C.S. EP/2 (All Saints').

43 This is on the assumption that the parish had around four hundred households, as seems to have been the case in 1665. That such a proportion of households was affected is the more likely since I have confined the analysis to male-headed households. Some additional households affected were headed by widows, but I felt obliged to exclude them from the count: some of them may have been widowed during the plague itself (in the period of defective registration) and this introduces a risk of counting some households twice. The morbidity rate – i.e. those who fell sick, even if they did not die – must have been higher still, but we have no way of measuring it. For a remarkable attempt to do so for the Salisbury outbreak of 1604, see Slack, *Impact of Plague*, p. 176.

44 This analysis includes households headed by widows. Once again, it is a minimum figure because of the gap in registration in July/early August.

45 Cf. Whickham, County Durham, where family reconstitution reveals that, in the plague of 1604, 55 per cent of fatalities came in family clusters, and in the plague of 1645, 59 per cent: Wrightson and Levine, "Death in Whickham", p. 141. Without full family reconstitution it is not possible to analyse the burials by age. However, of the burials in St John's, 39.5 per cent were of those described as son, daughter, or child; 8.3 per cent were of servants (probably young adults); 50.5 per cent were of adults (of which 56.6 per cent were men and 43.4 per cent women). For discussions

of the age structure of plague mortality, see Finlay, *Population and Metropolis*, pp. 122–30, and Slack, *Impact of Plague*, pp. 177–86.

46   D.U.L. DPRI/1/1636/G8/1–2.

47   D.U.L. DDR/EJ/CCD/2, Folder 20.i.1637–6.v.1637, fos 7, 9; N.C.S. EP 86/1 (St Nicholas').

48   D.U.L. DPRI/1/1636/S14/1–2; DPRI/1/1636/R12/1–6.

49   D.U.L. DPRI/1/1636/C6/1–10; DPRI/1/1637/H1/1–2; DPRI/1/1636/E3/1–3.

50   D.U.L. DPRI/1/1636/G12/1–3; DDR/EJ/CCD/2, Folder 20.i.1637–6.v.1637, fos 36v–37; DPRI/1/1636/C6/1–10. Mary and Elizabeth were both living when John Collingwood made his will on 26 October. He was the last Collingwood to be buried. Mary was one of the litigants disputing the will of Robert Grinwell in 1637.

51   D.U.L. DPRI/1/1636/E3/1–3; DPRI/1/1637/H1/1–2; N.C.S. EP 13/1–2 (St Andrew's); EP 73/3 (St John's). Between 23 August and 5 October, four named members of the Haddock family were buried at St Andrew's, and two servants of Ambrose Haddock were buried at St John's. Ambrose himself was buried at St Andrew's on 10 October. The spacing of the burial dates suggests that the infection may have reached the Haddocks more than once, a speculation supported by the administrator's accounts which mention payment "for clensing the houses severall tymes". No burials were recorded for the two remaining Ellison sisters, who must have been buried elsewhere.

CHAPTER 4   DILIGENCE AND CARE OF MAGISTRATES

1   Slack, *Impact of Plague*, pp. 209–12. The *Orders*, initially issued under the royal prerogative, continued to provide a uniform national model for combating plague until 1666.

2   Jenison, *Newcastles' Call*, p. 237.

3   For the role of viewers or searchers, see Slack, *Impact of Plague*, pp. 272–6, and R. Munkhoff, "Searchers of the Dead: Authority, Marginality, and the Interpretation of Plague in England, 1574–1665", *Gender and History*, 11 (1999).

4   D.U.L. DDR/EJ/CCD/2. Folder "Depositions *c.*22.vii.1637", fo. 104.

5   M.S.R. Jenner, "The Great Dog Massacre", in W.G. Naphy and P. Roberts, eds, *Fear in Early Modern Society* (Manchester and New York, 1997), p. 49.

6   Bourchier Richardson, *Plague and Pestilence*, pp. 30–1, citing an Allhallows' church book that is no longer extant. For the rationale behind this practice, see Slack, *Impact of Plague*, p. 30. Given the abundance of coal at Newcastle, it seems likely that coal fires were also kept burning as a means of dispelling the "miasma" held to carry the disease, as was reported by Defoe for the London outbreak of 1665: Defoe, *Journal of the Plague Year*, ed. Wall, pp. 210–12.

7   Jenison, *Newcastle's Call*, p. 237.

8   Slack, *Impact of Plague*, p. 188.

9   Jenison, *Newcastle's Call*, p. 35.

10   Fenwick, *Christ Ruling in Midst of his Enemies*, Epistle Dedicatory, A2v; Huntington Library, HM 69956, "Mss History of Newcastle by James Murray", fo. 181 (interlined).

11   Shrewsbury, *History of Bubonic Plague*, p. 368; *C.S.P.D., 1636–7*, p. 192; T.N.A. SP 16/378/58.

12   As is noted in Howell, *Newcastle-upon-Tyne and the Puritan Revolution*, p. 7, n. 7.

13   For the location of the office of the "Clarke of the Chamber", see Gray, *Chorographia*, p. 24. The exact number of vessels paying dues for ballast discharged, coal loaded, etc. was 1,397. In the whole six months from May to October 1636, 1,520 ships entered the river: T.W.A. 543/26, chamberlains' accounts. The detailed accounts run from May 1635 to October 1636. Contemporary totals for the accounting years October to October 1634–5 and 1635–6 are to be found on fos 93 and 264 respectively. After October 1636, the series of account books breaks off until 1642.

14   T.N.A. SP 16/362/90

15   T.W.A. 543/26, chamberlains' accounts, fos 185–248v, *passim*. For the landing of foodstuffs in August and September, see fos 227, 228, 231v, 234, 235, 238v, 241v, 242v, 243v, 245v, 249v. For the practice of paying "the poore" for shifting ballast, see e.g. fos 139v, 140v, 142v.

16 D.U.L. DPRI/1/1636/H2/2–4; DPRI/1/1637/F1/3.

17 D.U.L. DDR/EJ/CCD/11 (1618–26), fo. 106.

18 T.W.A. GU/TH/2/10, Trinity House Payments Book, 1634–9 (unfol.).

19 T.W.A. GU/Sh/3/1, GU/Sh/4/1 (Shipwrights'); GU/CW/17/2 (Cordwainers'); GU/CO/2/1 (Coopers'); GU/GP/2/1 (Goldsmiths', Plumbers', and Glaziers'). N.C.S. SANT/GUI/Ncl/4/2/1 (Glovers'); SANT/GUI/6/2/1 (Saddlers').

20 For the masons, see Bourchier Richardson, *Plague and Pestilence*, p. 31 (the original, T.W.A. GU/Ms/2/1, is currently unfit for production). For the Curriers', Feltmakers', and Armourers', see T.W.A. GU/CF/2/1 p. 24; GU/CF/2/2 (unpag.). One of the stewards of this company, John Bell, was buried in St Johns', together with his wife, on 30 August. Two of the three armourers who had signed guild orders in 1635 were buried in St Nicholas': Henry Gray (13 October, preceded by three of his children); John Hall (21 August, preceded by his wife and followed by one child).

21 T.N.A. SP 16/370/81; SP 16/386/78.

22 T.W.A. GU/BS/ 2/1, Barber-Surgeons' Minutes, 1616–86, unfoliated. In 1635, the Barber-Surgeons met two or three times a month, often with wine and music provided. Seven or eight of the approximately thirty members of the company usually attended each gathering. The May meetings had attendances of three and four. It seems likely that most of the sick either provided for themselves or relied on the services of "empirics" such as Elizabeth Wilkinson of St Andrew's parish, who was described in 1615 as one who "delt with medsonning and witching": D.U.L. DDR/EJ/CCD/1/10a–10b, fos 52v–53.

23 Jenison, *Newcastle's Call*, pp. 169–70. Among the "kind neighbours" was Berwick-upon-Tweed, which sent forty marks (around twenty-six pounds) as a contribution to the relief of Newcastle: J. Raine, "A Letter from the Corporation of Newcastle-upon-Tyne to the Mayor and Aldermen of Berwick", *Archaeologia Aeliana*, 2 (1832), pp. 366–7.

24 T.W.A. 543/26, Chamberlains' Accounts 1635–6, fo. 264.

25 For a full account of the 1633 riots, see Howell, *Newcastle-upon-Tyne and the Puritan Revolution*, pp. 53–61. A contemporary description and comment upon these events is found in the 1884 reprint of Gray's *Chorographia*, which included handwritten additions made by Gray to his own copy in the 1650s: W. Gray, *Chorographia, or A Survey of Newcastle upon Tyne*, ed. Andrew Reid (Newcastle, 1884), pp. 95–6.

26 Jenison, *Newcastle's Call*, p. 237.

27 Slack, *Impact of Plague*, pp. 26–8.

28 *Ibid.*, pp. 30, 45–7. That Newcastle, like other cities, routinely sought to keep the principal streets clean, is evidenced by payments made by the chamberlains in 1635 to "the scavenger for leadeing of rubbishe from the Bridge and other places", and "the porters for cleansinge the Sandhill and Loeth borne this yeare": T.W.A. 543/26, fos 142, 142v. The problem of the city's great public "middens" (see Ch. 3, n. 15 above) remained. For efforts to dispel "miasma" during the outbreak, see n. 6 above.

29 *Ibid.*, pp. 210, 215–16. Cf. J.F. Merritt, *The Social World of Early Modern Westminster: Abbey, Court, and Community* (Manchester and New York, 2005), pp. 298–301.

30 Slack, *Impact of Plague*, pp. 203–4, 220.

31 D.U.L. DDR/EJ/CCD/2, Folder 20.i.1637–6.v.1637, fo. 26; Folder depositions c.22.vii.1637, fos 47–47v, 108. Bourchier Richardson, *Plague and Pestilence*, p. 31; Welford, ed., *History of Newcastle and Gateshead*, vol. III, p. 339.

32 D.U.L. DDR/EJ/CCD/2, Folder 20.i.1637–6.v.1637, fos 26 (Edward Holmes), 9 (Clement Curry). Other examples can be found on fos 4, 6–6v, 7, 10, 16 17, 23, 23v, 33, 36v.

33 Paul Slack is sceptical as to how efficiently household quarantine could be enforced in large cities, and suggests that it was probably most rigorous in lesser outbreaks, and in the central parishes which were least severely affected: *Impact of Plague*, p. 278.

34 *Ibid.*, fo. 26. W.H.D. Longstaffe, ed., *Memoirs of the Life of Mr Ambrose Barnes*, Surtees Society, 50 (1867), p. 38. Barnes' experience was probably during the outbreak of 1647.

35 D.U.L. DDR/EJ/CCD/2, Folder: depositions c.22.vii.1637, fo. 108.

36 D.U.L. DDR/EJ/CCD/2, Folder 20.i.1637–6.v.1637, fo. 33. Stobbs scarcely had strength to stand by this time, which may have prevented his coming down to the

door, but it seems significant that Margaret needed to get a smith to help her get into the house. A tradition recorded later held that in 1636 "such was the miserable situation of the people that their victuals were forced to be bore up in Baskets to their windowes", implying that doors were sealed: Huntington Library, HM 69956, "Mss History of Newcastle by James Murray", fo. 181 (interlined).

37 D.U.L. DDR/EJ/CCD/2, Folder 20.i.1637–6.v.1637, fo. 11. For other examples where the location of the sick person is specified, see fos 2v, 4, 10, 17, 33. The statement on the location of beds is based upon a survey of all Newcastle inventories for 1636–7 which specify the contents of particular rooms.

38 D.U.L. DDR/EJ/CCD/2, Folder 20.i.1637–6.v.1637, fos 10, 16, 23v; Folder 19.v.1637–17.vi.1637, fo. 85. DPRI/1/1637/H17/3–4 (Inventory of Thomas Holmes).

39 A survey of those inventories for people dying in 1636 that specify rooms indicates that some 29 per cent of the houses inventoried consisted of 2–3 rooms and some 43 per cent of 4–5 rooms (some also having a loft or a cellar). The remainder had 6-10 rooms. Most houses were clearly two-storey buildings. In the Barcelona plague of 1651, sick persons were often kept in attics, with minimum contact with others in the house, save for the person actually nursing them: Amelang, trans. and ed., *A Journal of the Plague Year*, p. 49.

40 D.U.L. DDR/EJ/CCD/2, Folder 20.i.1637–6.v.1637, fos 18v–19, Folder 19.v.1637–17. vi.1637, fos. 96v–97. In the outbreak at Prato, Tuscany, in 1630–1, people were so reluctant to enter the town's extramural pest house that they had to be encouraged by the refusal of relief to sick people who remained at home: Cipolla, *Cristofano and the Plague*, p. 79. There is no evidence of such compulsion in Newcastle, though it remains possible that the city's relief expenditure was focused on the lodges.

41 T.W.A. Microfilm 1139 (Registers of Gateshead, St Mary's), fo. 163. Of the 200 plague burials listed for Gateshead, 72 took place in June and 82 in July, but only 27 in August and 19 in September.

42 Benwell was jurisdictionally part of the city parish of St John's. Thirty-six burials from Benwell were recorded in the register of St John's, many of them in family clusters. The riverside settlement of Elswick, however, and the area "without Westgate", both of which were also part of St John's, provided only six and three burials respectively. No burials from Fenham to the north-west, or Jesmond to the north-east, are separately noted in the register of St Andrew's; perhaps simply a matter of registration practice, but perhaps also because they lay sufficiently distant from the city to be effectively insulated. The failure of the register of Allhallows' means that nothing can be said of Byker and Heaton, lying to the east and north-east of Sandgate, beyond the Ouseburn. N.C.S. EP 73/3 (St John's); EP 13/1–2 (St Andrew's); EP 9/2 (All Saints' [Allhallows']).

43 No registers for the 1630s survive for the parishes of Longbenton and Gosforth to the north of the city, Newburn to the west, or Wallsend to the east. The message of those registers that survive, however, seems clear: Whickham saw a flurry of burials in mid-August (five members of the Blenkinshipp family) but nothing more serious. Ryton, Jarrow (which included South Shields), and Tynemouth (which included North Shields) saw no signficant rise in burials. Neither did Chester-le-Street, despite the existence of a Durham Quarter Sessions order of July 1636 alluding to "the reliefe of the infected" in that parish. T.W.A. Microfilms 899 (Whickham), 1091 (Ryton), 1092 (Jarrow, St Paul's), 1994 (Chester-le-Street); N.C.S. Microfilm 586 (Tynemouth, Christchurch); Durham County Record Office [henceforward D.C.R.O.] Q/S OB 2, pp. 208–9.

44 D.U.L. DPRI/1/1637/S15/1–2 (Gateshead); DPRI/1/1636/S18/1–4 (Gateshead); DPRI/1/ 1636/A4/1–2 (South Shields); DPRI/1/1637/R2/1 (Tynemouth); DPRI/1/1637/P8/1 (Chester-le-Street); DPRI/1/1636/H10/1 (Usworth in Washington); DPRI/1/1637/M1/1 (Haltwhistle); DDR/EJ/CCD/2, Folder 20.1.1637–6.v.1637, fos 26v (Corbridge), 29 (Harton, South Shields). For cases from Northumberland (notably Felton and Alnwick) in 1637, see D.U.L. DPRI/1/1637/H19/1–2; DPRI/1/1637/D8/1; DPRI/1/1637/M12/1; DPRI/1/1637/H3/1–2; DPRI/1/1637/R3/1–2; DPRI/1/1637/R6/1; DPRI/1/1637/T8/3–4; DPRI/1/1637/W10/3. I am grateful to Francis Gotto, of the Archives and Special Collections Department of Durham University Library, for sharing with me his list of plague-related wills and inventories, without which a survey of plague deaths outside Newcastle would have been prohibitively time-consuming.

45 For information on Bishopwearmouth in 1637, I am grateful to Dr Maureen Meickle. For the Durham justices' response to later threats, see D.C.R.O. Q/S OB 2, pp. 256, 276, 322.

46 This expression was used to describe the effects of the plague of 1647, as recalled by Ambrose Barnes: Longstaffe, ed., *Memoirs of the Life of Mr Ambrose Barnes*, p. 38.

47 For examples of these common phrases, see e.g. D.U.L. DDR/EJ/CCD/2, Folder 20.i.1637–6.v.1637, fos 9, 11v, 17v, 23v, 24, 33, 37.

48 D.U.L. DDR/EJ/CCD/2, Folder 1.ix.1633–26.iv.1634, fos 68v–69v. It was common for women to gather at neighbours' doors in this way. For another example from 1620, see DDR/EJ/CCD/1/11, fos 50, 80v: Jane Scolledg, Jane Askew, and Katherine Dawson all "sitting at Jane Scolledg her doore", while Ann Hall was "sitting at her owne dore there hard by".

CHAPTER 5 SENT FOR TO WRITE

1 D.U.L. DDR/EJ/CCD/2, Folder 20.i.1637–6.v.1637, fo. 23v. This incident took place in St Nicholas' parish, probably somewhere on the bank above The Close. Robert Moore's will shows that he owned property in the area, "on the west side of the long staires", and "on the Castle mote", though the location of his own "dwelling house" is not specified: D.U.L. DPRI/1/1636/M9/1–2.

2 All of these documents are in the Durham probate registry. Those Newcastle people who held property outside the diocese of Durham should have applied for probate at the Prerogative Courts of York or Canterbury. The records of both courts were searched. Neither of the two wills of Newcastle residents proved at York in 1636 and 1637 relates to the plague, though one of the administrations granted may be that of a plague victim. There are no Newcastle wills in the registers of the Prerogative Court of Canterbury for the years 1636–9. For Newcastle records at York, see *Index of Wills in the York Registry from 1636 to 1652*, Yorkshire Archaeological and Topographical Society Record Series, vol. IV (1888), p. 32, and *Index of Wills in the York Registry, A.D. 1627 to 1636: Administrations A.D. 1627 to 1652*, Yorkshire Archaeological Society Record Series, vol. XXXV (1905), pp. 106, 113, 243. I am grateful to Dr P. Withington for obtaining copies of the original documents for me. For the Prerogative Court of Canterbury, see T.N.A. PROB 11.

3 Of the 103 wills and inventories generated by plague deaths, twenty-five can be attributed to Ralph Tailor. Sixteen of these (ten wills and six inventories) are definitely his work since he signed the will or was named as one of the appraisers of an inventory and clearly wrote it. Nine more (four wills and five inventories) can be confidently attributed to him on the grounds that they follow his distinctive forms, employ his usual phrases, and are clearly in his hand. Each of these documents was carefully compared with "definite" wills or inventories written by Tailor, with particular attention being paid to the format, the language used, and the manner in which he wrote certain words and formed certain letters. Inevitably, an element of judgment is involved in these attributions, but every effort was made to resist the temptation to maximize them. Indeed, several unsigned wills that may well have been written by Tailor were eventually excluded on the grounds that small inconsistencies meant I did not feel sufficiently certain that they were indeed his work. Even if only the documents definitely written by Tailor were included, he would still stand out as by far the most active scribe during the epidemic.

4 Based on the evidence of the actual wills and of depositions describing will-making. Ralph Tailor's nearest rivals were Francis Slinger, John Netherwood, and John Carr, all of them professional penmen, who wrote three wills each. Carr died in the epidemic and his career was cut off (see n. 17 below), but there is no burial recorded for Netherwood, who operated in St Nicholas' and St John's parishes, and Slinger definitely survived.

5 Parishes of residence can be established from the evidence provided in wills, inventories, and depositions, and from registered burials. In the case of Allhallows', the absence of burial registration means that in a small number of cases individuals were judged likely to be from Allhallows' on the grounds of their occupation, e.g. "skipper" (of a keel), and the absence of a registered burial elsewhere. If these

doubtful cases were to be excluded, the proportion of Allhallows' victims with whom Tailor was involved would be even higher (57 per cent).

6 D.U.L. DPRI/1/1636/G8/1. The first identifiable plague will was that of John Reay, miller, of Sandgate, made on 21 May.

7 D.U.L. DPRI/1/1638/C2/1. For Plummer Chare, see Ch. 2, n. 27 above.

8 D.U.L. DDR/EJ/CCD/2, Folder 20.i.1637–6.v.1637, fos 10, 16.

9 D.U.L. DPRI/1/1636/E2/1–2 (Thomas Eden); DPRI/1/1636/M9/1–2 (Robert Moore); DPRI/1/1636/W9/1–6 (Cuthbert Woodman).

10 D.U.L. DRPI/1/1636/S14/1.

11 D.U.L. DPRI/1/1636/R12/1–2.

12 DPRI/1/1637/H17/3–4. He was involved in making two inventories of plague victims in October, four in November, one in December, and four in the early months of 1637.

13 D.U.L. DPRI/1/1637/M2/1.

14 See Ch. 3, n. 24 above. For the accusation against Stevenson, see Ch. 4, p. 49 above. Pringle's will was not included in the tally of 1636 plague wills, since it clearly relates to a subsequent recurrence of the disease.

15 The fragments of deposition books relate to four sessions of the court for February 1636/7, three for March, one for April, two for May, and one each for June and July 1637. Probably half the sessions held in the first seven months of 1637 are undocumented, and thereafter the record breaks off: D.U.L. DDR/EJ/CCD/2, Folder 20.i.1637–6.v.1637, fos 5, 9, 18v, 19, 16, 26v; Folder 19.v.1637–17.vi.1637, fo. 96v; Folder, depositions c.22.vii.1637, fos 47, 47v. For further discussion of testamentary litigation, see Ch. 11 below.

16 D.U.L. DPRI/4/14, Probate Act Book, April 1635–March 1637/8. Of those whose estates entered probate between October 1636 and June 1637, a quarter can be identified from wills, inventories, depositions, or administration papers as definite plague victims. The surviving probate bonds, which could also relate to the administration of the estates of intestates, cast further light on the impact of the plague. There are usually around forty bonds each year for Newcastle (e.g. thirty-five for 1630; forty-seven for 1638). No Newcastle bond survives for 1636. For 1637 there are 145 – an upsurge that was surely related to the massive mortality of the preceding year. Nevertheless, only nineteen of these relate to plague victims identifiable from wills, inventories, or depositions: D.U.L. Archives & Special Collections, Calendar of Probate Bonds. Since inventories should have been prepared for all estates entering probate, we can safely assume that most inventories made were discarded or have been lost.

17 Carr had written three plague wills in Allhallows' between May and July, including the first will to survive. He wrote his own will on 10 August and died shortly thereafter: D.U.L. DPRI/1/1636/C1/1. In August and September, the scrivener Francis Slinger, who survived the plague, wrote two wills in Allhallows', and Lactantius Sands wrote another.

18 Jenison, *Newcastle's Call*, p. 35.

19 D.U.L. DDR/EJ/CCD/2, Folder 20.i.1637–6.v.1637, fos 7, 9, 23, 26, 29, 33.

20 *Ibid.*, Folder 20.i.1637–6.v.1637, fo. 23v, Folder 19.v.1637–17. vi.1637, fo. 85; DPRI/1/1636/M9/1–5 (Robert Moore).

21 Wear, "Fear, Anxiety, and the Plague", pp. 347ff, 356.

22 Jenison, *Newcastle's Call*, pp. 222–5. This was followed by the story, from the Book of Chronicles, of how David had been "by fear of the destroying Angell restrained from *Gibeon*, where the Tabernacle of the Lord, and the Altar of burnt offering were at that season".

23 As is noted in Slack, *Impact of Plague*, p. 238. Slack provides a full discussion of contemporary attitudes towards the problem of flight on pp. 36, 40–4, and 236ff. For early seventeenth-century criticism of "run-aways", see J. Monteyne, *The Printed Image in Early Modern London: Urban Space, Visual Representations, and Social Exchange* (Aldershot and Burlington, VT, 2007), pp. 79, 85, 91.

24 For Jenison and Alvey, see Howell, *Newcastle-upon-Tyne and the Puritan Revolution*, p. 84ff.

25 D.U.L. DDR/EJ/CCD/2, Folder, Depositions c.22.vii.1637, fo. 47–47v. Doncaster was not unfamiliar with the plague. Six years earlier he had visited a suspected plague

victim and witnessed his will: DDR/EJ/CCD/1/12, fos 239v–240. For an earlier example of removal *within* the city to avoid the plague in the minor outbreak of 1610, see D.U.L. DDR/EJ/CCD/1/11, fos 70v–71. This would have been of little use after July 1636 as the whole city was engulfed by the epidemic.

26   Christopher Foster repeatedly signed pages of the St Nicholas' register throughout the epidemic: N.C.S. EP/86 (St Nicholas'), pp. 312, 313, 314, 315, 316. He witnessed (and probably wrote) wills on 10 and 12 August, both of which, intriguingly, were of men from St John's parish: D.U.L. DPRI/1/1637/W8/1–2; DPRI/1/1637/W9/1; N.C.S. EP 13/1–2 (St Andrews), p. 74.

27   On the extramural residences of some of the city's "inner ring", see Howell, *Newcastle-upon-Tyne and the Puritan Revolution*, p. 50.

28   T.N.A. SP 16/386/78.

CHAPTER 6 LIVEING A SCRIVENER IN THE SAME TOWNE

1   D.U.L. DDR/EJ/CCD/2, Folder 20.i.1637–6.v.1637, fos 10, 13; Folder 19.v.1637–17. vi.1637, fo. 85.

2   D.U.L. DPRI/1/1669/T1/1; DPRI/2/8, fos 167v–168.

3   D.C.R.O. EP/Du SM1 (St Margaret's, Durham), Microfilm MF 42/144. I am assuming that he was baptized within a week or two of his birth.

4   Based upon: D.C.R.O. EP/Du SM1 (St Margaret's, Durham); H. Robertson, ed., *The Registers of St Margaret's (Durham) in the County of Durham*, Durham and Northumberland Parish Register Society (Sunderland, 1904); *International Genealogical Index* for County Durham (microfiche available at D.C.R.O.). In his own will, Ralph Tailor was later to refer to "my sister Mary", wife of William Little, and to Katherine Wilson, "my sister", neither of whom appears in the register of St Margaret's (or in that of any other parish in Durham city). They may have been siblings baptized elsewhere, but it is also possible that he used the term "sister" to mean "sister-in-law", as was common at the time. That he employed this kind of usage is shown by the fact that he also referred to Roger Jobling as "my brother" and to George Swaddell, husband of his wife's daughter by an earlier marriage, as "my son": D.U.L. DPRI/1/1669/T1/1; DPRI/2/8, fos 167v–168.

5   D.U.L. DDR/EJ/CCD/2, Folder 19.v.1637–17.vi.1637, fo. 85; T.N.A. E134, 1649–50, Hil. 1.

6   D.U.L. DPRI/1/1634/T1/1 (Raph Taler); DPRI/1/1629/T1/1 (Miles Taler). Interestingly, Raph Taler senior could not sign his name, but his son Miles could.

7   For the naming of children after godparents, the choosing of paternal kin and persons of higher status as godparents, and the role of godparents, see S. Smith-Bannister, *Names and Naming Patterns in England, 1538–1700* (Oxford, 1997), pp. 30–53.

8   D.U.L. DPRI/1/1617/T2/1 (John Tayler senior); T.W.A. GU/BU/1, Butchers' Company Book (unfol.). In his own will Ralph Tailor left a bequest to the poor of the Butchers' Company: D.U.L. DPRI/2/8, fo. 167v. It must be mentioned, however, that he left a similar bequest to the poor of the Bakers and Brewers' Company, and that a prominent member of that company was another John Tailor, probably the brother of Peter Taylor of Allhallows', who died in 1628: N.C.S. SANT/GUI/Ncl/1/3/1, Bakers and Brewers' Accounts, 1637–94 (unfol.); D.U.L. DPRI/1/1628/T1/1–2. Perhaps they were all kinsmen in some degree.

9   D.U.L. DPRI/1/1617/T2/1 (John Tayler senior). William Jackson was described as sixty years old and living in "Lee Side" in 1633, when he gave evidence in a case which involved him recalling being witness to a lease made in 1606, at which time he had been the servant of a "counselor at law". He gave further evidence attesting to a signature in February 1637, at which time he was still claiming to be sixty! During the plague he is known to have written only one will, that of John Collingwood, dated 26 October 1636: D.U.L. DDR/EJ/CCD/2, Folder 17.viii.1632–1.xi.1633, fo. 39, Folder 20.i.1637–6.v.1637, fo. 5v; DPRI/1/1636/C6/1–2.

10   William West, *Symbolaeographia . . . or The Notarie or Scrivener* (London, 1590), book 1, sections 1, 2 (unpag.).

11   For these developments and their implications, see C.W. Brooks, *Pettyfoggers and Vipers of the Commonwealth: The "Lower Branch" of the Legal Profession in Early*

Modern England (Cambridge, 1986), pp. 79–84, 93–101, and ch. 5; C. Muldrew, *The Economy of Obligation: The Culture of Credit and Social Relations in Early Modern England* (Basingstoke and New York, 1998), esp. part I.

12 C.W. Brooks, *Law, Politics and Society in Early Modern England* (Cambridge, 2008), p. 308; C.W. Brooks, R.M. Helmholz, and P.G. Stein, *Notaries Public in England since the Reformation*, Society of Public Notaries of London (London, 1991), p. 84.

13 For the measurement of literacy and trends in the ability to sign one's name, see D. Cressy, *Literacy and the Social Order: Reading and Writing in Tudor and Stuart England* (Cambridge, 1980). The Durham diocese figures are given on pp. 146–7. In the depositions made by Newcastle people in 1637 in cases arising from the plague of 1636, 56 per cent of the male deponents (most of whom were craftsmen and tradesmen) were able to sign their names. None of the women could do so. For later developments, see R.A. Houston, "The Development of Literacy: Northern England, 1640–1750", *Economic History Review*, 2nd series, 35 (1982), in which the urban figures provided aggregate samples from York, Newcastle, Durham, and Carlisle.

14 Brooks, Helmholz, and Stein, *Notaries Public in England*, pp. 59, 77. The Scriveners' Company of Newcastle was not founded until 1675.

15 This was the rule adopted by the Newcastle Scriveners' Company when it was established in 1675, and it presumably reflected existing practice: T.W.A. GU/SC/1, Scriveners' Minute Book, 1675–1775.

16 M.H. Dodds, ed., *The Register of Freemen of Newcastle upon Tyne from the Corporation Guild and Admission Books Chiefly of the Seventeenth Century*, Newcastle upon Tyne Records Committee, III (Newcastle, 1923), p. 19.

17 Robert Jenison used this phrase when praising the city's educational sponsorship in *The Height of Israel's Heathenish Idolatrie*, Epistle Dedicatory, B2. For the need for at least basic Latin, see Brooks, Helmholz, and Stein, *Notaries Public in England*, p. 58. For the grammar school and writing school, see R. Tuck, "Civil Conflict in School and Town, 1500–1700", in B. Mains and A. Tuck, eds, *Royal Grammar School, Newcastle-upon-Tyne: A History of the School in its Community* (Stocksfield, 1986), p. 19. Tuck observes (p. 23) that John Lilburne was a pupil at the grammar school in the late 1620s, raising the possibility that Ralph Tailor was a schoolmate of the future Leveller leader.

18 These are the skills emphasized in two of the most popular printed "copy books" of the period, which may well have been used at the writing school: John de Beau Chesne, *A Booke Containing Divers Sortes of Hands* (London, 1571), unpag.; Martin Billingsley, *The Pens Excellencie or The Secretaries Delight* (London, 1618), B3. For a vivid account of learning to write and the use of "copy books" in a slightly later period, see S. Whyman, *The Pen and the People: English Letter Writers, 1660–1800* (Oxford, 2009), pp. 19–21, 24–7.

19 West, *Symbolaeographia*, book 2, section 2, and *passim*. West's book is essentially a compendium of legal instruments, each of which is defined and exemplified.

20 Brooks, Helmholz, and Stein, *Notaries Public in England*, pp. 94–5.

21 R. Bartlett, *The Hanged Man: A Story of Miracle, Memory, and Colonialism in the Middle Ages* (Princeton and Oxford, 2004), p. 106. For the role of notaries in continental European legal systems, see e.g. B.Z. Kadar, "The Genoese Notaries of 1382: The Anatomy of an Urban Occupational Group", in H.A. Miskimin, D. Herlihy, and A.L. Udovitch, eds, *The Medieval City* (New Haven and London, 1977); D.V. and F.W. Kent, *Neighbours and Neighbourhood in Renaissance Florence: The District of the Red Lion in the Fifteenth Century* (Locust Valley, NY, 1982), pp. 83, 110; Donna Merwick, *Death of a Notary: Conquest and Change in Colonial New York* (Ithaca, NY and London, 1999), pp. 2, 5, 17, 189–90.

22 Brooks, Helmholz, and Stein, *Notaries Public in England*, pp. 5, 8.

23 *Ibid.*, pp. 16–40, 67. For Newcastle's Admiralty Court, see Gray, *Chorographia*, p. 24.

24 Brooks, Helmholz, and Stein, *Notaries Public in England*, pp. 68–74.

25 D.U.L. DPRI/1/1636/C1/2–4.

26 Norman was still active in 1635, when he wrote a will, and in 1637, when he gave evidence in a testamentary case. His relationship to Carr and Clarke was described by Clarke in the same year: D.U.L. DPRI/1/1636/H11/1; DDR/EJ/CCD/2, Folder

20.i.1637–6.v.1637, fos 20, 21v. For an account of the making of a will by Clarke in Newcastle in 1627, when he was thirty-two, see DDR/EJ/CCD/1/12, fo. 62v.

27 D.U.L. DDR/EJ/CCD/2, Folder 17.viii.1632–1.xi.1633, fos 34v–35v. Slinger described how, after he had written the will, Brandling "did himself take it into his hand and redd it over himself and said it was very well" before signing and sealing it. Sands later wrote one plague will in September 1636, Slinger wrote three in August and September.

28 D.U.L. DDR/EJ/CCD/12, fos 42, 50.

29 Brooks, Helmholz, and Stein, *Notaries Public in England*, pp. 86, 89; West, *Symbolaeographia*, book 1, sections 2, 5. West added that too many failed to live up to this standard, and "for small gaine without blushing, will professe and undertake to effect any thing".

30 C. Brooks, "Apprenticeship, Social Mobility, and the Middling Sort, 1550–1800", in J. Barry and C. Brooks, eds, *The Middling Sort of People: Culture, Society, and Politics in England, 1550–1800* (Basingstoke and London, 1994), pp. 75–7. For the culture of urban freedom and citizenship, see P. Withington, *The Politics of Commonwealth: Citizens and Freemen in Early Modern England* (Cambridge, 2005), pp. 10–12, 14–15, 30, 87–94, 98–9, 114–19, 127–49, 189 (quoting p. 119). Withington provides specific Newcastle illustrations of the operative nature of these ideals on pp. 169–80.

31 Dodds, ed., *Register of Freemen of Newcastle upon Tyne*, p. 19: "Ra Tayler scrivener". We have no precise date or information on the identity of Ralph's master since the original Freeman's Register survives only from 1645. For earlier years Dodds was forced to rely upon a list of freemen's names, the "Freemens Alphabet 1409 to 1738", compiled by John Douglas, the town clerk, in 1710–38, from admissions books now lost.

32 D.U.L. DPRI/1/1636/A6/1–3; DPRI/1/1637/F9/2. A search of Newcastle wills and inventories for 1635 reveals no earlier documents bearing Ralph Tailor's name, though four other scriveners and notaries can be identified in these records: D.U.L. DPRI/1/1635, *passim*.

33 D.U.L. DPRI/1/1636/A6/1–3.

34 For the cultural significance of such things, see A. Butcher, "The Functions of Script in the Speech Community of a Late Medieval Town, *c.*1300–1550", in J. Crick and A. Walsham, eds, *The Uses of Script and Print, 1300–1700* (Cambridge, 2005), pp. 162, 167. Butcher also stresses (pp. 160–1) how the clerks who produced even mundane documents could "seek to impose their own individual skill and understanding upon these texts even as they construct them according to generic forms".

35 One can compare, for example, the wills written by John Netherwood for William Cooke, Robert Grinwell, and Robert Walker, or that prepared for Thomas Hayton by John Carr, with the accounts of the making of these wills contained in the court depositions: D.U.L. DPRI/1/1636/C10/1–2; DPRI/1/1636/G12/1–2; DPRI/1/1637/W1/1; DPRI/1/1637/H10/2; DDR/EJ/CCD/2, Folder 20.i.1637–6.v.1637, fos 4, 6–7v, 36v–37; Folder: depositions *c.*22.vii.1637, fos 103v–104.

36 D.U.L. DPRI/1/1636/1–2.

37 On one occasion, writing the will of Ann Carr on 28 June, he added a brief note of the regnal year in Latin: D.U.L. DPRI/1/1638/1. Thereafter he dropped this practice.

38 It is interesting that in the aftermath of the plague Ralph Tailor immediately resumed the writing of the wills he prepared in full formal style: e.g. DPRI/1/1637/E1/1–3 (Ralph Emerson, 28 January 1636/7); DPRI/1/1637/B11/1–5 (Richard Brown, 21 September 1637). But when he came to write the nuncupative will of the late plague victim William Pringle on 4 November 1637, he reverted to the memorandum style he had adopted in 1636: DPRI/1/1637/P9/1.

39 D.U.L. DDR/EJ/CCD/2, Folder 20.i.1637–6.v.1637, fos 10–10v, 13–13v; Folder 19.v.1637–17.vi.1637, fo. 85.

40 For their depositions, see *ibid.*, Folder 20.i.1637–6.v.1637, fos 20–1

41 *Ibid.*, fo. 20v.

42 For notarial signs and devices, see Brooks, Helmholz, and Stein, *Notaries Public in England*, pp. 47–50 and the accompanying illustrations.

CHAPTER 7 THE DIALECT OF HEAVEN

1 D.U.L. DDR/EJ/CCD/2, Folder 20.i.1637–6.v.1637, fo. 26.

2 Jenison, *Newcastle's Call*, pp. 31, 32, 33, 59–60, 61.

3 *Ibid.*, pp. 95–104. "Gods good creatures" was the usual expression used by moralists for food and drink. "Company keeping" usually referred to convivial gatherings, often associated with excessive drinking.

4 *Ibid.*, pp. 57–9.

5 *Ibid.*, pp. 12, 106, 155, 205–6, 240–1, 260–8.

6 Fenwicke, *Christ Ruling in Midst of his Enemies*, Epistle Dedicatory, A2v, A3, A4. Fenwick was alluding to Luke 19:42, and citing Jer. 13:27, which ends (in the Authorized or King James Version): "Woe unto thee, O Jerusalem! Wilt thou not be made clean? When shall it once be?"

7 *Ibid.*, Epistle Dedicatory, A3. Fenwick, who had a history of religious and political opposition to the Caroline regime, took the Scottish National Covenant on a visit to Edinburgh in 1638. He was investigated for this treasonable act by the Newcastle authorities in 1639 and fled to Scotland. Returning with the Scottish army of occupation in 1640, both he and his wife vigorously attacked the Arminian church establishment of Newcastle and Durham. With the withdrawal of the Scots and the outbreak of civil war, he was subject to disenfranchisement and confiscation of property at the hands of the royalist corporation: see Hopper, "Fenwick (Fenwicke), John", *Oxford D.N.B. Christ Ruling in Midst of his Enemies* was an appeal to parliament setting out his history and grievances. Newcastle was yet to suffer the further trial of the siege of 1644 and renewed Scottish occupation in 1644–6.

8 Jenison, *The Height of Israel's Heathenish Idolatrie*, Epistle Dedicatory, B3–C2, C4v. The generally positive tone of Jenison's ministry in the early 1620s is also reflected in the opening epistles and content of *Directions for the Worthy Receiving of the Lord's Supper* (London, 1624) and *The Christians Apparelling by Christ* (London, 1625).

9 *The Christians Apparelling by Christ*, Epistle Dedicatorie.

10 Jenison's sermons were later published as *Soled Comfort for Sound Christians* (1641), an unauthorized publication, with an epistle "To the Reader" recounting his experience and dated "10 November 1629". An authorized version with a further "Epistle" appeared as *Two Treatises* (London, 1642). For Jackson's significance as an anti-Calvinist theologian, and his career in Newcastle, 1625–32, see A.J. Hegarty, "Thomas Jackson", in *Oxford D.N.B.* The prominence of the higher clergy of the diocese of Durham in the rise of Arminianism is discussed in D. Newton, *North-East England, 1569–1625: Governance, Culture, and Identity* (Woodbridge, 2006), pp. 131–5, and a succinct account of the religious controversies in the city in the later 1620s and 1630s is given in C.R. Newman, "The Reformation Era in Newcastle, 1530–1662", in Pollard and Newton, eds, *Newcastle and Gateshead before 1700*, pp. 207–11.

11 R. Jenison, *The Cities Safetie: or a Fruitfull Treatise (and Usefull for these Dangerous Times)* (London, 1630), pp. 133–4, 136–7, 160–1, and *passim*. In discussing the plague, Jenison showed himself very familiar with the figures recorded in the London Bills of Mortality for 1602–3 and 1624–5, revealing a fascination with such records that was to reappear in *Newcastle's Call*.

12 Jenison, *The Cities Safetie*, p. 160.

13 Jenison, *Newcastle's Call*, Preface, a3v, a4, A9 (the pagination is inconsistent and incomplete), and pp. 96, 116, 142, 224–5. Jenison was certainly back in the city by late 1637 and remained a firm opponent of Arminian "innovation" until his suspension and then deprivation for nonconformity in 1639 and flight early in 1640 into exile in Danzig. See Shiels, "Jenison, Robert", in *Oxford D.N.B.* and Howell, *Newcastle-upon-Tyne and the Puritan Revolution*, pp. 96, 104, 108–11, 118.

14 G. Selement and B.C. Woolley, eds, *Thomas Shepard's Confessions*, Colonial Society of Massachusetts, LVIII (Boston, 1981), pp. 2–3, 7–9, 12, and *passim*. The confessions concerned are those of Edward Hall, John Sill, Joanna Sill, Robert Holmes, Elizabeth Cutter, Jane Wilkinson Winship, Jane Palfrey, and Ann Errington. For Shepard's career, see also M. Jinkins, "Thomas Shepard (1605–1649)" in *Oxford D.N.B.*, and for Glover, see Howell, *Newcastle-upon-Tyne and the Puritan*

Revolution, p. 82. Glover was accused of preaching seditious doctrine in 1634, but his whereabouts thereafter are uncertain. As early as May 1635, the leading Newcastle puritan John Blakiston, reflecting on the evil of the times, said of New England: "It is in all the best mens opinion a place likeliest for the people of God to escape unto, whom he gives liberty to remove." For this letter and other evidence of contact between Newcastle puritans and New England in the late 1630s, see Howell, *Newcastle-upon-Tyne and the Puritan Revolution*, pp. 92, 103.

15 Selement and Woolley, eds, *Thomas Shepard's Confessions*, pp. 150–1. The reference to Glover raises a question concerning the date of this "great sickness", but there was no other significant plague outbreak in Newcastle in the late 1620s and early 1630s. It is also not clear whether she met Glover himself or became subject to the influence of his followers in Heddon. Her preoccupation with using "a form of prayer" suggests that the sins of which she became convinced were those of conformity to the Anglican prayer book. The cause of her husband's death is unstated, but she came to New England as a young widow with two children and remarried there. By 1638, she was "Goodwife Willows", wife of George Willows.

16 I.e. she had taken the name of the Lord in vain (presumably by swearing) and she had failed to keep the Sabbath day holy.

17 Selement and Woolley, eds, *Thomas Shepard's Confessions*, pp. 144–6. She was apparently preceded to New England by her husband and three adult children and was there before 1639. Shepard recorded her confession, most of which concerns her renewed spiritual doubts and anguish *after* coming to New England, in c.1640. He called her "Old Goodwife Cutter".

18 *Ibid.*, pp. 142–3. Like Jane Palfrey, Holmes had come to regard his former acceptance of the Book of Common Prayer and the Homilies (officially approved sermons) of the Church of England as sinful. He remained deeply troubled and uncertain of his salvation, ending his confession, "Still I am doubting but I know I shall know if I follow on and if He damn me He shall do it in His own way." The text that comforted him in the plague was Isaiah 26:3: "Thou wilt keep him in perfect peace, whose mind is stayed on thee: because he trusteth in thee." A fourth confession, that of Ann Errington, another Jenison convert, who in her widowhood "desired hither to come thinking one sermon might do me more good than a hundred there", refers to how "when lecture sermons came after sickness I was very sad in my spirit but there was something spoke that came near to me". However, the placing of this recollection in her confession is such that she may have been recalling a "sickness" *after* her coming to New England rather than before: *ibid.*, p. 185.

19 *Ibid.*, p. 143.

20 T.N.A. SP 16/376/35. Liddell was not a member of Newcastle's puritan faction: Howell, *Newcastle-upon-Tyne and the Puritan Revolution*, p. 114.

21 In the pre-Reformation era, the city had supported around 120 clergy of all kinds. Thereafter clerical manpower fell drastically, despite the growth of the city's population: A.J. Pollard and D. Newton, "Introduction", in Pollard and Newton, eds, *Newcastle and Gateshead before 1700*, pp. xxxiv–xxxv. By 1636, Newcastle's clerical establishment consisted only of the vicar of Newcastle, four curates, and a lecturer. For their whereabouts and role during the plague, see Ch. 5, pp. 59–61 above.

22 D.U.L. DPRI/1/1636/H9/1–2. The scribe of Heslop's will, George Fetherstonhaugh, did not employ such language in the other will that he is known to have written. The words and the sentiments are clearly Heslop's. He was buried at St John's on 9 September.

23 D.U.L. DPRI/1/1636/W11/1–2. He still had a house in Newcastle and had presumably been visiting the city in the course of the coal trade when he fell sick in late August.

24 D.U.L. DPRI/1/1636/C9/1–2. He was buried at St Nicholas' on 11 July.

25 Quoting from D.U.L. DPRI/1/1636/C10/1 (William Cooke); DPRI/1/1636/R10/1 (George Robson); DPRI/1/1637/H10/1, 2 (Thomas and Katherine Hayton); DPRI/1/1637/H20/1–2 (Margaret Hutcheson).

26 See e.g. D.U.L. DPRI/1/1636/S12/1–2 (John Stobbs); DPRI/1/1636/R9/1 (William Robinson); DPRI/1/1636/G7/1 (Jane Glazenby); DPRI/1/1636/H2/1 (Gilbert Hall); DPRI/1/1637/L4/1 (John Laverrock).

27 See e.g. D.U.L. DPRI/1/1637/W8/1 (George Wilkinson); DPRI/1/1636/B8/1–2 (Michael Brown); DPRI/1/1636/E2/1–2 (Thomas Eden); DPRI/1/1637/F1/1–2 (Oswald Fayreallis); DPRI/1/1637/H8/1 (Barbara Havelock); DPRI/1/1636/1–2 (Robert Greenwell).

28 For the classic discussion of this issue, see M. Spufford, "Religious Preambles and the Scribes of Villagers' Wills in Cambridgeshire, 1570–1700", *Local Populations Studies*, 7 (1971) and the revised discussion in her *Constrasting Communities: English Villagers in the Sixteenth and Seventeenth Centuries* (Cambridge, 1974), pp. 320–44. See also C. Marsh, "In the Name of God? Will Making and Faith in Early Modern England", in G.H. Martin and P. Spufford, eds, *The Records of the Nation* (Woodbridge, 1990).

29 Slack, *Impact of Plague*, p. 287.

30 D.U.L. DDR/EJ/CCD/2, Folder 20.i.1637–6.v.1637, fos 2–3v; DPRI/1/1636/R11/1–2.

31 D.U.L. DDR/EJ/CCD/2, Folder 20.i.1637–6.v.1637, fos 16–17; DPRI/1/1636/W2/1–3.

32 D.U.L. DDR/EJ/CCD/2, Folder 20.i.1637–6.v.1637, fos 36v–37; DPRI/1/1636/G12/1–2.

33 D.U.L. DDR/EJ/CCD/2, Folder 20.i.1637–6.v.1637, fos 6–7v; DPRI/1/1637/W1/1.

34 D.U.L. DDR/EJ/CCD/2, Folder, depositions c.22.vii.1637, fo. 104; DPRI/1/1637/H10/1, 2.

35 D.U.L. DPRI/1/1636/H2/1.

36 Such references are sometimes to be found in depositions describing the making of wills. For an account of Thomas Harrison of nearby Whickham, who after making his will in 1603 "did for the most part of all the daie perfectly read praiers in a Booke", see Wrightson and Levine, "Death in Whickham", pp. 159–60, 161. London examples of one testator answering questions on the state of his soul in 1633, and of another reading prayers in 1636, can be found in Guildhall Library MS 9057/1, fos 14, 143. The absence of such references in a year for which so many accounts of the making of wills survive is striking.

37 Slack, *Impact of Plague*, pp. 240–1.

38 D.U.L. DPRI/1/1636/A6/1 (Margaret Ayre, 10 March 1636); DPRI/1/1637/E1/1 (Ralph Emerson, 28 January 1637); DPRI/1/1637/B11/1 (Richard Brown, 21 September 1637). He varied it a little for Richard Brown, substituting "bloodshed" for "passion" and "remission" for "remission pardon and forgiveness").

39 D.U.L. DPRI/1/1636/E2/1–2; DPRI/1/1636/H5/1–2; DPRI/1/1637/M2/1.

40 D.U.L. DPRI/1/1636/G8/1; DPRI/1/1636/H3/1–2.

41 A. Pettegree, *The Book in the Renaissance* (New Haven and London, 2010), p. 335.

CHAPTER 8 BEQUESTS AND LEGACIES

1 D.U.L. DPRI/1/1637/H15/1; DDR/EJ/CCD/2, Folder 19.v.1637–17.vi.1637, fos 95v–96. Henryson actually died in July 1637 and his earlier will was revised at that time and a new date inserted. Stobbs was buried at St Nicholas' on 21 September.

2 D.U.L. DDR/EJ/CCD/2, Folder 20.i.1637–6.v.1637, fo. 3. It was a simple enough task, since the total value of his goods came to little over nineteen pounds, eleven pounds were accounted for by "his pack and all his merchandises": DPRI/1/1636/R11/3. For chapmen, who dealt in small goods, often as peripatetic pedlars, see M. Spufford, *The Great Reclothing of Rural England. Petty Chapmen and their Wares in the Seventeenth Century* (London, 1984).

3 D.U.L. DPRI/1/1636/G7/1.

4 R. Hill, *The Pathway to Prayer and Pietie* (London, 1613), p. 148; D.U.L. DDR/EJ/CCD/1/10a–10b, fo.135.

5 D.U.L. DDR/EJ/CCD/2, Folder 20.i.1637–6.v.1637, fos 2v–3v (Robson), 23v–24 (Milburne).

6 For a fuller discussion of the law relating to nuncupative wills, see Ch. 11 below. That the expedients adopted in order to make the wills of plague victims were well established is evident from earlier accounts of how such wills were made. See e.g. D.U.L. DDR/EJ/CCD/1/12, fos 229v–230v, 239–40, 276v, 299–300. That on one occasion clarification was needed regarding which Bible was being bequeathed is evident from the wording in DPRI/1/1636/C5/1. Some of the specifics included in describing houses or goods probably served the same purpose.

7 D.U.L. DPRI/1/1636/H6/1–4. Robert's will was dated 1 October and Elizabeth's 18 October. His ends "By me Robert Harrison"; hers with her mark.

8 In 1634, Robert Moore had made his mark as an appraiser of the inventory of Lancelot Rayne: D.U.L. DPRI/1/1635/R1/3.

9 Inventories included goods, chattels, leases, and debts owed to the deceased, but not real estate: see Ch. 10 below for a fuller discussion. Of all plague victims whose gross inventoried estates are known, 45 per cent had estates of less than 40 pounds; 19 per cent had estates of 50–99 pounds; 21 per cent had estates of 100–199 pounds; and 15 per cent had estates of over 200 pounds. Ralph Tailor's clients included neither the poorest (those with estates of less than 15 pounds) nor the richest (those with estates of over 200 pounds). Their gross inventoried wealth ranged from approximately 17 to 176 pounds, with a median value of 68 pounds.

10 For conventional advice on the duties of testators, see e.g. Hill, *Pathway to Prayer and Pietie*, pp. 148–9. Under the Custom of the Province of York, testators' freedom to dispose of their goods was subject to certain restrictions. A married man with children, for example, must leave one-third of his goods to his widow and another third to his children. A married man with no children must leave half to his widow. Provision was also made for granting the "tuition" of minor children to a "tutor" who would have custody of the child's portion. See H. Swinburne, *A Briefe Treatise of Testaments and Last Wills* (London, 1611), pp. 101–20. My brief account of actual practice among Newcastle's testators in 1636 is based on all surviving wills for plague victims.

11 D.U.L. DPRI/1/1636/G8/1.

12 D.U.L. DPRI/1/1636/C10/1; DPRI/1/1636/H3/1–2. A deposition relating to a deathbed scene in 1617 suggests that the possibility of a posthumous child was often considered. When Robert Robinson of St Andrew's parish was making his will one of the witnesses asked him whether his wife was with child and he replied: "he was persuaded she was". On being further asked whether he should change the will, however, he declined, "sayinge there was ynough for her and itt to, meaninge his childe": DDR/EJ/CCD/1/10a–10b, fo. 199v. In a will of 1635, Thomas Errington of St John's parish left a portion of twenty pounds "unto my supposed child", which should revert to his wife and other children "failing my supposed child": DPRI/1/1635/E5/1.

13 D.U.L. DDR/EJ/CCD/2, Folder, depositions *c*.22.vii.1637, fo. 47v; DPRI/1/1636/C1/1; DPRI/1/1636/W1/1; DPRI/1/1636/C10/1; DPRI/1/1636/W9/1–2. For further examples of the appointment of tutors charged with the upbringing of minor children, see DPRI/1/1637/C8/1–4; DPRI/1/1637/F1/1–2; DPRI/1/1637/H4/1–2. Those so appointed were usually close male kin.

14 D.U.L. DPRI/1/1637/W1/1–4; DDR/EJ/CCD/2, Folder 20.i.1637–6.v.1637, fo. 7. Cf. the case of John Stobbs the younger. He was the nephew and heir of the childless widower John Stobbs senior. By the time Ralph Tailor wrote his will ten days after his uncle's burial, he seems to have had no surviving family and he gave all his goods to "my loveing frind Alexander Veich": DDR/EJ/CCD/2, Folder 20.i.1637–6.v.1637, fo. 33; DPRI/1/1636/S17/1–2.

15 D.U.L. DPRI/1/1636/C5/1; DPRI/1/1636/H2/1; DPRI/1/1638/C2/1.

16 D.U.L. DPRI/1/1636/S18/1–2. Swan's provision effectively rejected the legal doctrine of coverture by which all goods brought to a marriage by the wife became the property of the husband. It is perhaps the more remarkable in that the surviving list of the goods "unpraised" consists of a few items of clothing and some household utensils to a total value of less than two pounds.

17 Such expressions were common, but by no means universal. See e.g. DPRI/1/1636/C1/1; DPRI/1/1636/C9/1; DPRI/1/1637/H4/1; DPRI/1/1637/H10/2; DPRI/1/1637/M2/1; DPRI/1/1636/R3/1.

18 D.U.L. DPRI/1/1635, *passim*.

19 Almost all women left tokens regardless of their wealth. Among men whose gross inventoried wealth is known, half of those worth less than 20 pounds and three-quarters of those worth over 100 pounds left tokens. But almost nine tenths of those worth 20–100 pounds did so, and even among the relatively poor some men made many such small bequests.

20 D.U.L. DPRI/1/1636/G8/1.

21 D.U.L. DPRI/1/1636/M6/1. This list was relayed from a window.

22 D.U.L. DPRI/1/1637/W9/1.

23   D.U.L. DPRI/1/1637/W1/1, Robert Wright, mariner, similarly left tokens to his six apprentices, his maidservant, his own former master, Robert Brown of Newcastle, and his "loveing friend William Stagg of Wapping", a shipwright: D.U.L. DPRI/1/1636/W11/1–2.

24   D.U.L. DPRI/1/1637/H20/1–3; DPRI/1/1636/W2/1; DDR/EJ/CCD/2, Folder 20.i.1637–6.v.1637, fos 16–17v. Seven of the nine tokens left by Ann Milborne (listed above) also went to women. For the manner in which women's bequests commonly "served as gendered markers which sustained and maintained a sense of spiritual and material affinity between the dead and the living community", see J.S.W. Helt, "Women, Memory, and Will-Making in Elizabethan England", in B. Gordon and P. Marshall, eds, *The Place of the Dead: Death and Remembrance in Late Medieval and Early Modern Europe* (Cambridge, 2000).

25   D.U.L. DPRI/1/1636/C5/1.

26   D.U.L. DPRI/1/1636/M4/1.

27   D.U.L. DPRI/1/1636/M6/1; DPRI/1/1637/L4/1; DPRI/1/1637/W1/1. Jane Foster is identified as Ann's "keeper" in DDR/EJ/CCD/2, Folder 20.i.1637–6.v.1637, fos 23v–24.

28   DPRI/1/1636/C5/1–4. For Thomas' anxiety about Margaret's future, see p. 90 above.

29   D.U.L. DPRI/1/1636/H9/1.

30   N.C.S. EP 13/1–2, (St Andrew's), p. 9. Two women named Robson had been buried earlier in August, but neither was stated to be his wife. There were several Robson families in the parish. George himself was buried on 7 October (p. 13).

31   D.U.L. DPRI/1/1636/R10/1–2.

32   For these and other similar examples, see D.U.L. DDR/EJ/CCD/1/12, fos 4v, 9v, 47, 88, 89, 102v, 103, 139, 145, 177, 187, 197, 206, 228, 252v, 276v, 301; DDR/EJ/CCD/2, Folder, depositions *c*.22.vii.1637, fo. 108; DPRI/1/1635/C2/2, 5; DPRI/1/1636/C1/1; DPRI/1/1636/M9/1–2; DPRI/1/1636/H9/1–2; DPRI/1/1637/H10/1; DPRI/1/1637/W8/1–2; DPRI/1/1636/C10/1.

33   Though the wards remained units of defensive obligation and of taxation, they did not have a significant role in the political structure of the city. Aldermen did not represent wards. They were elected by the "Twenty-Four", who were chosen either by the guilds or by co-option. The Common Council consisted of the aldermen and the Twenty-Four, and the guild of all free burgesses. See Howell, *Newcastle-upon-Tyne and the Puritan Revolution*, pp. 35–9. The exceptional place of Pandon and Sandgate in people's sense of the city may derive from their topographical separateness and distinctive social characteristics. For a valuable discussion of the larger role of the sense of place in the physical, institutional, and social fabric of English "city commonwealths" in this period, see Withington, *Politics of Commonwealth*, ch. 4.

34   D.U.L. DPRI/1/1637/F9/1–2; DPRI/1/1637/W8/1–2.

35   The places of residence of those for whom he wrote wills usually emerge from the inventories of the testators, burial registers, or deposition evidence.

36   D.U.L. DPRI/1/1636/H7/1–2.

37   A point made in Calvi, *Histories of a Plague Year*, p. 108.

38   D.U.L. DPRI/1/1636/C1/1; DPRI/1/1637/H10/1–2; DPRI/1/1636/H3/1–2; DPRI/1/1636/M6/1.

39   D.U.L. DPRI/1/1637/C8/1–2.

40   Brooks, *Law, Politics, and Society*, p. 308.

CHAPTER 9   THE ATTENTIVE PRESENCE OF OTHERS

1   Jenison, *Newcastle's Call*, pp. 28, 35.

2   The phrase is Giulia Calvi's: *Histories of a Plague Year*, p. 143.

3   D.U.L. DDR/EJ/CCD/2, Folder 20.i.1637–6.v.1637, fos 16, 23v.

4   D.U.L. DPRI/1/1636/D3/1; DPRI/1/1636/H5.1–2; DDR/EJ/CCD/2, Folder 20.i.1637–6.v.1637, fo. 16; DPRI/1/1637/M2/1.

5   D.U.L. DPRI/1/1636/C6/1; DPRI/1/1636/W11/1–3.

6   D.U.L. DDR/EJ/CCD/2, Folder 20.i.1637–6.v.1637, fos 9, 17–17v. Cf. for similar examples, fos 4, 6, 11v, 23v, 33. Calvi observes that, in the records of Florence in 1630–1, "the continuous presence of neighbours always emerges in the testimonies,

as a sort of pause or comment in the story": *Histories of a Plague Year*, p. 142. It was the same in Newcastle.

7 M. Healy, " 'Seeing' Contagious Bodies", pp. 164–5; Jenison, *Newcastle's Call*, p. 237.

8 D.U.L. DDR/EJ/CCD/2, Folder 20.i.1637–6.v.1637, fos 2v, 3, 6, 9, 10, 11, 11v, 15v, 23, 23v, 24. There are many more examples.

9 For earlier examples, see D.U.L. DDR/EJ/CCD/1/11, fos 12, 13, 16v; DDR/EJ/CCD/1/12, fos 9, 64, 140.

10 D.U.L. DDR/EJ/CCD/2, Folder 1.ix.1633–26.iv.1634, fos 55–55v. For other similar examples from Newcastle and the region more generally, see DDR/EJ/CCD/1/11, fos 12, 13, 21; DDR/EJ/CCD/1/12, fos 40, 45v, 122v, 229v–230.

11 Hill, *Pathway to Prayer and Pietie*, pp. 140–5, 146–7. For the evidence that the curate of St Nicholas' attended dying people on at least two occasions, see Ch. 7, p. 61 above.

12 D.U.L. DDR/EJ/CCD/2, Folder 20.i.1637–6.v.1637, fos 4–4v, 9, 33–33v.

13 *Ibid.*, fos 6–6v, 10v–11v, 18v.

14 Robert Hill advised plague victims that "If it please [God] to recover you againe, you are like to be after far more healthful": *Pathway to Prayer and Pietie*, p. 146.

15 *Ibid.*, fos 5, 5v, 15v. That questions were later raised about their relationship is evident from the defensive statement of one witness that Isabel had indeed been suspected of "incontinency" in the past, "but she did purge herself thereof" – a reference to the church court procedure whereby people accused of sexual impropriety could "purge" themselves by producing people willing to swear to belief in their innocence.

16 D.U.L. DPRI/1/1637/H10/1; DDR/EJ/CCD/2, Folder 20.i.1637–6.v.1637, fo. 19.

17 D.U.L. DPRI/1/1637/L4/1, 3. John Hall similarly made the arrangements for Anthony Robson's stay in the lodges and "tooke great care of him": DDR/EJ/CCD/2, Folder 19.v.1637–17.vi.1637, fo. 96v.

18 D.U.L. DPRI/1/1636/E2/8; DPRI/1/1637/H8/3; DPRI/1/1636/H12/3; DPRI/1/1636/G7/2.

19 The term "to keep" was synonymous with "to nurse" or "to care for". Several years before the plague, for example, Isabella Forster, a young widow, "did attend upon and keep Elizabeth Elwood in her sicknes": D.U.L. DDR/EJ/CCD/2, Folder 1.ix.1633–26.iv.1634, fo. 55.

20 D.U.L. DPRI/1/1636/W9/1–2; DPRI/1/1637/M2/1.

21 There is one reference to a male keeper in the lodges on the town moor: William Gardiner, aged thirty-three, who seems to have been in the lodges already when he was hired to look after Anthony Robson. See n. 17 above.

22 D.U.L. DDR/EJ/CCD/2, Folder 20.i.1637–6.v.1637, fo. 33.

23 *Ibid.*, fos 3–3v, 4–4v, 7–7v, 23v, 37; Folder, depositions c.22.vii.1637, fo. 103v.

24 D.U.L. DPRI/1/1636/G7/2; DPRI/1/1637/L4/3. For wage rates in Durham and Newcastle, see D. Woodward, *Men at Work: Labourers and Building Craftsmen in the Towns of Northern England, 1450–1750* (Cambridge, 1995), pp. 261, 291. Male labourers were paid 8–10 pence a day in Newcastle in the 1630s. Women were paid sixpence a day in late seventeenth-century Durham. For payments to the poor for shifting ballast, see Ch. 4, p. 45 above.

25 D.U.L. DDR/EJ/CCD/2, Folder 20.i.1637–6.v.1637, fo. 37; DPRI/1/1636/C6/1–2.

26 Comparison of the dates of wills with known dates of burial shows that 63 per cent of testators were buried within five days of making their wills and 75 per cent within a week. Deposition statements in cases for which the original will does not survive indicate that almost all the testators concerned died within five days.

27 D.U.L. DDR/EJ/CCD/2, Folder 20.i.1637–6.v.1637, fo. 23; Folder, depositions c.22.vii.1637, fos 37, 103v–104; DPRI/1/1637/H10/1–2. Thomas' will is dated 8 July, though the witnesses all agreed that it had been declared on Thursday the 7th. Perhaps John Carr wrote it up neatly the following day. The extant will is a certified copy.

28 For this order and other attempts by urban authorities to restrict attendance at funerals in time of plague, see Slack, *Impact of Plague*, pp. 210, 234, 296–8.

29 The two women left gross estates of approximately 120 and 286 pounds respectively. That their funeral expenses were very similar despite the difference in inventoried wealth suggests the existence of a social norm: D.U.L. DPRI/1/1636/A6/3; DPRI/1/1637/M3/2. The administrator's accounts for John Curry, who also died before the plague, leaving a gross estate of approximately 130 pounds, show that his

funeral cost eleven pounds, ten shillings, an expenditure close to that of the two women: DPRI/1/1636/C13/1–2.

30 D.U.L. DDR/EJ/CCD/2, Folder 1.ix.1633–26.iv.1634, fo. 55v. For other local examples of the conception of a decent funeral as being "honestly brought forth", see Wrightson and Levine, "Death in Whickham", pp. 162–3.

31 D.U.L. DPRI/1/1636/W9/9; DPRI/1/1637/M2/3; DPRI/1/1636/G12/3; DPRI/1/1637/ F1/3; DPRI/1/1636/M6/2–4; DPRI/1/1636/R12/3; DPRI/1/1636/C6/2–10.

32 E.g. the expenses of William Robinson and his wife came to twenty-six shillings and eightpence in all. Those for James Dune, miller, were only fifteen shilling and fourpence: D.U.L. DPRI/1/1636/R9/2; DPRI/1/1637/D9/3.

33 D.U.L. DPRI/1/1635/G3/2; DPRI/1/1636/H5/2; DPRI/1/1635/M8/2; DPRI/1/1635/P2/1–3; DPRI/1/1635/R1/3; DPRI/1/1635/S15/1; DPRI/1/1635/S16/3–8; DPRI/1/1635/W5/1–3. Most of those concerned were of lower inventoried wealth than the cases in n.29 above. On guild funerals in both Newcastle and Durham in this period, see R. King, "The Sociability of the Trade Guilds of Newcastle and Durham, 1660–1750: The Urban Renaissance Revisited", in H. Berry and J. Gregory, eds, *Creating and Consuming Culture in North-East England, 1660–1830* (Aldershot and Burlington, VT, 2004), pp. 59–60, 62, 65–6.

34 See Hill, *Pathway to Prayer and Pietie*, p. 147; Jenison, *Newcastle's Call*, p. 35.

35 D.U.L. DPRI/1/1637/H10/3–4. The inventory of their son and heir Thomas Hayton the younger specifies two pounds, ten shillings spent on "the funeral expenses of the deceased and cleansing the house": DPRI/1/1637/H10/6. This kind of conflation of funeral and other expenses was common.

36 D.U.L. DPRI/1/1637/L4/3.

37 D.U.L. DPRI/1/1636/H2/2–4.

38 D.U.L. DPRI/1/1636/G7/2.

39 D.U.L. DPRI/1/1637/H4/2. Hall was a baker and brewer whose gross inventoried estate came to well over four hundred pounds. His house, however, was not a vast establishment, and it is unlikely that cleansing it cost more than a few pounds.

40 For the social and psychological importance of funerals and resistance to attempts by the authorities of London to curtail them during epidemics, see Slack, *Impact of Plague*, pp. 297–8.

41 N.C.S. EP/86 (St Nicholas'), pp. 313, 314; EP 13/1 (St Andrew's), pp. 13, 14.

42 *Ibid.*, pp. 3, 5, 6, 9, 11.

43 The examples quoted are from N.C.S. EP 73 (St John's), pp. 103, 105 and EP 13/1 (St Andrew's), p. 5. In St John's, 8.3 per cent of registered burials were of servants. In the poorer district of St Andrew's, they were less common, comprising only 2.3 per cent of burials.

44 N.C.S. EP 73 (St John's), *passim*, quoting pp. 101, 103, 104, 105.

45 N.C.S. EP 13/1 (St Andrew's), pp. 6, 9, 10, 12, 13. Penne and Crinstone were the only servants accorded their own names rather than those of their masters or mistresses.

46 *Ibid.*, pp. 5, 7, 8, 9, 10; EP 73 (St John's), pp. 106, 107, 109, 112. For an illuminating discussion of "imperfectly known" people in the records of the period more generally, see D.A. Postles, *Social Proprieties: Social Relations in Early Modern England (1500–1680)* (Washington, DC, 2006), ch. 2.

47 See Ch 3, n. 19 above.

48 For the anonymity of most of the later plague victims buried in St Andrew's in 1637–8, see Ch. 3, n. 24 above.

49 Camus, *The Plague*, p. 179.

50 The phrase quoted is Camus': *ibid.*, p. 181

51 D.U.L. DPRI/1/1637/H1/1–2.

52 D.U.L. DDR/EJ/CCD/2, Folder 20.i.1637–6.v.1637, fo. 26v; Folder, depositions c.22.vii.1637, fos 104, 108.

53 *Ibid.*, Folder 20.i.1637–6.v.1637, fos 2v, 3, 18v, 26.

54 *Ibid.*, fos 4, 9, 26, 36v.

55 *Ibid.*, fo. 37. Cf. fos 2v, 3, 4, 6v, 7, 23, 33, 37.

56 *Ibid.*, fo. 18v.

57 *Ibid.*, Folder 19.v.1637–17.vi.1637, fos 95v, 96; DPRI/1/1636/S12/1–2; N.C.S. EP/86 (St Nicholas'), p. 315.

58 Bourne, *History*, p. 54.
59 D.U.L. DDR/EJ/CCD/2, Folder 20.i.1637–6.v.1637, fos 10, 11v, 23v; DPRI/1/1637/M6/3; DPRI/1/1636/M9/1–2.
60 D.U.L. DDR/EJ/CCD/2, Folder 20.i.1637–6.v.1637, fos 10, 13; Folder 19.v.1637–17.vi.1637, fo. 85.
61 While English scriveners and notaries did not keep elaborate notarial registers, it was not unusual to keep a ledger noting legal instruments that had been prepared. They were able, when required, to give evidence regarding transactions completed years earlier. See Brooks, Helmholz, and Stein, *Notaries Public in England*, pp. 62–3, 65–6.

CHAPTER 10 HOUSHOLD STUFFE

1 D.U.L. DPRI/1/1636/E2/8. Cf. DPRI/1/1636/R11/3.
2 For recommendations on this issue, and the fear that such goods might remain a source of infection, see Slack, *Impact of Plague*, pp. 11, 19, 27, 35, 202, 210. Cf. Cipolla, *Cristofano and the Plague*, pp. 90–1. Cipolla takes the view that while some goods were destroyed, most were simply disinfected and then reused.
3 D.U.L. DPRI/1/1637/R12/1–2.
4 Welford, ed., *History of Newcastle and Gateshead*, vol. III, p. 339. For the functions of Trinity House, see Ch. 12, p. 151 below.
5 D.U.L. DPRI/1/1637/L4/3.
6 D.U.L. DPRI/1/1636/C5/2–4; DPRI/1/1636/G8/2.
7 D.U.L. DPRI/1/1636/G7/2; DPRI/1/1636/G12/3; DPRI/1/1636/H6/3; DPRI/1/1636/G8/2; DPRI/1/1637/W1/3; DPRI/1/1637/H10/3–4; DPRI/1/1636/F1/3.
8 D.U.L. DPRI/1/1637/H1/1. Cf. DPRI/1/1636/H12/3; DPRI/1/1636/G8/2. For the Haddocks and the Ellisons, see Ch. 3, pp. 41–2 above.
9 The phrase is Colin Jones': "Plague and its Metaphors", p. 111.
10 Swinburne, *Briefe Treatise of Testaments*, pp. 252–252v, 254v–256. Swinburne also discussed (pp. 253–254v) what items of a wife's personal *paraphernalia* might be omitted from her deceased husband's inventory, noting that in the northern province it was customary to reserve to a widow "not onely their apparrell, and a convenient bed, but a coffer, with divers things therein necessarie for their owne persons, which things usually have been omitted out of the Inventary, of their deceased husbands goods. Unlesse peradventure the husband were so farre indebted, as the rest of his goods would not suffice to discharge the same." For Swinburne's career and significance as an ecclesiastical lawyer, see S. Doyle, "Swinburne, Henry (c.1551–1624)", in *Oxford D.N.B.*
11 Swinburne, *Briefe Treatise of Testaments*, pp. 256–256v. One of the appraisers of the inventory of Ralph Smith of South Shields described how his goods "were by them indifferently apprised and according to their true worth as for his part he thinketh no man would have given any more for the same": D.U.L. DDR/EJ/CCD/1/12, 1626–31, fos 103v–104v.
12 Swinburne, *Briefe Treatise of Testaments*, p. 255. However, probate bonds issued on the grant of administration specified a date for the final presentation of the inventory and administrator's accounts.
13 D.U.L. DPRI/1/1636/A6/1–3; DPRI/1/1637/B11/1–5.
14 Based on the thirteen sets of Newcastle wills and inventories in DPRI/1/1635. Of the eleven inventories that can be matched with wills in the coalmining parish of Whickham, just upriver from Newcastle, in the years 1615–42, seven were made within a month of the testator's will; four of them within fourteen days: D.U.L. DPRI/1/1615–1642, *passim*.
15 D.U.L. DPRI/1/1637/H10/6 (Thomas Hayton jnr); DPRI/1/1637/M2/1–3 (Robert Mallabar).
16 D.U.L. DPRI/1/1637/W1/3.
17 D.U.L. DDR/EJ/CCD/2, Folder 20.i.1637–6.v.1637, fo. 3; DPRI/1/1637/H8/1–3.
18 D.U.L. DPRI/1/1636/C5/2–4.
19 Swinburne, *Briefe Treatise of Testaments*, p. 257.
20 There are in fact eighteen surviving inventories for the years 1636 and 1637 which were either definitely written by Ralph Tailor or can be confidently ascribed to him.

Two were made before the plague. Eleven were of plague victims. Five were of people who died in 1637 after the end of the plague.

21 Prior to the plague, he had written the inventory of Elizabeth Franklin on 8 April, and that of Margaret Ayre on 11 April 1636: D.U.L. DPRI/1/1636/A6/2–3; DPRI/1/1637/F9/3.

22 Swinburne, *Briefe Treatise of Testaments*, p. 256v.

23 What follows is based upon D.U.L. DPRI/1/1637/H17/3–4.

24 The "boll" used to measure grain in south Northumberland and County Durham at the time was equivalent to two Winchester bushels. A Winchester bushel comprised eight dry gallons. See G.V. Harrison, "Appendix 1. Agricultural Weights and Measures", in J. Thirsk, ed., *The Agrarian History of England and Wales. Vol V. 1640–1750. Part II. Agrarian Change* (Cambridge, 1985), pp. 820–1. Holmes was dealing commercially in grain. Two of the debts owing to him were from Elizabeth Robinson for "A boule of wheate meale" and "A boule of Rye meale".

25 The "chalder" or "chaldron" was the standard measure of coal.

26 For the transition from Roman to Arabic numerals in this period, the difficulties of calculating using Roman numerals, and the frequency with which arithmetical errors are encountered in contemporary inventories and accounts, see K. Thomas, "Numeracy in Early Modern England", *Transactions of the Royal Historical Society*, 5th series, 37 (1987), pp. 103, 106–7, 117–18, 120. With the exception of a small error in one of his subtotals, Ralph Tailor's calculations were accurate in both notations. He was clearly comfortable with both systems and (by the standards of the day) a fairly competent arithmetician.

27 D.U.L. DPRI/1/1636/M9/3–4. A third of inventories listed livestock, usually a cow (or two), or a horse or mare. There were still considerable open spaces within the city to accommodate animals and the freemen enjoyed common rights on the town moor.

28 D.U.L. DPRI/1/1637/H10/6. A "tempse" was a flour sieve. Hayton was a baker and brewer. Trenchers were wooden platters.

29 D.U.L. DPRI/1/1637/H8/2–3; DPRI/1/1637/M2/2–3.

30 Later, in his post-plague inventories, Ralph Tailor was to adopt a somewhat more elaborate style of presentation, with larger, bolder headings, using a thicker nib, and more generous spacing. Perhaps these handsome documents commanded a larger fee. See e.g. D.U.L. DPRI/1/1637/B7/1–3 (George Bindlosse, 6 September 1637); DPRI/1/1637/B11/2–5 (Richard Brown, 13 October 1637).

31 Based upon all surviving inventories for people dying in 1636 which provide sufficient detail of rooms, etc. For specific examples cited, see: D.U.L. DPRI/1/1636/W12/2–7 (Wynn); DPRI/1/1636/S19/2 (Symons); DPRI/1/1636/W1/2–4 (Waddell); DPRI/1/1636/C9/2 (Cooke). For the inventories as a whole, the figures for heated rooms (rooms containing fire irons) are: one room 42 per cent; two rooms 29 per cent; three or more rooms 29 per cent. The Hearth Tax returns for 1665 indicate that, in Newcastle as a whole, 62 per cent of households reported only one hearth, 14 per cent two hearths, and 24 per cent more than two. This suggests that (as might be expected) the inventoried population was drawn disproportionately from the middling and upper parts of the social scale. Hearth Tax figures from Howell, *Newcastle-upon-Tyne and the Puritan Revolution*, Appendix, Table III, p. 352.

32 D.U.L. DPRI/1/1637/D9/1–3. Dune would hardly have needed to make a will but for the fact that he owned a house in Carlisle, which he left to his sister's family there.

33 K. Thomas, *The Ends of Life: Roads to Fulfilment in Early Modern England* (Oxford, 2009), p. 126.

34 The inventories of rural households commonly reveal somewhat simpler, barer domestic interiors, much of the value of the inventories lying in farm goods and stock rather than in furnishings. For a detailed discussion of household goods in the nearby parish of Whickham, see Levine and Wrightson, *Making of an Industrial Society*, pp. 87–92, 101–4, 231–9. For urban–rural differences in a slightly later period, including a discussion of the north-east, see L. Weatherill, *Consumer Behaviour and Material Culture in Britain, 1660–1760* (London and New York, 1988), pp. 51–2, 75–90.

35 This and the subsequent discussions of domestic goods are based on analysis of all surviving inventories of inhabitants of Newcastle who made their wills in 1636.

36 D.U.L. DPRI/1/1636/E2/5; DPRI/1/1636/R3/2–3. Such items of plate were among the few goods of sufficient significance to be passed on as heirlooms in wills. Richard

Browne, for example, left one of his daughters "three Apostle spoones and one silver beaker", and another three apostle spoons and a silver beer bowl. Ralph Rowmaine left items of plate to each of his six children, one of whom was to receive "one cupp made of a nutt tipt with silver and with a silver stalke". Ralph Tailor wrote both wills. D.U.L. DPRI/1/1637/B11/1; DPRI/1/1636/R12/1–2.

37 D.U.L. DPRI/1/1636/H6/3–4; DPRI/1/W1/2–4.
38 These items were almost invariably owned by people whose household goods were of more than twenty pounds in value (62 per cent of the inventoried population). Among Ralph's clients, see e.g. D.U.L. DPRI/1/1636/R12/3–6 (Ralph Rowmaine); DPRI/1/1636/S19/2 (Ann Symons); DPRI/1/1636/E2/5 (Thomas Eden); DPRI/1/1637/E1/2–3 (Ralph Emerson). It is interesting to speculate on the significance of the fact that three-quarters of the people inventoried did not own a mirror. The members of these households presumably saw their own faces rarely, if ever. What might that imply for their sense of selfhood?
39 D.U.L. DPRI/1/1636/M9/3; DPRI/1/1637/E1/2–3.
40 D.U.L. DPRI/1/1636/R12/3–6. Thomas Wynn, merchant, also owned a "house clock" worth thirty shillings: DPRI/1/1636/W12/2–7. For hourglasses, see e.g. DPRI/1/1636/A6/2–3; DPRI/1/1636/M6/2–4. William Hall had "a fower hower glass" in his hall: DPRI/1/1637/H4/2. One of the victims of the plague was James Wilson, "clock-maker", of Denton Chare in St John's parish. He himself owned a clock, and there was another completed clock and "21 dyells" in his workshop. He does not, however, seem to have had more than a handful of customers among the craftsmen and tradesmen of the city: DPRI/1/1637/W9/1–2. Most people probably relied on public clocks or the tolling of bells to mark the hours.
41 D.U.L. DPRI/1/1637/B11/2–5 (Richard Browne); DPRI/1/1636/W12/2–7 (Thomas Wynn); DPRI/1/1636/E2/5 (Thomas Eden); DPRI/1/1637/F9/3 (Elizabeth Franklin); DPRI/1/1636/R3/2–3 (John Reed). The other owner of china was the widow Margaret Hutcheson, who had "eight small Cheeney dishes" as well as "seaven little painted dublers of earth" (a rare reference to decorated earthenware): DPRI/1/1637/H20/3.
42 Examples quoted are from D.U.L. DPRI/1/1637/F9/3 (Elizabeth Franklin); DPRI/1/1637/H17/3 (Thomas Holmes); DPRI/1/1636/W9/9 (Cuthbert Woodman); DPRI/1/1636/R12/3–6 (Ralph Rowmaine); DPRI/1/1636/C6/2–10 (John Collingwood); DPRI/1/1636/W2/2–3 (Mabel Walker); DPRI/1/1636/C5/2–4 (Thomas Clark); DPRI/1/1636/W1/2–4 (Matthew Waddell); DPRI/1/1636/R3/2–3 (John Reed).
43 Quoting examples from D.U.L. DPRI/1/1637/H17/3 (Thomas Holmes); DPRI/1/1636/R3/2–3 (John Reed); DPRI/1/1636/H6/3–4 (Robert Harrison); DPRI/1/1636/M9/3 (Robert Moore); DPRI/1/1636/A6/2–3 (Margaret Ayre).
44 D.U.L. DPRI/1/1636/E2/3–4, 5, 7.
45 Wynn's "Malt Loft" contained grain measures and a substantial quantity of hops, malt, and rye, as well as "one hundreth and a half of Codfish" (presumably dried), and "Thirty salmond potts" (he owned a lease of "a fishing", or fishery). His "Seller" contained liquid measures of various capacities ("pottle", "quart", "pint", "gill", and "half gill"), "foure funnels" and "Three Tuns of wine, Three hogsheads of sack, one pipe of white wine, one half hogshead of wine and twenty gallons of Read wine". The wine alone was worth over seventy-six pounds. D.U.L. DPRI/1/1636/W12/2–7.
46 D.U.L. DPRI/1/1636/C6/2–10. Collingwood, who lived in St Nicholas' parish, was clearly operating on a substantial scale, and presumably employing several journeymen – perhaps the "servants" whose funeral expenses were noted in the inventory. For a cordwainer conducting his business on a smaller scale, see the will and inventory of William Cooke of St John's parish: DPRI/1/1636/C10/1–10.
47 D.U.L. DPRI/1/1636/C9/2 (Cooke); DPRI/1/1636/S17/1–2 (Susan). The term "bumpkin" was originally derived from the Dutch *boomken*, meaning a little tree. John Susan, who dealt in grain as well as timber, and owned a keel and another boat, was probably one of a community of merchants of foreign origin established in Newcastle. He apparently lived in lodgings "at John Pythies dwelling by the Key Side", and was close to another merchant of unusual name, Gerhart Cock, whose family he remembered in his will. For Cock's (post-plague) will, see DPRI/1/1637/C5/1.
48 D.U.L. DPRI/1/1636/H6/3–4 (Robert Harrison); DPRI/1/1636/W1/2–4 (Matthew Waddell); DPRI/1/1637/B11/2–5 (Richard Browne); DPRI/1/1637/H17/3 (Thomas Holmes); DPRI/1/1636/M9/3–4 (Robert Moore); DPRI/1/1637/F9/3 (Elizabeth

Franklin); DPRI/1/1636/R3/2–3 (John Reed); DPRI/1/1637/M2/2–3 (Robert Mallabar); DPRI/1/1636/S19/2–3 (Ann Symons); DPRI/1/1636/E2/5 (Thomas Eden). Some money probably remained in houses still inhabited. The inventory of George Wilkinson, merchant and draper, mentions twenty-five pounds' "money found in his cupboard": DPRI/1/1637/W8/3.

49 John Collingwood's elaborate household furnishings were valued at over ninety-four pounds; Robert Harrison's were worth just over ten pounds, and William Dixon's only one pound. See D.U.L. DPRI/1/1636/C6/2–10; DPRI/1/1636/H6/3–4; DPRI/1/1637/D6/3–4.

50 Muldrew, *Economy of Obligation*, p. 116.

51 D.U.L. DDR/EJ/CCD/1/12 (1626–31), fos 120–1. Another defamation case arose from Thomas Simpson's alleged failure to pay a debt owed to Elinor Clarkson's former husband Thomas. Simpson claimed to have paid it to Thomas before his death, and Elinor's new husband, who did not believe him, sued him in the mayor's court: DDR/EJ/CCD/1/11 (1618–26), fos 101–101v. For the "culture of credit" in early modern England and the significance of small debt litigation, see Muldrew, *Economy of Obligation*, esp. parts II and III.

52 For probate accounts, see P. Spufford, M. Brett, and A.L. Erickson, eds, *Probate Accounts of England and Wales*, 2 vols, British Record Society (London, 1999); A. Erickson, "Using Probate Accounts", in T. Arkell, N. Evans, and N. Goose, eds, *When Death Do Us Part: Understanding and Interpreting the Probate Records of Early Modern England*, Local Population Studies Supplement (Oxford, 2000), ch. 5; Muldrew, *Economy of Obligation*, pp. 103–7, 117–18.

53 D.U.L. DPRI/1/1636/C13/1–2. The document is undated, but clearly preceded the plague. Curry may have died intestate: no will survives and Margaret paid a fee for letters of administration empowering her to settle her dead husband's estate.

54 D.U.L. DPRI/1/1636/C6/1–10; DPRI/1/1636/R11/2–5. Cf. the keelman Thomas Dods of Sandgate. His goods were few and simple. He was owed close to six pounds by six people, but himself owed over twelve pounds to another seven: DPRI/1/1636/D3/2–3.

55 D.U.L. DPRI/1/1636/S14/1–2. An earlier example of such forbearance was provided by Ralph Tailor's client the house carpenter Robert Moore. When the miller John Huntridge died in 1613 he owed Moore three pounds. Huntridge's widow, Elizabeth, was able to pay three-quarters of the sum owed. Seven years later she too was dead and Moore had still not received the rest, but he commented complacently that "he expecteth to have itt" from her second husband, Thomas Mills. DDR/EJ/CCD/1/11 (1618–26), fos 80–1.

56 D.U.L. DPRI/1/1636/H12/2 (Margery Holborn); DPRI/1/1636/C1/2–4 (John Carr); DPRI/1/1637/H4/2 (William Hall).

57 For the general problem of "desperate debts" and the potential "domino effect of failed obligations", see Muldrew, *Economy of Obligation*, pp. 175–80. The circumstances of the plague may well have exacerbated this problem.

58 D.U.L. DPRI/1/1636/H12/3 (Margery Holborn); DPRI/1/1636/E2/8 (Thomas Eden); DPRI/1/1637/H1/1–2 (Ambrose Haddock). Cf. the case of the cooper Richard Rutlidge, whose administrator had to pay for two funerals, the cleansing of the house, and the "tabling" [i.e. board] of Rutlidge's daughter Mary and one of his surviving apprentices after his death: DPRI/1/1637/R12/1–2.

59 D.U.L. DPRI/1/1636/R12/1–6. In addition to this he owned a house in the Maltmarket and a farm at Ovingham, Northumberland.

60 D.U.L. DPRI/1/1636/M4/2.

61 D.U.L. DPRI/1/1636/G7/1–2. In fact, over 90 per cent of her gross inventoried estate of fifty-four pounds remained available. "Dockter Genisonn" was almost certainly Robert Jenison DD.

62 D.U.L. DPRI/1/1636/C5/1–4. This was so even though his funeral costs were not accounted for.

63 D.U.L. DPRI/1/1636/R9/2.

64 D.U.L. DPRI/1/1637/D6/1–6. Dixon's will indicates that he owned a house in Newcastle, which may have been sold to meet some of his obligations and provide for his wife and four children.

65 D.U.L. DPRI/1/1637/H10/1–7.

66 D.U.L. DPRI/1/1636/W1/1–4 (Matthew Waddell); DPRI/1/1636/H6/1–4 (Robert and Elizabeth Harrison); DPRI/1/1636/G8/1–2 (William Grame); DPRI/1/1636/M9/1–2 (Robert Moore). Moore's heirs were at least fortunate in that he also owned several houses.

67 D.U.L. DPRI/1/1637/H17/1–5. For the subsequent litigation, see DDR/EJ/CCD/2, Folder 20.i.1637–6.v.1637, fos 10–10v, 15v–16.

CHAPTER 11 DISCORDS, VARIANCES, AND SUITES

1   D.U.L. DPRI/4/14, Probate Act Book, 1635–8.

2   For the sessions for which depositions survive, see Ch. 5, n. 15 above. Two further wills were filed along with interrogatories, indicating that witnesses must have been examined (though no depositions survive), and a third was filed with a deposition from a witness.

3   These are of course minimum figures. However, the Probate Act Book (D.U.L. DPRI/4/14) casts some light on what may be missing. Of the twenty-two disputed estates, twenty-one first appeared in the act book between October 1636 and July 1637 (all save one being commenced before April 1637). In addition, entries relating to a further eight people whose estates entered probate in these months (one of them a known plague victim) suggest that otherwise undocumented disputes took place. This indicates that we lack deposition or other evidence for just over a quarter of the testamentary causes that were initiated in these months. It remains possible that additional disputes may have emerged much later (especially in cases involving the right of minors) or been heard in other jurisdictions, but it was not considered feasible to pursue such possibilities for this study.

4   D.U.L. DDR/EJ/CCD/1/11, (1618–26), fos 11–102, *passim*; DDR/EJ/CCD/1/12 (1626–31), fos 28–260, *passim*. The Probate Act Book helps to put this into larger perspective. Overall, 243 people's estates entered probate in October 1636 to July 1637. Of these, twenty-nine cases seem to have occasioned litigation: only 12 per cent. Despite the greatly elevated level of litigation occasioned by the exceptional circumstances of 1636–7, the vast majority of probate applications apparently remained uncontroversial: D.U.L. DPRI/4/14.

5   Swinburne, *Briefe Treatise of Testaments*, pp. 264–6, quoting p. 265. For a helpful recent account of probate procedures, see T. Arkell, "The Probate Process", in Arkell, Evans, and Goose, eds, *When Death Do Us Part*, and for the importance of probate business to the ecclesiastical courts, see R.B. Outhwaite, *The Rise and Fall of the English Ecclesiastical Courts, 1500–1800* (Cambridge, 2006), ch. 4.

6   The precise figures for the executors' relationship to the deceased in these causes are as follows: widow, 4; son or daughter, 2; brother or sister, 3; brother-in-law, 2; aunt, 1; definitely unrelated, 3; unknown, 4.

7   The precise figures are: sons or daughters, 4; brothers or sisters, 3; "cozen", 1; non-kin, 2; unknown, 9. Some may even have been creditors of the deceased.

8   Swinburne, *Briefe Treatise of Testaments*, pp. 12, 2–2v, 6.

9   *Ibid.*, pp. 8, 127, 251v. Though insisting on this legal distinction, Swinburne acknowledged (p. 3) that in England "we use the termes of *Testament* or *Last will*, indifferently, or one for another". To avoid the frequent repetition of cumbersome terminology, I will for the most part continue to refer to "last wills and testaments" simply as "wills".

10 *Ibid.*, pp. 21, 7. Swinburne added (p. 26) that writing was not necessary for devising land held by urban burgage tenure.

11 *Ibid.*, pp. 133, 131v, 320, 10. He also advised (p. 210v) that scribal errors in words and phrases could be overlooked so long as the sense could be determined, for "the will and intent of the testator is preferred before formal or prescript wordes", and he outlined (pp. 319v–320) how best to determine the "conjectured meaning of the testator".

12 *Ibid.*, pp. 21, 23. A "Solemn Testament" observed all the formal solemnities of civil law, but, as Swinburne wrote, "of this kinds of Testaments we have no use in England" (p. 19).

13 *Ibid.*, pp. 212v, 27v–28.

14 *Ibid.*, pp. 25–25v.

15 *Ibid.*, p. 28. He explained that "This kinde of Testament is commonly made, when the Testator is now very sicke, weake, and past all hope of recovery. For (as one reporteth) it is received for an opinion among the ruder and more ignorant people, that if a man should chance to be so wise, as to make his will in his good health, when hee is strong and of good memory; having time and leisure, and might aske counsel (if any doubt were) of the learned; that then surely he should not live long after. And therefore they deferre it until such time, when it were more convenient to applie themselves to the disposing of their soules, then of their lands and goods. And in consideration hereof it is, that Testaments are so much favoured to be made in such perilous times; namely for that the Testator cannot conveniently stay to ask counsel of such points as be doubtfull in law."

16 *Ibid.*, pp. 212v–213.

17 *Ibid.*, pp. 63v–65v.

18 D.U.L. DDR/EJ/CCD/2, Folder 20.i.1637–6.v.1637, fos 16–18; DPRI/1/1636/W2/1–3. The will had been written up from notes some time after Mabel's death and the name of the executor inserted at that time at the direction of the witnesses. The key interrogatory was whether the witnesses "did heare the said testator give all the residue of her goods to the said Barbarie and make her sole executrix of her will" or not. They could answer "yes" to only the first part of the question. But the court accepted the implication of Barbara's appointment and the will stood. A further copy of the will survives in N.C.S. EP 86/362 (St Nicholas') with a note of its probate acceptance.

19 D.U.L. DDR/EJ/CCD/2, Folder 20.i.1637–6.v.1637, fo. 4; DPRI/1/1636/C10/1, 4, 6, 8, 9. This ill-worded will contained further ambiguities concerning the bequest of a second house and the guardianship of unnamed children, and the testimony focused on the will-making and the accuracy with which the words spoken by Cooke and relayed by Barbara Hall to the scribe had been recorded. Since Margaret Cooke brought the challenge, however, it seems likely that the dispute related to the provision made for her future.

20 D.U.L. DDR/EJ/CCD/2, Folder 20.i.1637–6.v.1637, fos 2–3v; DPRI/1/1636/R11/1–5. The will was written up long after William's death. The interrogatories suggest that other kin also claimed that a more elaborate distribution of his goods had been made, though given his indebtedness it seems unlikely that there was much to squabble over. On the problems occasioned by conditional legacies, see Swinburne, *Briefe Treatise of Testaments*, p. 136ff.

21 *Ibid.*, p. 282v.

22 D.U.L. DPRI/1/1637/H1/1–2. She was clearly aware of the maxim "one witness is as none": Swinburne, *Briefe Treatise of Testaments*, p. 206v.

23 D.U.L. DDR/EJ/CCD/2, Folder 20.i.1637–6.v.1637, fos 18–19v, 23v, 26; Folder 19.v.1637–17.vi.1637, fos 96v–97. In these cases the evidence given relates to the procedures followed, rather than to any specific allegation. No will actually survives for Young, Robson, or Wiggham. The single deposition filed with the will of John Susan and the interrogatories filed with that of Robert Wright similarly focus on whether the will was properly made: DPRI/1/1636/S17/1–8; DPRI/1/1637/W11/1–7.

24 D.U.L. DDR/EJ/CCD/2, Folder 20.i.1637–6.v.1637, fos 10v, 13, 20. See Ch. 6, pp. 73–4 above. The procedures to be followed to establish "if it be *certaine and undoubted* that the testament is written with the testators own hand", including "the proofe made by comparing of hands", are described in Swinburne, *Briefe Treatise of Testaments*, p. 211.

25 Swinburne, *Briefe Treatise of Testaments*, p. 321; D.U.L. DDR/EJ/CCD/2, Folder 20.i.1637–6.v.1637, fos 10–10v, 15v–16; DPRI/1/1637/H17/5. The will was approved. William Robson's aggrieved kin seem also to have alleged that his will was incomplete: see n. 20 above.

26 D.U.L. DDR/EJ/CCD/2, Folder 20.i.1637–6.v.1637, fos 5–5v, 6–7, 15v. The will Moody was said to have made is not extant. For Walker's will, see DPRI/1/1637/W1/1.

27 D.U.L. DDR/EJ/CCD/2, Folder 20.i.1637–6.v.1637, fos 10v–11, 12; DPRI/1/1637/M6/1–4.

28 Swinburne, *Briefe Treatise of Testaments*, pp. 9–10, 326ff. This was the case when the provisions of a second will contradicted those of the first. If they did not do so, the second will simply functioned as a codicil.

29 D.U.L. DDR/EJ/CCD/2, Folder 20.i.1637–6.v.1637, fos 33–34v; Folder 19.v.1637–17. vi.1637, fos 95v–96; DPRI/1/1636/S12/1–2 (John Stobbs); DPRI/1/1636/S17/1–3 (John Stobbs jnr); DPRI/4/14, fo. 271v. This case remains puzzling. John Stobbs' first will survives in the probate records and presumably prevailed. No copy of the second will survives. Yet three witnesses testified to the making of the second will, which Stobbs requested to be committed to writing "immediatlie" and which was apparently written down by George Robson (the musician) and witnessed by three others, two of whom survived to give evidence in 1637. Meanwhile, according to Margaret Hyndmers' testimony, George Lambe had approached her through an intermediary to tell her that if she deposed that she had seen another will naming Lambe and John Stobbs junior as joint executors "he would pay her as Royally as ever she was paid in her life". She refused. One wonders whether Lambe was so persistent because he had become a business partner of his former master. Exactly what transpired, and on what grounds Lambe apparently won, remains a mystery. The surviving depositions were spread over several months and others relating to the case may be missing. Perhaps the court was not convinced that John Stobbs was of sound mind at the making of the second will.

30 D.U.L. DPRI/1/1636/W9/1–8.

31 Swinburne states that if a testator is forbidden or prevented from altering an earlier testament, then the earlier testament is voided: *Briefe Treatise of Testaments*, pp. 337v–338. In this instance, however, the second will was written on the word of only one witness. This would not usually be sufficient to secure its acceptance by the court, though Swinburne did allow (pp. 206–206v) that in exceptional circumstances this might be possible.

32 This was alleged in one of the entries in the Probate Act Book: D.U.L. DPRI/4/14, fo. 203v.

33 Swinburne, *Brief Treatise of Testaments*, pp. 40, 63v–64v. In Swinburne's opinion (p. 41v), the presumption of reason was such that evidence of witnesses deposing that a person was of sound mind should outweigh the evidence of those claiming the contrary. Specific proofs of insanity were required.

34 D.U.L. DPRI/1/1637/H10/5; DPRI/1/1636/M9/5.

35 In the Mills case it was stated in response to the interrogatories that "Raph Taylor writt the shedale or will articulate this day" (18 February) at the request of Margaret Humphrey. As noted above, no depositions survive in the Woodman case, but there was clearly a dispute and the notarized copy of Cuthbert's first will has the note "iurat" (sworn) beside Ralph Tailor's name and those of several of the others who had witnessed it. D.U.L. DDR/EJ/CCD/2, Folder 20.i.1637–6.v.1637, fos 11–12; DPRI/1/1636/W9/1–2.

36 What follows is influenced by the arguments of J.T. Rosenthal, *Telling Tales: Sources and Narration in Late Medieval England* (University Park, PA, 2003), esp. his Introduction and ch. 1, and by Fentress and Wickham, *Social Memory*, pp. ix–x and ch. 1.

37 For an illuminating discussion of these and other aspects of deposing in the church courts, see L. Gowing, *Domestic Dangers: Women, Words, and Sex in Early Modern London* (Cambridge, 1996), ch. 7, esp. pp. 235–9.

38 L.C. Orlin, *Locating Privacy in Tudor London* (Oxford, 2007), p. 3

39 Rosenthal, *Telling Tales*, p. xxiv.

40 The precise figures are: not known, 16.3 per cent; known only by sight, 5.8 per cent; known one year or less, 9.3 per cent; known 2–4 years, 13.9 per cent; known 5–9 years, 15.1 per cent; known 10–14 years, 16.3 per cent; known over 15 years, 23.3 per cent. The latter included those known "since infancy", which meant at least twenty years, since no witness was under twenty years old.

41 Rosenthal, *Telling Tales*, p. 3.

42 *Ibid.*, p. xxiii.

43 The fact that 30 per cent of both the men and the women were under thirty is in telling contrast to the predominance of elderly people in depositions taken in this period in court cases relating to such issues as local customs. In such matters the old carried authority. In the recorded events of the plague, however, the most active participants seem to have been the relatively young.

44 Swinburne, *Briefe Treatise of Testaments*, pp. 206v–207v. For the frequent assumption that the testimony of the poor was suspect, see A. Shepard, "Poverty, Labour, and the Language of Social Description in Early Modern England", *Past and Present*, 201 (2008), esp. pp. 52–3, 57, 81–5, 92–5. For the related issue of how the poor were obliged to present themselves in order to be deemed credible and "deserving" when petitioning for relief, see S. Hindle, *On the Parish? The Micro-Politics of Poor Relief in Rural England c.1550–1750* (Oxford, 2004), pp. 157–64, 379–428.

45 D.U.L. DDR/EJ/CCD/2, Folder 20.i.1637–6.v.1637, fos 11–11v. For some earlier examples of the challenging of the credibility of poor witnesses, especially poor women, in the Durham courts, see DDR/EJ/CCD/1/12 (1626–31), fos 222v, 252v–253, 299v–301.

46 Swinburne was very firm on this point: "A woman is also a good witness in this case by the lawes Ecclesiasticall: And whatsoever divers do write, that a woman is not without all exception, because of the inconstancy and frailty of the feminine Sexe, whereby they may the sooner be corrupted: yet I take it that their testimony is so good, that a Testament may be proved by two women alone, being otherwise without exception." He added: "A poore man likewise, being an honest man, is not forbidden to be a witnesse." See *Briefe Treatise of Testaments*, pp. 207v–208.

47 Cf. Munkhoff, "Searchers of the Dead", *passim*, on the power vested in poor women appointed to view the dead, identify plague, and thereby initiate quarantine.

48 If the depositions illustrate, as they do, many of the points of law discussed by Henry Swinburne, they do so not only because they were partly shaped to address those issues, but also because these were precisely the types of problem that often arose in reality. Swinburne endeavoured not only to provide an original synthesis of legal authorities on testamentary law, but to do so in a manner that would help to adjudicate the kinds of dispute with which he was familiar from his long experience as an ecclesiastical judge in the Province of York.

CHAPTER 12 RALF TAYLOR NOTARIE PUBLICKE

1 For contemporary appreciation of this role of "stayers" as against "run-aways", see Monteyne, *Printed Image in Early Modern London*, p. 91.

2 These were the testators for whom he wrote wills, the witnesses of those wills, and the appraisers with whom he prepared inventories. Those people whose inventories he wrote but whom he is not recorded as having met (because he did not also write their wills) are not included. The figures for his recorded encounters are of course minimum figures, since people may have been present at the making of wills and inventories whose presence was not recorded, and he presumably met additional people on occasions for which no record survives. What follows is based upon an index of all those known to have been encountered by Ralph Tailor between March and December 1636 and the evidence provided by the probate records of the further connections of those individuals.

3 Ralph's fourteenth plague will, that of Ann Mills, was written up later, and he is not known to have actually met her.

4 Later examples of Michael Moore's signature show that he wrote a very laboured hand. He probably preferred others to do his writing for him. In the case of Mabel Walker, the notes he took were subsequently written up as a nuncupative will by William Preston.

5 Whether Elizabeth and Ann Tailor were relatives of Ralph Tailor cannot be established on the available evidence.

6 D.U.L. DPRI/1/1636/E2/1–9. The sale lists are items 3–4 and 7. No other sale record of this kind survives in the probate records relating to the plague. Five of the buyers were actually beneficiaries of Thomas Eden's will. One of them, Isabel Harrison, was a former servant of Eden who had witnessed his will and was left five pounds. She spent a total of twenty-four shillings on pots, pans, a chair, and a variety of soft furnishings.

7 All parish registers of the city were searched from 1630 onwards, using T.W.A. microfilms: MF 249 (All Saints' [Allhallows']); MF 263 (St Nicholas'); MF 528 (St John's); MF 279 (St Andrew's). There is also no evidence of the grant of a licence

to marry (information from Margaret McCollum of Durham University Library Department of Archives and Special Collections, 4 June 2008).

8 In St Nicholas' parish, for example, there were only six marriages between May and October 1636 (half of them in June before the plague erupted in that parish) but twenty-six between November 1636 and April 1637 despite the interruption occasioned by Lent. The comparable figures for St John's parish were fourteen between May and October 1636 (mostly in May and June) and an extraordinary fifty-six in the six months from November. St Andrew's witnessed a similar surge of marriages between November 1636 and February 1637.

9 At the front of the Allhallows' register book is a note of the years covered by the volume in a contemporary hand. The clerk noted under burials that "1636 is wanting", and under marriages that "ye Register for 1636 is wanting", meaning April 1636 to March 1637 under the old system of dating. Registration was resumed on 25 March 1637, but the events that had taken place during the preceding year were never entered up. The register of St John's contains a badly faded entry of the marriage on 26 November 1636 of a man named "Tayler" whose abbreviated forename began with "R". However, it seems to me most likely that it is "Rich." (Richard), and the bride's name was Elizabeth, whereas Ralph Tailor's bride was probably called Grace.

10 T.W.A. MF 250 (All Saint' [Allhallows']). I am assuming that Grace was Ralph's first wife, since neither this register not its predecessor (MF 249) contains any earlier reference to the burial of a woman described as the wife of Ralph Tailor.

11 Welford, "Newcastle Householders in 1665", pp. 71, 72, 73. All three wards were part of Allhallows' parish. For the proportion of households with six or more hearths, see Howell, *Newcastle-upon-Tyne and the Puritan Revolution*, pp. 12–13.

12 The will survives as a fair copy on parchment and a registered copy: D.U.L. DPRI/1/1669/T1/1; DPRI/2/8, fos 167v–168. Both are copies of an original that was returned to the executrix, whose receipt also survives: DPRI/1/1669/T1/2. There is no accompanying inventory. Interestingly, his widow signed the receipt with her initials only, which may indicate that she could read but could not write confidently.

13 T.N.A. SP 16/386/78. His point was that they were not liable for taxation for 1636–7.

14 D.U.L. DPRI/1/1637/A4/1–2 (Henry Anderson); DPRI/1/1637/B7/1–2 (George Bindlosse); DPRI/1/1637/B11/1–5 (Richard Browne); DPRI/1/1637/E1/1–3 (Ralph Emerson); DPRI/1/1637/M3/2 (Jane Mawe); DPRI/1/1637/P9/1 (William Pringle); DPRI/1/1637/L2/1–2 (Nicholas Lambton). For the lease, see *Proceedings of the Society of Antiquaries of Newcastle upon Tyne*, 3rd series, 8 (1917), p. 116, and for a further will proved in 1638, *Archaeologia Aeliana*, 3rd series, 13 (1916), p. 31. I have not attempted to search the probate records beyond 1637 for evidence of Ralph's continuing activity. The time and labour involved in attempting to search every surviving document for over thirty years would hardly be justified by the outcome. Probate documents can never have been more than part of his work, and probably not the most significant part after 1636, though the part most likely to have been preserved.

15 For the final phase of Jenison's career in Newcastle, see Howell, *Newcastle-upon-Tyne and the Puritan Revolution*, pp. 220–39, quoting p. 236. Howell comments (p. 222) on the "almost messianic violence" of Jenison's sermons in 1646.

16 T.N.A. PROB 11/226, Will of Robert Jenison DD. He also recalled his "unjust suspension by the high commissioners of Yorke and my abode for five yeeres and a halfe with my familye att Danzigke".

17 He is mentioned once in Howell's meticulously documented *Newcastle-upon-Tyne and the Puritan Revolution*, but only as a witness in the postwar defence of the city's monopoly powers over the Tyne. He does not appear in Longstaffe, ed., *Memoirs of the Life of Mr Ambrose Barnes*, which alludes to many of the most prominent figures of Interregnum Newcastle.

18 He was not alone in this. Roger Howell Jnr notes that while successive shifts of power at the centre brought purges of the city's corporation, a substantial core of office holders survived all changes of regime: "Newcastle and the Nation: The Seventeenth-Century Experience", in Barry, ed., *Tudor and Stuart Town*, pp. 281–3.

19 Dodds, ed., *Register of Freemen of Newcastle upon Tyne*, pp. 36–7.

20 T.W.A. BC.RV/1/3, River Court Book, fos 5, 5v, 19v, 43v, and *passim*.
21 T.N.A. Exchequer Depositions, E 134, 1649–50, Hil. 1. He was the first of thirteen witnesses to be examined by the commissioners taking depositions in the suit brought by the city against Thomas Cliffe for breach of its monopoly over the trades of the Tyne valley, and specifically the privileges of the Shipwrights' Company. These issues were later incorporated into the comprehensive attack on Newcastle's monopoly powers over the Tyne launched by Ralph Gardner, with the result that Ralph Tailor's deposition was briefly (and inaccurately) abstracted in R. Gardiner (sic), *Englands Grievance Discovered in Relation to the Coal Trade* (London, 1655), p. 84, which describes him as "Steward of the Carpenters of Newcastle", perhaps an error for "Shipwrights". For the Cliffe and Gardner cases, see Howell, *Newcastle-upon-Tyne and the Puritan Revolution*, pp. 300–12, and *Monopoly on the Tyne, 1650–58: Papers Relating to Ralph Gardner*, ed. R. Howell Jnr, Society of Antiquaries of Newcastle-upon-Tyne (1978).
22 D.U.L. DPRI/1/1669/T1/1; DPRI/2/8, fos 167v–168; N.C.S. SANT/GUI/Ncl/1/3/1, Bakers' and Brewers' Accounts, 1637–94, unfoliated. The references to Ralph Tailor are to be found in the accounts for 1649–50, 1653–4, and 1656–7. One of the officers of the company also referred to in these accounts was a certain John Tailor, who died in 1654–5.
23 T.W.A., Calendar of the Common Council Book of Newcastle, 1656–1722, fo. 61; GU/TH/37/1, Trinity House Admissions Book, unfoliated, 23 February 1664/5; *C.S.P.D., 1667*, p. 547; D.U.L. DPRI/1/1669/T1/1; DPRI/2/8, fos 167v–168. He lived in the district of the city described by Bourne as "chiefly inhabited by such as have their living by Shipping": Bourne, *History*, p. 133. For Trinity House, which survives to this day in Broad Chare, see G. McCombie, "The Development of Trinity House and the Guildhall before 1700", in Newton and Pollard, eds, *Newcastle and Gateshead before 1700*.
24 He is known to have acted for a Newcastle merchant in obtaining the original of a family will from the Durham registry in 1653. In 1655, he was party to an unsuccessful deal to lease lands in Ryton parish from the widow of a sequestrated royalist. In 1656, he was one of the commissioners appointed by the court of Chancery in Westminster to take depositions in a suit commenced in that court. He witnessed, and perhaps drew up, an indenture for the sale of houses in Pandon in 1659, and he was involved in securing marriage licences as late as 1664. See J.C. Hodgson, ed., *Wills and Inventories from the Registry at Durham Part III*, Surtees Society, 112 (1906), p. 91; R. Welford, ed., *Records of the Committee for Compounding etc. with Delinquent Royalists in Durham and Northumberland*, Surtees Society, 111 (1905), p. 358; *Calendar of Chancery Depositions, "Before 1714" Series*, in *The British Archivist*, Miscellanea 1–5 (1913), No. 3, p. 24; *Archaeologia Aeliana*, 3rd series, 13 (1916), pp. 21–2; D.U.L. Durham Diocesan Records, Index of Marriage Bonds, pp. 6, 12. I owe the marriage bond references to Margaret MacCollum. Were it practicable to search every surviving record of the area for this period, one can be confident that further evidence of his notarial and business activities would surface.
25 D.U.L. DPRI/1/1644/G1/1–3. The accompanying inventory had a gross value of £21.13s.4d., against which was set the sum of £4. 10s. 2d. "Disbursed for charges dureing the time of ther sicknesse and the cleansers wages", leaving "for the childs filiall portion" the sum of seventeen pounds, three shillings, which was in the hands of three named men. A note of the appointment of Katherine Elwood, and the probate bond accompanying the inventory and Tailor's letter, had both been dated 20 March 1644 (i.e. 1645). Clearly the court had responded to Ralph's suggestion, and the fact that his letter was retained in the record suggests that in the circumstances the expedient adopted in this case was not considered particularly contentious.
26 D.U.L. DPRI/1/1669/T1/1; DPRI/2/8, fos 167v–168.
27 For the presentment, see "Ecclesiastical Proceedings after the Restoration", *Proceedings of the Society of Antiquaries of Newcastle-upon-Tyne*, 3rd series, 4 (1909–10), pp. 27–8.
28 T.W.A. MF 250 (All Saints' [Allhallows']). He had married Margaret Colier on 29 January 1667/8.

29 A search of the parish registers, and especially the renewed registration at Allhallows' from 1637, reveals no entry relating to the baptism or burial of children attributed to Ralph Tailor. This seems to confirm that he was childless. The identifications of the kin named in his will are made with reference to the 1675 will of his widow Margaret: D.U.L. DPRI/2/9, fo. 163. Ralph Tailor did leave a token to one Mary Comyn, "my Grand child", but given the fact that he did not will his property to her, it seems very unlikely that she was his direct descendant. I suspect, given the nature of the token, that this may be a copying error, and that she was one of his godchildren.

30 For the language of kinship in early modern England, see N. Tadmor, *Family and Friends in Eighteenth-Century England: Household, Kinship, and Patronage* (Cambridge, 2001), ch. 4.

31 The guilds with which Ralph Tailor was associated had concentrations of members in these wards: the Bakers and Brewers in Austin Tower and Pandon Tower; the Butchers in Plummer Tower and Austin Tower; the Shipwrights in Sandgate. Trinity House was located in Broad Chare, and Masters and Mariners were concentrated in Wall Knoll, Sandgate, and Pandon Tower wards. See Langton, "Residential Patterns in Pre-Industrial Cities", p. 195.

32 These identifications are made with the aid of: D.U.L. DPRI/2/9, fo. 163 (will of Margaret Taylor, widow); Welford, "Newcastle Householders in 1665"; A. Green, E. Parkinson, and M. Spufford, eds, *County Durham Hearth Tax Assessment, Lady Day 1666*, British Records Society, Hearth Tax Series, vol. 4 (2006); Dodds, ed., *Register of Freemen of Newcastle upon Tyne*; Howell, *Newcastle-upon-Tyne and the Puritan Revolution*. It is of interest that, with the exception of one of her two daughters, her sister, the husbands of these two women, and Mr Matthew of Durham, there is no overlap between the people mentioned in Ralph Tailor's will and those acknowledged in that of his widow six years later.

33 It cannot be identified today. It was probably removed when Allhallows' was demolished in the late eighteenth century and rebuilt as the present All Saints' church.

34 For subsequent plague outbreaks in the 1640s, see Bourchier Richardson, *Plague and Pestilence*, p. 35ff and Howell, *Newcastle-upon-Tyne and the Puritan Revolution*, p. 320; William Ellis, *News from Newcastle* (London, 1651). In 1649, William Gray referred to the earliest waggonway in his *Chorographia*, p. 35, and by the time of Ralph Tailor's death several were in operation. See Levine and Wrightson, *Making of an Industrial Society*, pp. 51–4.

EPILOGUE

1 P. Abrams, *Historical Sociology* (Shepton Mallett, 1988), p. 191; W.H. Sewell, *The Logics of History: Social Theory and Transformation* (Chicago, 2005), p. 218 (and for fuller discussion of Sewell's conception of events as transformative, see also pp. 8, 9, 100–2, 226–8).

2 For the disappearance of the plague in England, see Slack, *Impact of Plague*, ch. 12.

3 Huntington Library, HM 69956, Vol. II, fo. 181; Brand, *History and Antiquities*, vol. 2, pp. 455–6. In both cases the plague was mentioned in the course of annalistic listings of principal events, and succeeded by lengthy accounts of Newcastle's part in the Bishops' Wars and the Civil Wars.

4 Bourchier Richardson, *Plague and Pestilence*, pp. 26–34. He knew Jenison's and Fenwick's tracts, and had also researched parish records and those of Trinity House and several of the guilds. Thereafter Welford's *History of Newcastle and Gateshead*, pp. 337–9, added some further details in 1887, Dendy's note on "The Plague in Newcastle" published Coulson's figures in 1905, and in 1967 Roger Howell considered the scale and impact of the mortality in the introductory chapter of *Newcastle upon Tyne and the Puritan Revolution*, pp. 6–7. For a stimulating discussion of the "forgetting" of a more recent demographic disaster, see A.W. Crosby, *America's Forgotten Pandemic: The Influenza of 1918*, 2nd edn (Cambridge, 2003), ch. 15.

5 West, *Symbolaeographia*, book 1, section 1, "Of Instruments", unpag.

6 The phrase quoted is from Henry Swinburne's description of his own research: *Briefe Treatise of Testaments*, "Epilogue", unpag.

7 I am influenced by Peter Burke's argument that an alternative approach to the history of events is to "focus on events not for their own sake, but for what they reveal about the culture in which they took place": P. Burke, "History of Events and the Revival of Narrative", in P. Burke, ed., *New Perspectives on Historical Writing* (Cambridge, 1991), p. 234.

8 Alice Munro, "Meneseteung", in *Friend of my Youth*, Penguin edn (Toronto, 1991), p. 73. Munro was describing local and family historians.

9 Orlin, *Locating Privacy in Tudor London*, p. 14.

10 Jones, "Plague and its Metaphors", pp. 117–18.

11 D. Arnold, "Cholera and Colonialism in British India", *Past and Present*, 113 (1986), p. 151.

12 Slack, *Impact of Plague*, esp. ch. 11, quoting pp. 288, 293–4.

13 Quoted in P. Withington, "Two Renaissances: Urban Political Culture in Post-Reformation England Reconsidered", *Historical Journal*, 44 (2001), p. 248.

14 Camus, *The Plague*, p. 308.

15 Gray, *Chorographia*, p. 15.

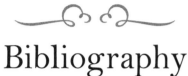

Bibliography

1. MANUSCRIPT SOURCES

Durham County Record Office [D.C.R.O.]

EP/Du SM1	Parish registers of St Margaret's, Durham [MF 42/144].
Q/S OB	Quarter Sessions Order Books.

Durham University Library, Archives and Special Collections [D.U.L.]

DDR/EJ/CCD	Consistory Court Depositions.
DPRI/1	Original Wills and Inventories.
DPRI/2/8–9	Probate Registers, 1665–70, 1670–5.
DPRI/4/14	Probate Act Book, 1635–8.

Calendar of Probate Bonds [typescript].

Guildhall Library, London

MS 9057/1	Archdeaconry Court Examinations and Depositions, 1632–6.

Huntington Library

HM 69956	Manuscript History of Newcastle-upon-Tyne by James Murray

Northumberland Collections Service [N.C.S.]

EP 9/1–6	Parish Registers of Newcastle, All Saints' (Allhallows'), 1600–87.
EP 13/1–2	Parish Registers of Newcastle, St Andrew's, 1597–1687.
EP 52/1A	Parish Registers of Christchurch, Tynemouth [MF 586].
EP 73/2–4	Parish Registers of Newcastle, St John's, 1600–74.
EP 86/1–2	Parish Registers of Newcastle, St Nicholas', 1558–1678.
EP 86/361–3	Wills among Parish Records of Newcastle, St Nicholas'.
SANT/GUI/Ncl/1/3/1	Bakers' and Brewers' Company Accounts, 1637–94.
SANT/GUI/Ncl/4/2/1	Glovers' Company Minute Book, 1636–77.
SANT/GUI/Ncl/6/2/1	Saddlers' Company Minute Book, 1593–1708.

The National Archives [T.N.A.]

E134, 1649–50, Hil. 1	Exchequer Depositions

| PROB 11 | Prerogative Court of Canterbury, Wills. |
| SP 16 | State Papers Domestic, Charles I. |

Tyne and Wear Archives [T.W.A.]

Calendar of the Common Council Book of Newcastle, 1656–1722.

543/26	Newcastle-upon-Tyne Chamberlains' Account Book, 1635–6.
BC.RV/1/3	River Court Book, 1654–7.
D/NCP/3/1	Plan of the Ancient Boundaries of the Town and County of Newcastle-upon-Tyne by Thomas Oliver (1852).
D/NCP/3/23	Parishes of Newcastle c.1900.
GU/BS/2/1	Barber Surgeons' Company, Minutes, 1616–86 [MF 129].
GU/BR/3/1	Bricklayers', Wallers', and Plasterers' Company, Minute Book, 1636–60.
GU/BU/1	Butchers' Company Book, 1626–1784 [MF 2068].
GU/CF/2/1–2	Curriers', Feltmakers', and Armourers' Company Books, 1581–1802, 1635–1856.
GU/CO/2/1	Coopers' Company Order Book, 1576–1671 [MF 1265].
GU/CW/17/2	Cordwainers' Company Order Book, 1566–1900 [MF1269].
GU/GP/2/1	Goldsmiths', Plumbers' and Glasiers', etc Company Book, 1598–1671 [MF 1273].
GU/SC/1	Scriveners' Company, Minute Book, 1675–1775.
GU/Sh/3/1	Shipwrights' Company Enrollment Book, 1613–1812 [MF 1278].
GU/Sh/4/1	Shipwrights' Company Order Book, 1622–1908 [MF 1278].
GU/TH/2/10	Trinity House Payments Book, 1634–9.
GU/TH/37/1	Trinity House Admissions Book, 1606–1738.
GU/TH/9/1	Trinity House Order Book, 1604–89.
MF 249 & 250	Microfilm of Parish Registers of Newcastle, All Saints' [Allhallows'].
MF 263	Microfilm of Parish Registers of Newcastle, St Nicholas'.
MF 279	Microfilm of Parish Registers of Newcastle, St Andrew's.
MF 528	Microfilm of Parish Registers of Newcastle, St John's.
MF 899	Microfilm of Parish Registers of Whickham.
MF 1091	Microfilm of Parish Registers of Ryton.
MF 1092	Microfilm of Parish Registers of Jarrow, St Paul's.
MF 1139	Microfilm of Parish Registers of Gateshead, St Mary's.
MF 1994	Microfilm of Parish Registers of Chester-le-Street.

2. EARLY PRINTED BOOKS (PRE-1800)

Beau Chesne, J. de, *A Booke Containing Divers Sortes of Hands* (London, 1571).

Billingsley, M., *The Pens Excellencie or The Secretaries Delight* (London, 1618).

Bourne, H., *History of Newcastle-upon-Tyne or, The Ancient and Present State of That Town* (Newcastle upon Tyne, 1737).

Brand, J., *The History and Antiquities of the Town and County of Newcastle upon Tyne* 2 vols (London, 1789).

Camden, W., *Britannia* (London, 1607 edn).

Camden, W., *Britain, or A Chorographical Description of the Most Flourishing Kingdomes, England, Scotland, and Ireland*, trans. P. Holland (London, 1637 edn).

Ellis, W., *News from Newcastle* (London, 1651).

Fenwicke, J., *Christ Ruling in Midst of his Enemies* (London, 1643).

Gardiner, R., *Englands Grievance Discovered in Relation to the Coal Trade* (London, 1655).

G[ray], W[illiam], *Chorographia, or A Survey of Newcastle upon Tyne* (Newcastle, 1649).

Hill, R., *The Pathway to Prayer and Pietie* (London, 1613).

Jenison, R., *The Height of Israels Heathenish Idolatrie in Sacrificing their Children to the Devill* (London, 1621).

Jenison, R., *Directions for the Worthy Receiving of the Lord's Supper* (London, 1624).

Jenison, R., *The Christians Apparelling by Christ* (London, 1625).

Jenison, R., *The Cities Safetie or A Fruitfull Treatise (and Usefull for These Dangerous Times)* (London, 1630).

Jenison, R., *Newcastle's Call: to her Neighbour and Sister Townes and Cities throughout the Land* (London, 1637).

Jenison, R., *Soled Comfort for Sound Christians* (London, 1641).

Jenison, R., *Two Treatises* (London, 1642).

Speed, J., *The Theatre of the Empire of Great Britaine* (London, 1611).

Swinburne, H., *A Briefe Treatise of Testaments and Last Wills* (London, 1611 edn).

West, William, *Symbolaeographia . . . or The Notarie or Scrivener* (London, 1590).

3. Editions of Manuscripts and Early Printed Books, Calendars, and Indexes

Amelang, J.S., trans. and ed., *A Journal of the Plague Year: The Diary of the Barcelona Tanner Miquel Parets, 1651* (New York and Oxford, 1991).

Archaeologia Aeliana, 3rd series, 13 (1916) [Miscellaneous documents relating to districts of the city of Newcastle-upon-Tyne].

Bédoyère, G. de la, ed., *The Diary of John Evelyn* (Woodbridge, 1995).

Brereton, W., "The Journal of Sir William Brereton, 1635", in J.C. Hodgson, ed., *North Country Diaries (Second Series)*, Surtees Society, 124 (1915).

Calendar of Chancery Depositions, "Before 1714" Series, in *The British Archivist*, Miscellanea 1–5 (1913).

Calendar of State Papers Domestic, Charles I, 1636–7, 1637, 1637–8.

Calendar of State Papers Domestic, Charles II, 1667.

Defoe, D., *A Journal of the Plague Year*, ed. C. Wall, Penguin Classics edn (London, 2003).

Dendy, F.W., "The Plague in Newcastle", *Proceedings of the Society of Antiquaries of Newcastle-upon-Tyne*, 3rd series, 1 (1905).

Dodds, M.H., ed., *The Register of Freemen of Newcastle upon Tyne from the Corporation Guild and Admission Books Chiefly of the Seventeenth Century*, Newcastle upon Tyne Records Committee, III (Newcastle, 1923).

"Ecclesiastical Proceedings after the Restoration", *Proceedings of the Society of Antiquaries of Newcastle-upon-Tyne*, 3rd series, 4 (1909–10).

Gray, W., *Chorographia or A Survey of Newcastle upon Tyne*, ed. Andrew Reid (Newcastle, 1884).

Green, A., Parkinson, E., and Spufford, M., eds, *County Durham Hearth Tax Assessment, Lady Day 1666*, British Records Society, Hearth Tax Series, vol. 4 (2006).

Hodgson, J.C., ed., *Wills and Inventories from the Registry at Durham Part III*, Surtees Society, 112 (1906).

Howell, R., Jnr, ed., *Monopoly on the Tyne, 1650–58. Papers Relating to Ralph Gardner*, Society of Antiquaries of Newcastle-upon-Tyne (1978).

Index of Wills in the York Registry from 1636 to 1652, Yorkshire Archaeological and Topographical Society Record Series, vol. 4 (1888).

Index of Wills in the York Registry, A.D. 1627 to 1636. Administrations A.D. 1627 to 1652, Yorkshire Archaeological Society Record Series, vol. 35 (1905).

Longstaffe, W.H.D., ed., *Memoirs of the Life of Mr Ambrose Barnes*, Surtees Society, 50 (1867).

Proceedings of the Society of Antiquaries of Newcastle upon Tyne, 3rd series, 8 (1917). ["Miscellanea"].

Raine, J., ed., "A Letter from the Corporation of Newcastle upon Tyne to the Mayor and Aldermen of Berwick", *Archaeologia Aeliana,* 2 (1832).

Robertson, H., ed., *The Registers of St Margaret's (Durham) in the County of Durham,* Durham and Northumberland Parish Register Society (Sunderland, 1904).

Selement, G., and Woolley, B.C., eds, *Thomas Shepard's Confessions,* Colonial Society of Massachusetts, 58 (Boston, 1981).

Welford, R., ed., *Records of the Committee for Compounding etc. with Delinquent Royalists in Durham and Northumberland,* Surtees Society, 111 (1905).

Welford, R., ed., "Newcastle Householders in 1665", *Archaeologia Aeliana,* 3rd series, 7 (1911).

Wickham Legg, L.G., ed., *A Relation of a Short Survey of 26 Counties* (London, 1904).

4. BOOKS AND ARTICLES

Abrams, P., *Historical Sociology* (Shepton Mallett, 1988).

Amelang, J.S., "Introduction: Popular Narrative and the Plague", in J.S. Amelang, trans. and ed., *A Journal of the Plague Year: The Diary of the Barcelona Tanner Miquel Parets, 1651* (New York and Oxford, 1991).

Arkell, T., "The Probate Process", in T. Arkell, N. Evans, and N. Goose, eds, *When Death Do Us Part: Understanding and Interpreting the Probate Records of Early Modern England,* Local Population Studies Supplement (Oxford, 2000).

Arnold, D., "Cholera and Colonialism in British India", *Past and Present,* 113 (1986).

Bartlett, R., *The Hanged Man: A Story of Miracle, Memory, and Colonialism in the Middle Ages* (Princeton, NJ and Oxford, 2004).

Biraben, J.N., *Les hommes et la peste en France et dans les pays européens et méditerranéens* (Paris, 1975–6).

Bourchier Richardson, G., *Plague and Pestilence in the North of England* (Newcastle, 1852).

Britnell, R., "Medieval Gateshead", in A.J. Pollard and D. Newton, eds, *Newcastle and Gateshead before 1700* (Chichester, 2009).

Brooks, C., "Apprenticeship, Social Mobility, and the Middling Sort, 1550–1800", in J. Barry and C. Brooks, eds, *The Middling Sort of People: Culture, Society, and Politics in England, 1550–1800* (Basingstoke and London, 1994).

Brooks, C.W., *Pettyfoggers and Vipers of the Commonwealth: The "Lower Branch" of the Legal Profession in Early Modern England* (Cambridge, 1986).

Brooks, C.W., *Law, Politics, and Society in Early Modern England* (Cambridge, 2008).

Brooks, C.W., Helmholz, R.M., and Stein, P.G., *Notaries Public in England since the Reformation,* Society of Public Notaries of London (London, 1991).

Burke, P., "History of Events and the Revival of Narrative", in P. Burke, ed., *New Perspectives on Historical Writing* (Cambridge, 1991).

Butcher, A., "The Functions of Script in the Speech Community of a Late Medieval Town, c.1300–1550", in J. Crick and A. Walsham, eds, *The Uses of Script and Print, 1300–1700* (Cambridge, 2005).

Calvi, G., *Histories of a Plague Year: The Social and the Imaginary in Baroque Florence,* trans. D. Biocca and B.T. Ragan, Jnr (Berkeley and Oxford, 1989).

Camus, A., *The Plague,* trans. S. Gilbert, Vintage International edn. (New York, 1991).

Champion, J.A.I., ed., *Epidemic Disease in London* (Centre for Metropolitan History Working Papers Series, No. 1, 1993).

Cipolla, C.M., *Cristofano and the Plague: A Study in the History of Public Health in the Age of Galileo* (London, 1973).

Cipolla, C.M., *Faith, Reason, and the Plague in Seventeenth-Century Tuscany,* trans. M. Kittel (New York and London, 1979).

Cressy, D., *Literacy and the Social Order: Reading and Writing in Tudor and Stuart England* (Cambridge, 1980).

Crosby, A.W., *America's Forgotten Pandemic: The Influenza of 1918,* 2nd edn (Cambridge, 2003).

Doyle, S., "Swinburne, Henry (c.1551–1624)", in *Oxford Dictionary of National Biography.*

Erickson, A.L., "Using Probate Accounts", in T. Arkell, N. Evans, and N. Goose, eds, *When Death Do Us Part: Understanding and Interpreting the Probate Records of Early Modern England*, Local Population Studies Supplement (Oxford, 2000).

Fentress, J., and Wickham, C., *Social Memory* (Oxford, UK and Cambridge, MA, 1992).

Finlay, R., *Population and Metropolis: The Demography of London, 1580–1650* (Cambridge, 1981).

Ginzburg, C., and Poni, C., "The Name and the Game: Unequal Exchange and the Historiographical Marketplace", in E. Muir and G. Ruggiero, eds, *Microhistory and the Lost Peoples of Europe*, trans. E. Branch (Baltimore, MD and London, 1991).

Gowing, L., *Domestic Dangers: Women, Words, and Sex in Early Modern London* (Cambridge, 1996).

Gray, M.W., "Microhistory as Universal History", *Central European History*, 34 (2001).

Harbottle, B., "The Medieval Archaeology of Newcastle", in A.J. Pollard and D. Newton, eds, *Newcastle and Gateshead before 1700* (Chichester, 2009).

Harbottle, B., Ellison, M., et al., "An Excavation in the Castle Ditch, Newcastle-upon-Tyne, 1974–6", *Archaeologia Aeliana*, 5th series, 9 (1981).

Harrison, G.V., "Appendix 1. Agricultural Weights and Measures", in J. Thirsk, ed., *The Agrarian History of England and Wales. Vol V. 1640–1750. Part II. Agrarian Change* (Cambridge, 1985).

Hatcher, J., *The History of the British Coal Industry. Vol. 1, Before 1700: Towards the Age of Coal* (Oxford, 1993).

Healey, M., "Discourses of the Plague in Early Modern London", in J. Champion, ed., *Epidemic Disease in London* (Centre for Metropolitan History Working Papers Series, No. 1, 1993).

Healey, M., " 'Seeing' Contagious Bodies in Early Modern London", in D. Grantley and N. Taunton, eds, *The Body in Late Medieval and Early Modern Culture* (Aldershot, 2000).

Hegarty, A.J., "Thomas Jackson", in *Oxford Dictionary of National Biography*.

Helt, J.S.W., "Women, Memory, and Will-making in Elizabethan England", in B. Gordon and P. Marshall, eds, *The Place of the Dead: Death and Remembrance in Late Medieval and Early Modern Europe* (Cambridge, 2000).

Heslop, D.H., "Newcastle and Gateshead before A.D. 1080", in A.J. Pollard and D. Newton, eds, *Newcastle and Gateshead before 1700* (Chichester, 2009).

Hindle, S., *On the Parish? The Micro-Politics of Poor Relief in Rural England c.1550–1750* (Oxford, 2004).

Hopper, A.J., "Fenwick (Fenwicke), John", in *Oxford Dictionary of National Biography*.

Houston, R.A., "The Development of Literacy: Northern England, 1640–1750", *Economic History Review*, 2nd series, 35 (1982).

Howell, R., Jnr., *Newcastle-upon-Tyne and the Puritan Revolution: A Study of the Civil War in North England* (Oxford, 1967).

Howell, R., Jnr., "Newcastle and the Nation: The Seventeenth-Century Experience", in J. Barry, ed., *The Tudor and Stuart Town: A Reader in English Urban History* (London and New York, 1990).

Jenner, M.S.R., "The Great Dog Massacre", in W.G. Naphy and P. Roberts, eds, *Fear in Early Modern Society* (Manchester and New York, 1997).

Jinkins, M., "Thomas Shepard (1605–1649)", in *Oxford Dictionary of National Biography*.

Jones, C., "Plague and its Metaphors in Early Modern France", *Representations*, 53 (1996).

Kadar, B.Z., "The Genoese Notaries of 1382: The Anatomy of an Urban Occupational Group", in H.A. Miskimin, D. Herlihy, and A.L. Udovitch, eds, *The Medieval City* (New Haven, CT and London, 1977).

Kent, D.V. and F.W., *Neighbours and Neighbourhood in Renaissance Florence: The District of the Red Lion in the Fifteenth Century* (Locust Valley, NY, 1982).

King, A.C., and Pollard, A.J., " 'Northumbria' in the Later Middle Ages", in R. Colls, ed., *Northumbria: History and Identity, c.547–2000* (Chichester, 2007).

King, R., "The Sociability of the Trade Guilds of Newcastle and Durham, 1660–1750: The Urban Renaissance Revisited", in H. Berry and J. Gregory, eds, *Creating and Consuming Culture in North-East England, 1660–1830* (Aldershot and Burlington, VT, 2004).

Langton, J., "Residential Patterns in Pre-Industrial Cities: Some Case Studies from Seventeenth-Century Britain", in J. Barry, ed., *The Tudor and Stuart Town: A Reader in English Urban History* (London and New York, 1990).

Langton, J., "Urban Growth and Economic Change: From the Late Seventeenth Century to 1841", in P. Clark, ed., *The Cambridge Urban History of Britain. Vol. II, 1540–1840* (Cambridge, 2000).

Levi, G., "On Microhistory", in P. Burke, ed., *New Perspectives on Historical Writing* (Cambridge, 1991).

Levine, D., and Wrightson, K., *The Making of an Industrial Society: Whickham, 1560–1765* (Oxford, 1991).

Marsh, C., "In the Name of God? Will Making and Faith in Early Modern England", in G.H. Martin and P. Spufford, eds, *The Records of the Nation* (Woodbridge, 1990).

McCombie, G., "The Development of Trinity House and the Guidhall before 1700", in A.J. Pollard and D. Newton, eds, *Newcastle and Gateshead before 1700* (Chichester, 2009).

Merritt, J.F., *The Social World of Early Modern Westminster: Abbey, Court, and Community* (Manchester and New York, 2005).

Merwick, D., *Death of a Notary: Conquest and Change in Colonial New York* (Ithaca, NY and London, 1999).

Monteyne, J., *The Printed Image in Early Modern London: Urban Space, Visual Representations, and Social Exchange* (Aldershot and Burlington, VT, 2007).

Muir, E., "Introduction: Observing Trifles", in E. Muir and G. Ruggiero, eds, *Microhistory and the Lost Peoples of Europe*, trans. E. Branch (Baltimore, MD and London, 1991).

Muldrew, C., *The Economy of Obligation: The Culture of Credit and Social Relations in Early Modern England* (Basingstoke and New York, 1998).

Munkhoff, R., "Searchers of the Dead: Authority, Marginality, and the Interpretation of Plague in England, 1574–1665", *Gender and History*, 11 (1999).

Munro, A., "Meneseteung", in *Friend of my Youth*, Penguin edn (Toronto, 1991).

Munro, I., "The City and its Double: Plague Time in Early Modern London", *English Literary Renaissance*, 30 (2000).

Newman, C.R., "The Reformation Era in Newcastle, 1530–1662", in A.J. Pollard and D. Newton, eds, *Newcastle and Gateshead before 1700* (Chichester, 2009).

Newton, D., *North-East England, 1569–1625: Governance, Culture, and Identity* (Woodbridge, 2006).

Orlin, L.C., *Locating Privacy in Tudor London* (Oxford, 2007).

Outhwaite, R.B., *The Rise and Fall of the English Ecclesiastical Courts, 1500–1800* (Cambridge, 2006).

Palliser, D.M., ed., *The Cambridge Urban History of Britain. Vol. I, 600–1540* (Cambridge, 2000).

Pettegree, A., *The Book in the Renaissance* (New Haven, CT and London, 2010).

The Plague Reconsidered, supplement to *Local Population Studies* (1977).

Pocock, D., "Place Evocation: The Galilee Chapel in Durham Cathedral", *Transactions of the Institute of British Geographers*, new series, 21 (1996).

Pollard, A.J., and Newton, D., "Introduction", in A.J. Pollard and D. Newton, eds, *Newcastle and Gateshead before 1700* (Chichester, 2009).

Postles, D.A., *Social Proprieties: Social Relations in Early Modern England (1500–1680)* (Washington, DC, 2006).

Rosenthal, J.T., *Telling Tales: Sources and Narration in Late Medieval England* (University Park, PA, 2003).

Rushton, P., "Gateshead 1550–1700 – Independence against All the Odds?", in A.J. Pollard and D. Newton, eds, *Newcastle and Gateshead before 1700* (Chichester, 2009).

Scott, S., and Duncan, C.J., *Biology of Plagues: Evidence from Historical Populations* (Cambridge, 2001).

Sewell, W.H., *The Logics of History: Social Theory and Transformation* (Chicago, 2005).

Sheils, W.J., "Jenison, Robert", in *Oxford Dictionary of National Biography*.

Shepard, A., "Poverty, Labour, and the Language of Social Description in Early Modern England", *Past and Present*, 201 (2008).

Shrewsbury, J.F.D., *A History of Bubonic Plague in the British Isles* (Cambridge, 1970).

Slack, P., *The Impact of Plague in Tudor and Stuart England* (London, 1985).

Smith-Bannister, S., *Names and Naming Patterns in England, 1538–1700* (Oxford, 1997).

Spufford, M., "Religious Preambles and the Scribes of Villagers' Wills in Cambridgeshire, 1570–1700", *Local Population Studies*, 7 (1971).

Spufford, M., *Constrasting Communities: English Villagers in the Sixteenth and Seventeenth Centuries* (Cambridge, 1974).

Spufford, M., *The Great Reclothing of Rural England. Petty Chapmen and their Wares in the Seventeenth Century* (London, 1984).

Spufford, P., Brett, M., and Erickson, A.L., eds, *Probate Accounts of England and Wales*, 2 vols, British Record Society (London, 1999).

Tadmor, N., *Family and Friends in Eighteenth-Century England: Household, Kinship, and Patronage* (Cambridge, 2001).

Thomas, K., "Numeracy in Early Modern England", *Transactions of the Royal Historical Society*, 5th series, 37 (1987).

Thomas, K., *The Ends of Life: Roads to Fulfilment in Early Modern England* (Oxford, 2009).

Thompson, E.P., "Anthropology and the Discipline of Historical Context", *Midland History*, 1 (1972).

Tuck, R., "Civil Conflict in School and Town, 1500–1700", in B. Mains and A. Tuck, eds, *Royal Grammar School, Newcastle-upon-Tyne: A History of the School in its Community* (Stocksfield, 1986).

Twigg, G., "Plague in London: Spatial and Temporal Aspects of Mortality", in J.A.I. Champion, ed., *Epidemic Disease in London* (Centre for Metropolitan History Working Papers Series, No. 1, 1993).

Wear, A., "Fear, Anxiety, and the Plague in Early Modern England: Religious and Medical Responses", in J.R. Hinnels and R. Porter, eds, *Religion, Health, and Suffering* (London and New York, 1999).

Weatherill, L., *Consumer Behaviour and Material Culture in Britain, 1660–1760* (London and New York, 1988).

Welford, R., ed., *History of Newcastle and Gateshead. Vol. III, Sixteenth and Seventeenth Centuries* (London, 1887).

Whyman, S., *The Pen and the People: English Letter Writers, 1660–1800* (Oxford, 2009).

Withington, P., "Two Renaissances: Urban Political Culture in Post-Reformation England Reconsidered", *Historical Journal*, 44 (2001).

Withington, P., *The Politics of Commonwealth: Citizens and Freemen in Early Modern England* (Cambridge, 2005).

Woodward, D., *Men at Work: Labourers and Building Craftsmen in the Towns of Northern England, 1450–1750* (Cambridge, 1995).

Wrightson, K., and Levine, D., "Death in Whickham", in J. Walter and R. Schofield, eds, *Famine, Disease, and the Social Order in Early Modern Society* (Cambridge, 1989).

Wrigley, E.A., and Schofield, R.S., *The Population History of England, 1541–1871* (London, 1981).

Wrigley, E.A., "Urban Growth and Agricultural Change: England and the Continent in the Early Modern Period", *Journal of Interdisciplinary History*, 15 (1985).

Index